MODERN CHINESE REAL ESTATE LAW

Law, Property and Society

Series Editor:
Robin Paul Malloy

The Law, Property and Society series examines property in terms of its ability to foster democratic forms of governance, and to advance social justice. The series explores the legal infrastructure of property in broad terms, encompassing concerns for real, personal, intangible, intellectual and cultural property, as well as looking at property related financial markets. The series is edited by Robin Paul Malloy, and book proposals are welcome from all interested authors.

Robin Paul Malloy is E.I. White Chair and Distinguished Professor of Law, and the Kauffman Professor of Entrepreneurship and Innovation at Syracuse University College of Law, USA. He is Director of the Center on Property, Citizenship, and Social Entrepreneurism. He is also Professor of Economics (by courtesy appointment) in the Maxwell School of Citizenship and Public Affairs, Syracuse University. Professor Malloy writes extensively on law and market theory and on real estate transactions and development. He has authored eight books (one now in its third edition and another in its second edition), and edited seven additional books. He has also written more than 30 scholarly articles, and contributed to 12 other books. His recent books include: LAW AND MARKET ECONOMY (2000, in English and translated into Spanish and Chinese); LAW IN A MARKET CONTEXT (2004); and REAL ESTATE TRANSACTIONS 3RD EDITION (with James C. Smith, 2007).

Modern Chinese Real Estate Law
Property Development in an Evolving Legal System

GREGORY M. STEIN
University of Tennessee College of Law, USA

ASHGATE

© Gregory M. Stein 2012

All rights reserved. No part of this publication may be reproduced, stored in a retrieval system or transmitted in any form or by any means, electronic, mechanical, photocopying, recording or otherwise without the prior permission of the publisher.

Gregory M. Stein has asserted his right under the Copyright, Designs and Patents Act, 1988, to be identified as the author of this work.

Published by
Ashgate Publishing Limited
Wey Court East
Union Road
Farnham
Surrey, GU9 7PT
England

Ashgate Publishing Company
Suite 420
101 Cherry Street
Burlington
VT 05401-4405
USA

www.ashgate.com

British Library Cataloguing in Publication Data
Stein, Gregory M., 1961-
  Modern Chinese real estate law : property development in an
  evolving legal system. -- (Law, property and society)
  1. Real property--China. 2. Land tenure--Law and
  legislation--China. 3. Real estate business--China.
  I. Title II. Series
  346.5'1043-dc23

Library of Congress Cataloging-in-Publication Data
Stein, Gregory M., 1961-
  Modern chinese real estate law : property development in an evolving legal system / Gregory M. Stein.
     p. cm. -- (Law, property and society)
  Includes bibliographical references and index.
  ISBN 978-0-7546-7868-7 (hardback) -- ISBN 978-0-7546-9714-5 (ebook)
  1. Real property--China. 2. Land use--Law and legislation--China.
  I. Title.
  KNQ683.S74 2011
  346.5104'3--dc23

2011036990

ISBN 9780754678687 (hbk)
ISBN 9780754697145 (ebk)

MIX
Paper from
responsible sources
FSC® C018575

Printed and bound in Great Britain by the
MPG Books Group, UK.

In loving memory of

*Edwin R. Stein (1930–2010)
and
Rita A. Kelleher (1915–2010)*

Contents

Acknowledgments   ix

PART I: INTRODUCTION

1   The Excitement of Modern China   3

2   Contrasting China with the West:
Background History, Preliminary Observations, and Conclusions   17

PART II: THE OPERATION OF CHINA'S REAL ESTATE MARKET

3   The Land Use Right:
Owning the Right to Use Land Without Owning the Land   27

4   Ownership Entities:
Who Owns Land, and How Do They Own It?   45

5   Choosing Where to Build:
The Private Market and Government Pressure   53

6   Demolishing Existing Structures, Relocating Current Residents   61

7   Lenders and Loans: Where Does All the Money Come From?   75

8   Preselling and Reselling of Residential Units   103

9   Commercial Construction and Commercial Leasing   119

10   Infrastructure:
Building and Paying for Roads, Bridges, Subways, and Airports   133

PART III: LAW AND DEVELOPMENT IN CHINA

11   China's Other "Other Path":
Confounding the Predictions of Development Economics   149

| 12 | Harmonizing Law and Development Theory with China's Actual Progress | 169 |

PART IV: CONCLUSION

| 13 | Will the Miracle Continue? | 201 |

Index 205

Acknowledgments

Acknowledgement sections customarily contain expressions of gratitude to those who helped the author write the book. These expressions are more warranted here than is ordinarily the case. As the book itself will make clear, I did not depend as heavily as is typical on traditional doctrinal legal resources, such as cases, statutes, and treatises. This is true for the simple reason that sources such as these are only beginning to be written in the field of Chinese real estate law. My research instead relies extensively on interviews with dozens of Chinese and Western experts on Chinese real estate law. Without their kindness, generosity, and willingness to speak to an inquisitive stranger, I could not have written this book.

Nearly everyone I met was willing to share their views on the Chinese real estate business and Chinese real estate law. They were quite forthright and generally were more than willing to offer criticisms of Chinese law, government, and business practices. Sadly, I cannot thank many of these people by name. In some cases, the people I interviewed expressly asked that I not identify them. Others indicated that I could do so, but I have opted to disregard this suggestion. Rather than naming these people individually, I want to express my deepest thanks to the many people who met with me and shared their insights in an environment in which doing so may create considerable personal and professional risk. This group also includes people who provided me with introductions to other experts and Chinese friends who were willing to serve as translators.

Fortunately, there are others who supported me in various ways to whom I can offer my thanks more personally. The University of Tennessee and its College of Law have been enormously supportive of my teaching and research in China. Deans Tom Galligan, John Sobieski, and Doug Blaze provided moral and financial support. My work was also supported by the W. Allen Separk Faculty Scholarship Fund and the Ben R. Winick Legal Research Fund. My law school colleagues provided many useful suggestions at a series of faculty forums, as did colleagues from the Southeastern Association of Law Schools at its annual meeting in Palm Beach, Florida; the Asian Real Estate Society at its annual meeting in Macau; the University of Missouri; and the Association for Law, Property, and Society, jointly sponsored by the law schools at Georgetown and Syracuse Universities, at its annual meeting at Georgetown Law School.

The UT colleagues and friends with whom I spent time in China—Tim Rogers, Ken Stoner, Yang Zhong, Ilona Leki, Barbara Klinkhammer, John Cofer, Steve Catlett, Gail Bier, and Michael Swift—were great companions and wonderful sounding boards. The terrific staff at the Law College were tremendously helpful in so many ways, including Tammy Neff, Neal Fischer, Sean Gunter, Cindy Farabow,

Beth Ford, Teresa Peterson, Mary Ann James, and CJ Ottinger. Several of my former students provided great assistance of different kinds, including Derrick and Wendy Free, Hannah and Jeff Metzger, Heath Clark, Bill Collins, and Patrick Fiel.

A large number of Fulbrighters and other travelers to China offered me much valuable advice. Thanks to Joyce Palomar, Hon. John Rogers, Stephen Alton, Wenona Whitfield, Dan Guttman, Steve Barnes, Kathy Manning, Jim Connelly, Jeff and Andrea Koch, Susan Sterett, Kathryn Mohrman, Ron Schramm, Gerry Rosenberg and Bonnie Koenig, Dan Borgia, and Andrea McElderry. Thanks as well to the many helpful people affiliated with the Fulbright Scholar Program, the United States Department of State, the American Embassy in Beijing, and the American Consulate in Shanghai, including Dan Saint-Rossy, Bill Shine, David Adams, Salome Hernandez, Peter Gibel, and Peter Cuthbert.

The administration and faculty at Shanghai Jiaotong University Law School were extremely gracious hosts, and I extend my thanks to Deans Tong Zhiwei, Zheng Chengliang, and Ji Weidong, and faculty members including the late Zhou Wei, Wang Hongqin, Xiao Kai, Xu Duoqi, Wang Xi, Xu Donggen, Xu Xiaobing, and Yang Li. Other Chinese scholars were also wonderful hosts. I received helpful guidance from colleagues at three universities with which the University of Tennessee has exchange programs: Li Fengzhang of Shanghai University, Yang Suiquan and Chen Jierong of Sichuan University, and Shen Weixing of Tsinghua University. Han Tie of Nankai University was extremely helpful during a conference jointly sponsored by that university and the Fulbright program. And the faculty and administration of Renmin University of China School of Law, including Dean Han Dayuan and Ding Xiangshun, co-sponsored an outstanding conference in Beijing along with Indiana University School of Law, Indianapolis, Dean Gary Roberts, and Tom Wilson.

A number of Western scholars provided helpful comments, suggestions, and reviews of my work at different stages of this project. I am grateful to Ben Liebman, Don Clarke, Robin Malloy, Rashmi Dyal-Chand, Graham Ferris, Bill Buzbee, Dale Whitman, Jay Weiser, Wilson Freyermuth, Carol Brown and Paul Harris, and Danny and Lisa Bogart.

In addition, my thanks to several American and Chinese scholars who helped to introduce me to Chinese real estate law, or who suggested Chinese experts who might be willing to meet with me. In particular, I am grateful to Pat Randolph, Lou Jianbo, Mo Zhang, John Smagula, Fran Ansley, and Gerald and Jackie Fryxell. And my apologies to anyone I have neglected to include here.

My work in this book draws on several articles that I have previously published in academic journals and elsewhere. My thanks to the editors of the *UCLA Pacific Basin Law Journal*, the *Missouri Law Review*, *Probate and Property*, the *Berkshire Encyclopedia of China*, the *Cornell Real Estate Review*, and the *San Diego International Law Journal* for their fine editorial review and cite-checking, and for deciding to publish my work in the first place!

Finally, I could not have written this book without Jeanette Kelleher's ideas, suggestions, reviews of drafts, support, encouragement, and love.

PART I
Introduction

Chapter 1
The Excitement of Modern China

The Excitement of Modern China

China's development during the past quarter-century has been astonishing. Outside observers marvel at China's ability to maintain double-digit economic growth year after year while expressing concern about the West's rising trade imbalance with this important partner.[1] Western consumers enjoy lower and lower prices for Chinese-made goods ranging from T-shirts to iPads, while American manufacturers decry the ability of Chinese factories to underprice their few surviving American competitors. Trading partners welcome China into the World Trade Organization[2] while wondering what effect that nation's economic expansion will have on the price and availability of critical commodities, particularly oil.[3] Meanwhile, China is in the puzzling position of developing raucous free markets while still nominally subscribing to Communist ideology.[4]

---

1 See, e.g., *Bamboo Capitalism*, THE ECONOMIST, Mar. 12, 2011, at 13 (lead article in issue entitled "Bamboo Capitalism: The Rise of Entrepreneurial China" that contains four stories devoted to China); *How to Make China Even Richer*, THE ECONOMIST, Mar. 25, 2006, at 11 (lead article in issue entitled "Special Issue on China's Reform Tasks: How to Make China Even Richer" that contains eight stories devoted to China); Fareed Zakaria et al., *Does the Future Belong to China?*, NEWSWEEK, May 9, 2005, at 26 (lead article in issue entitled "Special Report: China's Century" that contains nine stories devoted to China).

2 See generally RANDALL PEERENBOOM, CHINA'S LONG MARCH TOWARD RULE OF LAW 492–96 (2002) (discussing the immediate effects and the likely future implications of China's accession to the World Trade Organization, along with continuing reasons for concern).

3 See, e.g., Clifford Krauss, *Charting China's Energy Explosion*, N.Y. TIMES "GREEN" BLOG, Nov. 9, 2010, http://green.blogs.nytimes.com/2010/11/09/charting-chinas-energy-explosion/ ("China's push for rapid economic development will dominate global energy markets and be the single biggest force in spurring higher oil prices and carbon dioxide emissions linked to climate change over the next quarter-century"); Jad Mouawad, *Outlook on the Economy: With Oil Prices Off their Peak, Are Supplies Assured?*, N.Y. TIMES, Dec. 5, 2005, at C10 ("In 2004, global oil consumption rose 3.7 percent, ... a pace that surprised analysts and oil executives. China alone accounted for a third of that growth, its demand for oil up 15 percent."); Keith Bradsher & Christopher Pala, *China Ups the Ante in its Bid for Oil*, N.Y. TIMES, Aug. 23, 2005, at C1 ("One of China's state-owned oil companies may still be smarting from its failure to acquire Unocal this summer. But another Chinese oil giant showed on Monday that this country is still snapping up assets to satisfy its hunger for energy.").

4 See XIANFA [CONSTITUTION] pmbl. (2004) (China) ("The basic task of the nation is to concentrate its efforts on socialist modernization by following the road of Chinese-style socialism.").

Nowhere is this tension more evident than in China's real estate sector. Real estate developers are building award-winning office towers, modern shopping malls, and five-star hotels, and tens of millions of urban families are scraping together the money to buy their own apartments.[5] These developers have been meeting these residential needs by replacing decaying urban housing stock while also adding new units to house the tens of millions of workers who have migrated from rural areas to cities. The nation has also built or rebuilt its infrastructure, from roads and bridges to subway systems and airports.

Shanghai, China's key financial center located near the mouth of the Yangtze River, is said to be the home to one-fifth of the world's construction cranes, which local residents refer to as China's national bird.[6] Developers are ordering structural steel at a rate that is causing shortages and price increases around the globe. Shanghai residents speak of little else but their desire to purchase residential apartments as soon as possible, so as not to miss out on a bonanza that may not recur in their lifetimes.[7] All of this activity is particularly remarkable given that the government is firmly controlled by a single political party that remains Communist at least in name, Communist doctrine continues to prohibit the private ownership of real property, and all land in China thus remains owned by the state or by agricultural collectives. This doctrinal confusion does not seem to be holding back the real estate market, particularly in China's major cities, which have been flourishing for most of the last two decades.

---

5 See, e.g., Yan Song & Chengri Ding, *Conclusion*, in URBANIZATION IN CHINA: CRITICAL ISSUES IN AN ERA OF RAPID GROWTH 287, 287 (Yan Song & Chengri Ding eds., 2007) ("China will complete in several decades the urbanization process that took Western developed countries several hundred years."); David Barboza, *China Builds its Dreams, and Some Fear a Bubble*, N.Y. TIMES, Oct. 18, 2005, at A1 ("This year alone, Shanghai will complete towers with more space for living and working than there is in all the office buildings in New York City").

6 Many observers are particularly struck by this prevalence of construction cranes in Shanghai. *See, e.g.*, PAMELA YATSKO, NEW SHANGHAI: THE ROCKY REBIRTH OF CHINA'S LEGENDARY CITY 26 (2001) ("Shanghai embarked in 1992 on what has to be one of the biggest building sprees the world has ever seen. From the top of the Hilton Hotel, which in 1995 was still one of the tallest buildings in the city, the horizon yielded more tower cranes in every direction than the eye could count.").

7 The changes in China's real estate markets since the late 1980s are noteworthy. *See* Li Ling Hin, *Pricing of Land in China's Reforms*, in THE IMPACT OF CHINA'S ECONOMIC REFORMS UPON LAND, PROPERTY AND CONSTRUCTION 49, 55 (Jean Jinghan Chen & David Wills eds., 1999) (noting that "[b]efore 1987 the portion of the real estate industry in the GNP of the PRC was only around 3–4 percent, which was substantially lower than most of the East European socialist countries."). Even as early as 1999, the changes were dramatic. "The emergence of real estate markets in China to their current stage of development has been nothing short of astonishing particularly in the absence of any concept of market structure." Keith McKinnell & Anthony Walker, *China's Land Reform and the Establishment of a Property Market: Problems and Prospects*, in THE IMPACT OF CHINA'S ECONOMIC REFORMS UPON LAND, PROPERTY AND CONSTRUCTION, *supra*, at 26, 46.

The Dearth of Property Laws in the 1980s and 1990s

Westerners tend to assume that a stable legal system is a precondition to this type of robust development and that property is the "guardian of all other rights." After all, why would anyone make a substantial investment in Chinese real estate if the nation did not appear to afford legal protection to property rights, did not make clear what an owner's contractual remedies were, did not have a developed bankruptcy law, and provided a judiciary that was less than transparent?

Nonetheless, while China has adopted numerous written laws and regulations since the 1980s, property law has lagged behind other areas of civil law. The first Chinese law focusing specifically on property rights did not become effective until October 1, 2007, which means that China's breakneck real estate development during the preceding two decades occurred in a nation with no published law of real estate.[8] China has only haltingly begun to adhere to international rule-of-law standards.[9] Moreover, there still is heavy reliance in China on *guanxi*, or personal relationships and connections.[10] Chinese property rights also are limited by communitarian considerations in ways that are unfamiliar and surprising to many Westerners. China had few laws regulating property during this time of extraordinary growth, and property law as it has actually been practiced diverges from these published legal rules. Thus, those who have been buying, selling, and lending against Chinese real estate during this era have been operating in a world of significant legal uncertainty.[11]

Despite this shortage of laws relating to property, private and public investors have spent hundreds of billions of dollars investing in real estate in a nation that, during most of this period, had no formal property law. Investors purchased and improved assets without knowing just how much legal protection those assets

---

8 Wuquan Fa [Property Rights Law] (promulgated by the Standing Comm. Nat'l People's Cong., Mar. 16, 2007, effective Oct. 1, 2007) (China). While the Property Rights Law bears an effective date of 2007, China had previously enacted other laws affecting certain legal rights to property. *See infra* notes 334–42 and accompanying text.

9 *See, e.g.*, PEERENBOOM, *supra* note 2, at 20 ("[T]he notion that the PRC economy will be able to sustain economic growth without further legal reforms that bring the system into greater compliance with the basic requirements of a thin conception of rule of law is doubtful.").

10 For a more detailed discussion of *guanxi*, see *infra* notes 37–40 and accompanying text.

11 Yan Song, Gerrit Knaap & Chengri Ding, *Housing Policy in the People's Republic of China: An Historical Review*, *in* EMERGING LAND AND HOUSING MARKETS IN CHINA 163, 175 (Chengri Ding & Yan Song eds., 2005) ("Progress is impeded by the lack of an appropriate legal framework .... China's privatization has emphasized deregulation and decentralization, but a comprehensive legal framework for regulation of economic behavior in the emerging housing market has not yet formed."); *cf.* AMY L. SOMMERS & KARA L. PHILLIPS, REAL PROPERTY IN CHINA: A GUIDE TO FOREIGN INVESTMENT 35 (suggesting that the ambiguity in China's legal system has helped to foster innovative practices).

enjoyed, while banks lent money with only imperfect assurance that they would be repaid. How can a huge nation modernize so rapidly and dramatically when its legal system furnishes so much ambiguity? And how can all of this happen in a nation that still purports to subscribe to socialist ideology?

The Goals of this Book

This book offers a detailed account of how the Chinese real estate market actually operates in practice, from both legal and business perspectives. My goals are twofold. First, I seek to establish and describe how the Chinese real estate market, with so few written laws, actually functions. How do real estate professionals operate on such a large scale when they are not sure what the applicable law is or how it will be applied? Second, I aim to address the broader question of how a huge nation can achieve such dramatic levels of economic development so rapidly while its legal system is still so unsettled. In what ways does China force us to reconsider the traditional model of economic growth and expansion, which assumes that legal and institutional development is a prerequisite to economic growth?

In four visits to China since 2003, I have interviewed dozens of Chinese and Western experts who are currently taking part in what can be described without exaggeration as one of the greatest real estate booms in world history.[12] My conversations with these real estate developers, bankers, government officials, judges, practicing lawyers, real estate consultants, economists, real estate agents, law professors, business professors, law students, and recent homebuyers provide critical insights into how a major nation is quickly transforming itself from an economic backwater into a self-styled "socialist market economy."

Although I also rely on more traditional methods of legal scholarship throughout this book, a straightforward doctrinal approach would be incomplete and misleading. I quickly realized that I could develop an accurate grasp of how China's real estate market operates in practice only from those who are working in that market. Chinese real estate and business laws are still in an early stage of development, Chinese legal and economic institutions are evolving rapidly, and there is an intensely strong cultural tradition of reliance on personal relationships rather than rule-of-law principles. My goal is to establish how particular aspects of Chinese real estate practice are maturing with what appears to be tremendous success against the backdrop of a young legal system.[13]

---

12   China's growth is not restricted to the real estate sector. *See, e.g.*, C. FRED BERGSTEN, BATES GILL, NICHOLAS R. LARDY & DEREK MITCHELL, CHINA: THE BALANCE SHEET—WHAT THE WORLD NEEDS TO KNOW NOW ABOUT THE EMERGING SUPERPOWER 17 (2006) (describing China's recent revival as "one of the greatest transformations in modern history").

13   "The economic bird has already escaped from its cage, the economic plan, but the legal bird remains in its own cage, although it is stirring and the dimensions of the cage

Research Methods

This book examines Chinese real estate law as it operates in the field, focusing on both legal and business issues. I first had the opportunity to visit China during the spring of 2003, when I served as a Fulbright Scholar at Shanghai Jiaotong University Law School. Amazed by the staggering amount of real estate development in Shanghai, I became curious as to how China was succeeding in building new structures and rebuilding crumbling infrastructure so quickly in a partial legal vacuum. I had never before seen real estate development on the scale I observed during this initial stay and knew immediately that I wanted to understand how this nation—with a legal system, history, and cultural background so dramatically different from those of the United States and other Western nations—was managing to accomplish a complete rebuilding of its structures and infrastructure so rapidly.

I quickly learned that China's legal system, particularly as it pertained to real property, was both new and rapidly changing. China at that time did not yet have a comprehensive property law on the books. Furthermore, the legal landscape was evolving so rapidly that the few legal resources that did exist became obsolete almost immediately.

In addition, the legal academy in China still was recovering from the excesses of the Cultural Revolution, which left China with a shortage of legal academics. Most of the scholars I met seemed to be interested in other legal disciplines, and the burgeoning property field had barely started to attract academic attention. This means that there are few experts in property law and real estate finance in China even as the nation is grappling with important structural questions about how to harmonize private ownership of property with Communist principles.

Those Chinese citizens who have developed expertise in the emerging legal and business systems of China are more likely to be profiting from it than writing treatises about it. In fact, when I began to meet with real estate experts in China, more than one of my counterparts expressed gratitude that I had undertaken this project and indicated how great a need there is for more written material in this field. Many outstanding scholars write about real estate, or about real estate law, or about recent developments in China, and I have relied on their excellent work throughout this book. But I found few scholars—in China or in the West—who have developed expertise in the combined topic of Chinese real estate law. As a result of this shortage, many of my sources in China were extremely curious to hear what I had learned from others with whom I had already spoken and insistent that I send them copies of my finished work. One real estate developer expressed his frustration that not only are there no useful published sources in the field of Chinese real estate law, there also is no one else conducting research with a goal of creating any such sources.

---

may be changing." STANLEY B. LUBMAN, BIRD IN A CAGE: LEGAL REFORM IN CHINA AFTER MAO 2 (1999).

This scarcity of written information led me to conclude that the best way to comprehend the current real estate climate in China and the massive changes in recent decades is to speak to the professionals who are operating within the country. These are the only people who have the expertise and insight that might be found in the United States in a law school faculty or in a bar association library. I returned to China three more times in the ensuing years with the goal of interviewing as many people as I could who were knowledgeable about Chinese real estate law and business as actually practiced.

During these visits, I interviewed more than fifty experts in the real estate field. Legal experts with whom I spoke included practicing lawyers, law professors, judges, government officials in legal positions, and law students. I also met with non-lawyer business experts such as real estate developers, bankers, consultants focusing on the real estate sector, economists, professors of business, real estate agents, and government officials in non-legal positions. Most of these experts are Chinese—some of whom have studied or lived in the West—with the rest being Westerners currently residing in China. Nearly all of the specialists I met were able to converse in English at some level, but in several cases I made use of a translator, including some meetings with persons who speak reasonably good English but felt more comfortable with a translator present. Many of the people with whom I spoke are recent homebuyers themselves.

The classic example of field research into the development of informal norms is Robert Ellickson's *Order Without Law*.[14] Ellickson observes that "rural residents in [California's] Shasta County were frequently applying informal norms of neighborliness to resolve disputes even when they knew that their norms were inconsistent with the law."[15] He concludes from this that, "[i]n many contexts, law is not central to the maintenance of social order."[16] Following Ellickson's suggestion, I sought out a wide range of viewpoints to the greatest extent possible. "Instead of interviewing many persons who saw the problem from the same perspective, I sought out lesser numbers representing many different perspectives."[17]

Finding reliable sources is always a challenge, and this problem is particularly acute in China. As Donald Clarke has observed, "Fieldwork can yield interesting and original results, but unfortunately it typically does not yield representative statistics unless great care is taken in selecting the objects of study."[18] As he explains:

---

14   ROBERT C. ELLICKSON, ORDER WITHOUT LAW (1991).

15   *Id.* at viii.

16   *Id.* at 280; *see also* Robert C. Ellickson, *Of Coase and Cattle: Dispute Resolution Among Neighbors in Shasta County*, 38 STAN. L. REV. 623, 654–55 (1986) (presenting an earlier version of his field-research results).

17   Ellickson, *supra* note 16, at 655.

18   Donald C. Clarke, *Empirical Research into the Chinese Judicial System*, *in* BEYOND COMMON KNOWLEDGE: EMPIRICAL APPROACHES TO THE RULE OF LAW 164, 180 (Erik G. Jensen & Thomas C. Heller eds., 2003) (citation omitted).

> By piecing together information from [a variety of] sources, Chinese and foreign scholars have been able to assemble a picture of certain aspects of the Chinese legal system. That picture is by no means complete. But fleshing it out requires a great deal of thought about what information needs to be gathered and how it can be gathered effectively.[19]

At the same time, my selection of experts was far from random: I intentionally attempted to reach specialists in various different real estate sub-fields, I sought out the most knowledgeable authorities I could identify in each of these sub-fields, and some people declined my interview requests. Furthermore, my sample was skewed by the obvious reality that all of my interview subjects were people comfortable meeting with an inquisitive foreigner. Thus, "cooperative people were undoubtedly somewhat overrepresented in the sample."[20]

I generally asked my initial questions from a long list I had prepared before my first interview, but this list evolved throughout the months of my field research. In addition, I tailored the questions to the expertise of the particular interviewee, both in my pre-interview preparation and as each interview progressed along its unique trajectory. All interviews were face-to-face, with pre-interview logistics and follow-up discussions typically conducted by telephone, e-mail, or text message. I opted not to record my interviews, out of a belief that this approach might encourage more frankness from my counterparts.

While I do not rely on doctrinal legal sources to the degree that is common in many legal monographs or law review articles, this book is also not a journalistic or anthropological account. To the extent I have been able to identify more traditional doctrinal works, I have consulted and used these sources as a method of corroborating or challenging the information I gleaned from my interviewees. These works include both primary sources, such as the Chinese Constitution and Chinese statutes, and secondary sources, and I cite these works throughout this book. My overall goal was to merge my field work with more traditional research into a coherent and accurate picture of China's real estate market. Where I have unearthed discrepancies between interviews and published sources, I have so noted. These discrepancies may reflect the fact that the application of published laws in China, as described to me by my counterparts, can vary significantly from the text of those laws.[21] Or they might merely reveal faulty memories, intentional

---

19 *Id.* at 167.

20 Ellickson, *supra* note 16, at 655. For an extremely thoughtful discussion of the biases inherent in this type of information-gathering about the Chinese legal system, see Benjamin L. Liebman, *Watchdog or Demagogue? The Media in the Chinese Legal System*, 105 COLUM. L. REV. 1, 11–14 (2005). Liebman observes that personal introductions are critically important when conducting field research in China, a fact that unavoidably leads to biases that can affect research results. *Id.* at 13.

21 Even when written laws apply in China, they are not always readily accessible. *See, e.g.*, PEERENBOOM, *supra* note 2, at 246 ("The lack of centralized records makes it

misinformation, or other inaccuracies on the part of the speaker, the published source, or me.

A newcomer to the law of most Western nations can learn much by reading statutes, cases, treatises, and academic articles. China offers fewer resources of these types, and written sources do not completely capture the current state of the Chinese legal system. Thus, the book that follows necessarily differs from many of the more traditional works that appear in American legal scholarship. This book is not intended to be an authoritative doctrinal treatise on its subject; by necessity, it is impressionistic. It focuses on Shanghai, with secondary emphasis on Beijing, and thus primarily reflects the current state of real estate law and business in these two major cities. A small percentage of the people I met with were not particularly forthcoming, although I nearly always was surprised at how willing these experts were to meet with a total (and foreign) stranger and to discuss often proprietary aspects of their work. Their forthrightness frequently included direct criticism of government policies, a brave act in a nation where such conduct can subject the speaker to government harassment or worse.

My occasional need to use a translator when interviewing my counterparts introduced barriers, though not always the precise ones I had anticipated. The number of Chinese professionals who speak some level of English is growing. Several people suggested to me that China soon will have more English speakers than the United States, although the average level of fluency for these speakers is plainly much lower. However, because real estate markets are inherently so domestic, real estate lawyers have fewer occasions than other professionals to cross paths with foreign business people and lawyers and thus less need to be able to converse in English. My experience suggests that Chinese real estate lawyers and professionals had somewhat lower levels of English proficiency than many other Chinese lawyers and professionals.

Conversely, many educated Chinese who are fluent in English have little familiarity with Western real estate concepts and terminology. This occasionally led to translation barriers of a different sort. Originally, I assumed that speaking through a translator would lead to two primary barriers. First, it would create a leak of information that is transmitted from speaker to translator and then to listener, as any childhood player of "Telephone" would expect. Second, there would be the accompanying delays that tend to stilt conversation and reduce spontaneity and casual interaction. In fact, the main barrier was that my translators were often less familiar with real estate finance concepts than either of the two people for whom they were translating. My real estate counterpart and I frequently had to have side discussions with our common translator to ensure that he or she was properly

---

difficult to know exactly what rules apply at any given time in any given place.") (footnote omitted). And even when these laws are available, they may be vague, as is often the case in other civil law countries. *Id.* at 251. On the overall growth of law and legislation in China in recent years, see Stanley Lubman, *Looking for Law in China*, 20 COLUM. J. ASIAN L. 1, 6–7 (2006).

comprehending and translating the real estate concepts and terms that the two of us were more familiar with using, albeit in different languages.

Several of the people with whom I spoke requested that I not attribute their comments to them. One person specifically asked me not to take written notes during our conversation, which took place in a public coffee-house; I reconstructed the conversation in my notebook immediately after our meeting concluded. Out of respect for the generosity of my conversation partners, and in recognition of the fact that some of them have strong reasons for not wanting attribution, I have decided to refer to all of my contacts anonymously. In addition, I have occasionally and intentionally been opaque in describing a professional affiliation or a specialty. Although most people I met with expressed no reservations about my identifying them, I do not wish to expose any individual who was kind enough to spend time meeting with me and sharing their expertise to any sort of negative repercussions.

My aim in this book is to provide an up-to-date description of how the actors in the world's most explosive real estate market actually function. China's real estate professionals are still conducting their business in an unruly environment, with the rules evolving as they proceed. That evolution sometimes comes as a response to their prior activities. These professionals cannot fall back on conventional wisdom in a field in which no one has more than a few years of experience, and there are few senior experts who can serve as mentors. They also must conduct business under an authoritarian one-party government that severely limits freedom of expression while attempting to merge free markets and strict government control into a system of "socialism with Chinese characteristics."[22] The legal structure is far from transparent, enforcement of the laws that are on the books is inconsistent, corruption by government officials is widespread, and the rule of law is viewed by some as a Western concept that does not dovetail well with Chinese traditions.[23]

In short, this is a field survey of how the participants in a major and surging industry operate against a background of significant legal and policy ambiguity. I believe this portrayal to be accurate, but I expect that it is incomplete. I assume

---

22 *See, e.g.*, McKinnell & Walker, *supra* note 7, at 46–47 (comparing recent changes in Chinese behavior with the stasis in institutional structure, and quoting Deng Xiaoping's comment, "'The existing political system has now proved to be a formidable constraint to furthering the course of economic reform.'"); *infra* notes 46–54 and accompanying text (discussing the evolving language of the Chinese Constitution regarding the role of socialism).

23 *See, e.g.*, Lubman, *supra* note 13, at 11 ("The rule of law was alien and unknown [in China] throughout thousands of years of authoritarian rule."). Western observers today generally seem to believe that China is well on the road to accepting at least a thin core of rule-of-law principles. Peerenboom also notes, however, that some scholars, particularly those from the Critical Legal Studies school, believe that Western imposition of rule-of-law concepts on China is a thinly veiled attempt to oppress and inflict injustice. Peerenboom, *supra* note 2, at 164. *But see* Albert H.Y. Chen, An Introduction to the Legal System of the People's Republic of China 3–4 (3d ed. 2004) (maintaining that similar arguments "can probably be more effectively applied to self-proclaimed Marxist-Leninist states than to the Western states of advanced capitalism.").

that this description soon will become obsolete, and I remind the reader that I am attempting to depict Chinese real estate law and business as it is actually practiced, not as it is officially written.

Roadmap

The overall structure of the book is as follows. Part I of the book, which includes this chapter and Chapter 2, offers introductory material and some background information, along with my preliminary observations and conclusions. Part II, encompassing Chapters 3 through 10, discusses specific sub-topics within Chinese real estate law and practice and examines each of these sub-topics in detail. These chapters are designed to provide a thorough analysis of how Chinese experts have been managing to function so successfully in a nation with a rapidly changing legal system. Part III, which consists of Chapters 11 and 12, shifts the focus considerably, by discussing conventional law and development theory and its application within China. The traditional theory holds, as noted above, that a firmly established legal structure is an essential precondition to significant economic development. These chapters ask how the theory can be reconciled with China's experience during the past quarter-century. Finally, Part IV offers some conclusions.

More specifically, this chapter has provided an introduction to the overall subject of this book. It has attempted to impart a sense of the wonder that a first-time visitor to China is likely to experience today. That visitor may well ask how an ostensibly socialist nation can exhibit so many of the outward characteristics of a Western country with a firmly established, capitalist economic system. This chapter has also described my research methods and why I selected them and concludes here with a roadmap to the rest of the book.

Chapter 2 completes the introductory portion of the book. It provides an extremely brief description of modern Chinese history. It then proceeds to set forth some initial observations, along with my preliminary conclusions. I present these conclusions at the outset, so that the reader can test them throughout the book as I continue to present the evidence I gathered during the course of my field research in the ensuing chapters.

Chapter 3 is the first of the eight chapters in Part II to examine individual components of the Chinese real estate system. This chapter kicks off the discussion by describing and analyzing the Chinese land use right, which is the fundamental building block of the Chinese real property system. The essential difference between Chinese property law and that of Western nations is that private citizens may not own land in China. The new property law officially recognizes the land use right, a device by which private parties may acquire the right to use government-owned land for up to seventy years. The land use right is designed to harmonize the socialist principle of communal land ownership with the reality that much modern Chinese real estate development has been triggered by the profit motive. Any discussion of modern China's real estate system must begin with the land use right.

Chapter 4 turns to the real estate development entities that have become prevalent in China. Public–private joint ventures have come to play a key role in the Chinese real estate market. The private partner typically provides expertise and capital while the public partner contributes land use rights for desirable land. In this way, government entities enjoy some of the profits from developing valuable real estate while also maintaining control over the use of the land within their jurisdiction. This chapter will discuss the legal foundation for these partnerships by describing and discussing the different legal entities that can own and develop real estate in China. It also will provide contrasts with the parallel business entities prevalent in Western legal systems.

The first question these new businesses are likely to face is selection of a site, which is the subject of Chapter 5. Because China's market in land is controlled so completely by the government, those who wish to develop property cannot simply acquire land and then build on it. Rather, developers must work with government entities that wish to see certain types of development in certain places. This process often requires the developer to compromise with government bodies that have agendas that are unrelated to the success of a particular real estate project. Chapter 3 described the legal significance of the land use right, while Chapter 4 presented the ways in which public and private entities jointly participate in the development process. Chapter 5 continues this discussion by focusing on the issues developers face when they wish to obtain land use rights to desirable sites.

One of the most provocative issues in modern Chinese real estate law is the fate of established residents who presently live on parcels that real estate professionals wish to redevelop. This is the subject of Chapter 6. As desirable downtown land is cleared to make way for upscale residences, hotels, and office buildings, those who reside in the existing tenements are forced to exit and receive only modest stipends in exchange. Left with only small cash awards, these urban dwellers are forced to move to the outskirts of their cities. This process also leads to the destruction of stable, if poor, neighborhoods. The controversial process of demolition and relocation has led to violent public protests in China. Chapter 6 will examine the process as it is supposed to work and the problems and protests to which it has led.

Chapter 7 continues the examination of Chinese real estate law in actual practice by focusing on the lending process. The Chinese banking system, unlike parallel systems in the West, is dominated by state-owned and state-controlled lending institutions. Rather than looking solely at the economics of a proposed project, as shareholders of Western banks demand, these institutions focus as well on the social and political desirability of a potential new development. This can lead to construction of buildings that are politically necessary and socially worthwhile. However, the rental or sales proceeds from these developments may prove inadequate to repay their developers' loans. In short, Chinese banks are instruments of state policy, providing the financial resources needed for development but displaying little concern with the bottom line.

Chapter 8 turns its attention to urban residential units and the process by which buyers acquire them. Demand for these units has been so intense that developers often can sell the units before even breaking ground on construction. These developers are in a position to demand that their buyers pay a significant portion of the purchase price as construction is progressing. This presale structure creates significant problems for buyers and their lenders. A purchaser of a new unit must come up with a large portion of the purchase price before the unit is ready for occupancy, while still having to pay the carrying costs for her current residence. And to the extent this purchaser plans to borrow the acquisition funds, she does not yet own a unit that she can mortgage to her lender. The presale process thus raises important legal and financial questions for all parties involved in the process of urban residential development.

From the residential construction process, Chapter 9 turns to the processes of commercial construction and commercial leasing. This chapter examines the actual construction process in China and discusses differences between Chinese and Western methods. The discussion emphasizes the speed with which Chinese projects can be designed and built and provides contrasts with the corresponding Western approach. The chapter also compares Chinese and Western commercial leases.

Chapter 10 concludes Part II, which is the portion of the book that focuses on different fields within the overall real estate umbrella. It also completes the discussion of construction by turning to infrastructure. The chapter begins by noting once again the hazy line between public and private construction in a nation in which the notion of private property is so new. From there, the chapter turns to the construction of infrastructure. In an effort to modernize rapidly, China has had to renovate and expand its infrastructure to a significant degree. In the last two decades, for example, Shanghai has built a modern airport, a multi-line subway system, bridges and tunnels across the Huangpu River, and numerous double-decker highways. This chapter focuses on the financing of these huge infrastructure projects, including discussion of the "Build–Operate–Transfer" process that is also beginning to be employed in some Western nations.

The next two chapters of the book constitute Part III. These chapters introduce and analyze law and development theory. Chapter 11 begins by examining the traditional theory of law and development. Stated most succinctly, this theory holds that legal and institutional development must precede economic growth. Without stable laws, particularly property and contract laws, investors will not have sufficient confidence to invest, and the economic system will not be in a position to mature. Yet the chapters in Part II consistently highlighted the extent to which China has been able to revitalize its real estate market during the past two decades. This renaissance has occurred despite the absence of a strong real estate law, the scarcity of other important rule-of-law institutions, heavy reliance on personal connections, and considerable corruption.

Chapter 11 examines the theory itself and some of the leading commentary on it. Some of this commentary appears to argue that the type of development recently observed in China could never happen. The chapter then revisits many of the topics discussed in Part II, as a means of appraising the extent to which recent Chinese economic history seems to contradict the theory's predictions, at least superficially.

Chapter 12 continues the discussion of law and development theory by seeking to harmonize China's recent development with the predictions of the theory. To the extent that the two are not in accord, the chapter seeks possible explanations as to why China seems to disprove the model so far. The theory may be wrong. The theory may be partially correct but in need of refinement. China may, in fact, be behaving as the theory predicts. China may be too different from the Western nations in which the theory developed for the theory to apply well there. China may still have too many of the features of a Communist nation to be a suitable test case for the theory. And most generally of all, the theory is just a theory, and no generalized model such as this can be expected to fit any given nation perfectly.

Part IV, consisting of Chapter 13, offers my concluding thoughts. It summarizes the different ways in which written laws and actual practices have merged to create a particularized Chinese system that has been surprisingly successful so far. It revisits the preliminary conclusions I set forth in Chapter 2 and tests them against the evidence I developed in Part II. And it looks to the future and suggests possible reforms from which China might benefit.

Chapter 2
Contrasting China with the West: Background History, Preliminary Observations, and Conclusions

Background History

Show me a Chinese centenarian and I will show you a person who has lived through unbelievable change in her lifetime. She will have been born soon after the fall of the Qing Dynasty, with the Last Emperor succumbing to the republican revolution of 1911.[24] A quarter-century of upheaval followed, marked by four years of a shaky republic, twelve years of regional control by warlords, and the establishment of the Nationalist government in 1928, alongside the growth of the Communist Party.[25] Nationalist control of much of China gradually eroded as invading forces from Japan gained ground. The Japanese ruled the northern and eastern portions of China for nearly a decade.[26] Four years of uncertainty and civil war followed the departure of the Japanese.[27] Then came more than a quarter-century of Mao Zedong's rule. These years were difficult and often brutal, and they were marked ultimately by the nationalization of all land in China.

Jonathan Spence observes that early land reform efforts were extremely violent but intentionally incomplete.[28] Although some Chinese land was nationalized immediately after the establishment of the People's Republic in 1949, much

---

24 The revolution "was triggered by an accidental bomb explosion" on October 9, 1911. JONATHAN D. SPENCE, THE SEARCH FOR MODERN CHINA 262 (1990). Puyi, the last emperor of the Qing Dynasty, abdicated on February 12, 1912. *Id.* at 267; PATRICIA BUCKLEY EBREY, THE CAMBRIDGE ILLUSTRATED HISTORY OF CHINA 266 (1996).

25 EBREY, *supra* note 24, at 266–67, 273–78. For a discussion of the early days of the Chinese Communist Party, see JOHN KING FAIRBANK & MERLE GOLDMAN, CHINA: A NEW HISTORY 275–78 (enlarged ed. 1998); for a discussion of Mao Zedong's rise, see *id.* at 301–05.

26 SPENCE, *supra* note 24, at 443–83; EBREY, *supra* note 24, at 282, 284–86. At the peak of Japan's power, a majority of China's population lived in land controlled by Japan. FAIRBANK & GOLDMAN, *supra* note 25, at 312.

27 SPENCE, *supra* note 24, at 484–513; EBREY, *supra* note 24, at 286–90.

28 SPENCE, *supra* note 24, at 490–92 (estimating that at least one million landlords and family members of landlords were killed during the early stages of Chinese land reform, but noting that rich peasants often were left alone so that adequate food production could be maintained).

of it was not, especially in urban areas. As late as 1955, the private sector still provided two-thirds of the housing stock in Shanghai.[29] The final stages in the land nationalization process arguably did not occur until 1982, six years after the death of Mao Zedong.[30]

This progression of land nationalization started to reverse itself with the death of Mao and the subsequent ascension to power of Deng Xiaoping. Having completed its nationalization of the ownership of all real property in China, the government now took steps to allow private citizens to control the use of land, by granting long-term land use rights to those who wished to develop the real estate. The Chinese Constitution of 1982 was amended in 1988 to allow for the creation of transferable land use rights, and the Land Administration Law was adopted in 1986 and revised in 1998 and 2004.[31] A market-based economy also began to reappear during this time. In his final years at China's helm, Deng sparked the re-ignition of China's economy with his "reform and opening" policy, and the Chinese economy has grown at breakneck speed since the early 1990s.

Shanghai, a major international city that had been stuck in neutral for decades, began to re-emerge during the 1990s. In the years since Deng catalyzed the reopening of China's economic system, Shanghai has seen the construction of nine of the world's one hundred tallest buildings, including the Shanghai World Financial Center, the tallest building in mainland China and the third tallest in the world, for now.[32] The government initiated the development of the Pudong New Area, just across the Huangpu River from downtown Shanghai, in effect building a city of nearly three million people right next to the previously existing city of Shanghai in less than fifteen years.[33] Shanghai is stunning not just for its new steel-

---

29 Song, Knaap & Ding, *supra* note 11, at 164.

30 PATRICK A. RANDOLPH JR. & LOU JIANBO, CHINESE REAL ESTATE LAW 11 (2000) (observing that some Chinese scholars contend that the nationalization of all land in China was not completed until 1982).

31 For a more detailed discussion of these legal developments, see *infra* notes 46–54 and accompanying text; *see also* Dale A. Whitman, *Chinese Mortgage Law: An American Perspective*, 15 COLUM. J. ASIAN L. 35, 37–40 (2001) (offering a thorough and succinct summary of relevant Chinese real estate law principles).

32 *Official World's 200 Tallest High-Rise Buildings*, EMPORIS, http://www.emporis.com/en/bu/sk/st/tp/wo/ (last visited July 18, 2011). Of the world's 200 tallest buildings, 22 are in Dubai, 16 are in Hong Kong, 15 are in New York, 14 are in Chicago, and 13 are in Shanghai. *Id.* Emporis ranks Shanghai's skyline as the world's seventh most impressive, behind those of Hong Kong, New York, Chicago, Singapore, São Paulo, and Seoul, using a somewhat arbitrary formula that assigns progressively larger numbers of points for taller and taller buildings. *Emporis Skyline Ranking*, EMPORIS, http://www.emporis.com/en/bu/sk/st/sr/ (last visited July 18, 2011).

33 "[T]otal housing investment in Shanghai in 1997 was more than 190 times that in 1978." Xing Quan Zhang, *Development of the Chinese Housing Market*, *in* EMERGING LAND AND HOUSING MARKETS IN CHINA, *supra* note 11, at 183, 183. For a more detailed discussion of the rapid development of Pudong, see *infra* notes 328–33 and accompanying text.

and-glass structures or its handful of signature skyscrapers, but for its astonishing number of ordinary thirty- and forty-story buildings packed together. It is a city both vertical and horizontal, expanding relentlessly upward and outward at the same time and at an ever-accelerating pace.

Preliminary Observations and Conclusions

Before beginning the more detailed discussion of the coming chapters, it will be valuable for me to set forth here several of my preliminary observations about China's real estate markets, as a means of highlighting the themes of the discussion that follows. These points merit emphasis at the outset, because they differ significantly from what a Western lawyer or business person might predict based on their domestic experience. Thus, these observations serve to remind the reader that the assumptions an American or other Western expert might bring to the more detailed discussion that follows will not necessarily apply in China.

First, it is important to remember that all legal structures and institutions in this area of Chinese law are new and still evolving. Nothing about modern Chinese real estate law is time-tested. "Legal reform has been driven by economic reform, and virtually every element of Chinese law today was either revived or newly created in the course of two decades of extraordinary economic and social change that have begun to transform Chinese society."[34] As a result, lawyers and real estate developers frequently operate by trial and error.[35] One lawyer told me that there was so much money to be made in the early days of the real estate market that "if you mess up, try something else." Another attorney spoke about how lawyers would find a model that works and then stick with it.

This is an important point for Western lawyers and other professionals to keep in mind, because it often is so different from their own experience. A Western lawyer typically studies with law professors who may have decades of expertise in their field. In China, few of those experienced law professors existed until quite recently, given the condition of the Chinese educational system during the 1960s and 1970s. And if that professor does happen to exist, she would not have been a professor of real estate law in a nation that affirmatively did not recognize private rights in land during that era. Thus, the Chinese lawyer often must figure things out for himself.

---

34 LUBMAN, *supra* note 13, at 102; *see also* PEERENBOOM, *supra* note 2, at 268 ("Inevitably, rules change more often during periods of transition, leading to instability and inconsistency"). One pair of commentators describe the Chinese market as of 1999 as an "embryo." McKinnell & Walker, *supra* note 7, at 48.

35 "In China today ... rules are being adopted even while new transactions are themselves emerging and before much experience has been accumulated about them." LUBMAN, *supra* note 13, at 175; *see also* SOMMERS & PHILLIPS, *supra* note 11, at 30–32 (describing China's incremental approach to reform of its real estate market).

Second, and following from the first point, there are few seasoned experts in the field of real estate. Just as many of the legal structures and institutions in China are fairly new, so are many of China's lawyers. The most senior real estate professionals in China have plied their trade for perhaps fifteen or twenty years and have experienced only good times. This lack of experience and Gold Rush mentality is visible throughout the real estate market.[36] I asked one developer how he figured out what to do when he undertook his first project. He responded that as he developed his expertise, he relied on feelings, hunches, luck, and timing. These attributes, while unquestionably valuable, would not by themselves have enabled him to qualify for a loan in the United States.

The Chinese law student who graduates from school without having benefited from the same academic mentoring as his Western counterpart may next join a law firm in which every partner has been practicing law for at most two decades. These partners have less legal experience of their own on which to draw and less time in which they might have served as mentors to junior colleagues in need of training and guidance. Moreover, a senior lawyer who has witnessed only strong economic times is unlikely to be adequately prepared for the inevitable downturn.

Third, there is a much greater reliance on personal relationships (*guanxi*) than in Western nations. *Guanxi* refers to the complex web of personal and professional interactions enjoyed by two colleagues. "In China, rights and duties are contextual, depending on the relationship of individuals to each other, and each conflict must be addressed in terms of the alternative consequences with a view to finding a basis for cooperation and harmony."[37] These relationships are significantly more important in China than in the West. "[T]he Chinese emphasis on relationships (guanxi) seems to have had a strength and durability for thousands of years that make it more powerful and pervasive than comparable Western emphases."[38]

The importance of personal interactions in China runs headlong into international demands that China adhere more strongly to rule-of-law principles. Foreign insistence on this issue garners much attention in China but often is given little more than lip service.[39] As Albert Chen notes:

---

36 This same comment could be made about numerous other areas of Chinese life. For example, most automobile drivers have been operating a motor vehicle for a few years or less, and the staid-looking 45-year-old driver of the Shanghai GM sedan that is bearing down on you probably has no more experience behind the wheel and no better judgment than the typical American teenager.

37 LUBMAN, *supra* note 13, at 19 (footnote omitted).

38 *Id.* at 304.

39 In a foreword to an earlier edition of Albert H.Y. Chen's extremely valuable treatise on Chinese law, Jerome Cohen writes, "Mr. Chen keeps a sharp eye on the gap between law and life, between theory and practice. This is an indispensable element in accurately portraying any system, but particularly one where the gap is often very great and so too is the government's effort to conceal it." CHEN, *supra* note 23, at x (quoting from the Foreword to the First Edition, which was published in 1992, by Jerome Alan Cohen).

[T]here is a significant gap between the law-in-the-books and the law-in-action, between enacted rules and actual practice, and between the officially professed ideals and objectives of the legal system on the one hand, and on the other hand its practical management, operation and impact on those who come into contact with it.[40]

"Rule of law" is viewed by many Chinese as a Western construct designed to preserve Westerners' current advantage; it has not yet won its battle against "rule by man."

Fourth, the Chinese legal system is surprisingly undeveloped given how advanced the Chinese property markets have become. In Stanley Lubman's words, "Chinese economic success defies conventional theory, which requires, as one economist has observed, that 'To function anywhere near its potential, any economic system must have property rights that are much better defined and enforced than is true of China's mixed economic system today.'"[41] A casual observer viewing Shanghai's skyline for the first time would assume that Chinese property law has matured significantly since Mao's death, but this assumption is only partly accurate.[42] Those who work within China's real estate market often can only guess how problems that might arise in the future will be resolved.[43] In short, "formal legal institutions ... have to struggle against the cultural and social forces in Chinese society that tend to weaken and undermine property rights."[44]

Legal changes, though rapid, have often been incremental, responding only to the most immediate needs.[45] In a phrase attributed to Deng Xiaoping, the process of reform is comparable to "crossing the river by feeling the stones." Rather than adopting laws and regulations prospectively—an enormous task for a huge country that has been modernizing its legal and economic systems rapidly and dramatically—the Chinese government sometimes drafts them to address

---

40   *Id.* at 202. Chen continues by noting that closing this gap constitutes an important part "of the ongoing project of building a sound legal system for China." *Id.*

41   LUBMAN, *supra* note 13, at 117 (footnote omitted). Lubman continues, "Neither the game nor its rules ... seem to be free from ambiguity." *Id.* at 174. More generally, "because of the absence of a unifying concept of law and a considerable fragmentation of authority, China does not have a legal *system.*" *Id.* at 317 (emphasis in original). *But see* PEERENBOOM, *supra* note 2, at 565–68 (vehemently contesting this last argument).

42   "[T]he question of legal efficacy, or the gap between the law as stated in the statute book and actual behaviour on the part of officials and citizens, presents probably the most serious obstacle for the developers of the Chinese legal system." CHEN, *supra* note 23, at 115–16 (footnote omitted).

43   *See, e.g.*, SOMMERS & PHILLIPS, *supra* note 11, at 35 (noting the challenges that the absence of predictability can pose for sophisticated real estate transactions).

44   LUBMAN, *supra* note 13, at 118.

45   *See, e.g.*, PEERENBOOM, *supra* note 2, at 558–59 (noting the parallels between incremental economic reforms during the 1990s and incremental legal reforms more recently).

the crisis du jour. Meanwhile, China's creative business community continues to formulate new ways to approach new problems without waiting for formal government action. Market participants devise novel economic arrangements that subsequent legal developments expressly permit, or at least tacitly tolerate. As one lawyer put it, "Formerly, if the law doesn't expressly allow it, we won't do it. Now, if the law doesn't expressly prohibit it, we will do it." The business community frequently seems to be prodding the government to act, and China's legal system must struggle mightily to keep up. In short, formal law lags behind actual practice.

Fifth, and closely related to the previous point, China seems to be confounding the predictions of traditional law and development theory. As already noted in the introductory chapter, this theory presupposes that a stable body of law must precede significant levels of economic development. China appears at first glance to disprove these forecasts. The discussion below will introduce the traditional theory and illustrate the many ways in which China is not behaving as the theory predicts. For a variety of reasons that are also explored below, the theory's expectations and the reality of China may not truly be as out of synch as they might at first appear. China, after all, is an unusual nation, and some of China's unique features go a long way toward explaining why this nation appears not to be following the pattern that the theory anticipates.

Sixth, despite some movement by China toward a freer and less regulated market, those who operate within the Chinese legal and economic system still must tolerate a far greater level of government involvement, intrusion, and interference than Western real estate professionals typically experience. The government possesses numerous mechanisms for controlling the operation of markets, and it is quite prepared to use them. Meanwhile, Chinese citizens have been more willing than their Western counterparts to accept this type of government behavior.

More generally, there is a strong linkage between political institutions and the market. Government officials are not particularly responsive to public pressure. There is an overall lack of transparency within the Chinese legal system, including among the judiciary. Citizens have come to take it for granted that the legal effects of an individual's actions may be difficult to predict. In addition, different levels of government do not always agree on the appropriate ways to regulate real estate markets. Local and provincial governments, for instance, enjoy most of the benefits of rapid real estate development, while the central government will bear much of the brunt if a real estate bubble ever bursts.

This high level of government control of the real estate market manifests itself in other ways that threaten to upset social stability. For example, agricultural collectives often lose their property in exchange for compensation that is calculated on the assumption that the highest and best use for the land is agricultural. The government that requisitions the land then can sell land use rights to commercial developers at the current market price for urban property. Thus, the government profits significantly by displacing poor farmers in favor of commercial real estate developers. Long-time urban dwellers may lose their older housing in similar fashion if it is located in neighborhoods that have become ripe for commercial development.

Seventh, Chinese government bodies at all levels are spending phenomenal sums to modernize the nation, particularly its infrastructure. Some of these outlays take the form of direct spending, as when a city uses its own revenues to build a new road. Others take the form of loans, as when a government-backed lending institution provides funds to a separate entity for construction of a bridge, whether or not it expects the loan to be repaid. To some extent, these huge cash expenditures are possible because China serves as the factory floor for so much of the world, selling large quantities of goods to Western consumers. But government bodies also have access to enormous amounts of cash by virtue of their ability to sell off the right to use government-owned land for a fixed period of time. It is important to recognize at the outset that much of this real estate is publicly owned because the government nationalized the private property of previous generations of Chinese landowners without providing fair compensation to them.

Finally, Chinese legal and economic institutions continue to evolve dramatically and rapidly. Chinese citizens are developing more expertise in both business and legal matters. The government of China regularly reverses course and then doubles back again. And foreigners continue to exert influence, both through personal business activities and institutional law reform efforts. There is no indication that the pace of this change in China will slow in the coming years.

PART II
The Operation of China's Real Estate Market

Chapter 3

The Land Use Right: Owning the Right to Use Land Without Owning the Land

The Legal Basis for the Land Use Right

In 1988, China amended Article 10 of its Constitution to read, "The right to the use of land may be transferred in accordance with the law."[46] This provision does not permit the private ownership of land. In fact, the sentence immediately prior to the one just quoted, which dates back to the 1982 adoption of this Constitution, was retained with only conforming changes and now reads: "No organization or individual may appropriate, buy, sell or lease land, or unlawfully transfer land in other ways."[47] And the first two sentences of Article 10 of the Constitution indicate that urban land is owned by the state and that rural and suburban land is owned either by the state or by collectives.[48]

The 1988 amendment does, however, allow the government to grant land use rights for a specific term.[49] Taken together, these provisions make it clear that all land is state- or collective-owned, but that the state now is constitutionally empowered to transfer the right to use land. The central government may exercise ownership rights directly or may act through county and city governments as its surrogates, and it is generally these local-level governments that grant land use rights.[50] This enhanced legal status for property rights was further buttressed by another constitutional amendment in 2004, with the new language stating

---

46 XIANFA art. 10 (2004); *see generally* Gregory M. Stein, *Acquiring Land Use Rights in Today's China: A Snapshot from on the Ground*, 24 UCLA PAC. BASIN L.J. 1, 41–42 (2006).

47 XIANFA art. 10 (2004); *see also* Ming Fa Tong Ze [General Principles of the Civil Law] (promulgated by the Standing Comm. Nat'l People's Cong., Apr. 12, 1986, effective Jan. 1, 1987), art. 73 (China) (stating, "State property shall be owned by the whole people" and "State property is sacred and inviolable").

48 XIANFA art. 10 (2004).

49 In many cases, there are significant differences in authority and policy among local governments, provincial and municipal governments, and the central government. In cases where this difference is significant, I will refer to a specific level of government. When I use the more generic term "government," I am intentionally using it more inclusively to refer to government at any level.

50 *See* RANDOLPH & LOU, *supra* note 30, at 68–70.

that the government must provide compensation when it expropriates land.[51] The Land Administration Law reflects these constitutional changes and provides additional legal support for the granting of land use rights.[52] However, the statutory structure supporting such transfers was not particularly well developed until China's adoption of the Property Rights Law in 2007.[53] In fact, the Property Rights Law itself still leaves important questions unanswered, as the remainder of this chapter will discuss.

Prior to the 1988 constitutional change, some jurisdictions had experimented by leasing the right to use land to private entities. To the extent these precursors to the land use right were legally binding at all, they were enforceable only as contract rights; not until the 1988 constitutional amendments could users of property obtain more stable real estate rights. Albert Chen cites this as an example of a phenomenon that is fairly common in modern China, namely the rapid implementation of desirable new policies that lack any basis in the law existing at the time, followed by the law playing "catch-up."[54] In a legal system evolving as rapidly as China's, it is nearly impossible for policies and laws to develop precisely in tandem. Moreover, local government officials likely were taking advantage of the pre-1988 legal uncertainty to benefit themselves.

The Tension Between Private Property and Marxist Doctrine

By clarifying that private citizens could acquire land use rights but could not actually own the land itself, the Constitution "avoided abandoning the Marxist

---

51 XIANFA art. 10 (2004) ("The State may, in the public interest and in accordance with the provisions of law, expropriate or requisition land for its use and shall make compensation for the land expropriated or requisitioned."); *see generally* SOMMERS & PHILLIPS, *supra* note 11, at 23–30 (providing an overview of these constitutional changes and subsequent statutory developments).

52 *See, e.g.*, Tudi Guanli Fa [Land Administration Law] (promulgated by the Standing Comm. Nat'l People's Cong., June 25, 1986, revised Dec. 29, 1988, Aug. 29, 1998 & Aug. 28, 2004, effective Aug. 28, 2004), art. 2 (China) ("No units or individuals may encroach on or transfer land, through buying, selling or other illegal means. The right to the use of land may be transferred in accordance with law.").

53 Wuquan Fa [Property Rights Law]. Adoption of the Property Rights Law also necessitated the passage of amendments to various existing laws, to conform them to this newer law. *See, e.g.*, Chengshi Fangdichan Guanli Fa [Law on the Administration of Urban Real Estate] (promulgated by the Standing Comm. Nat'l People's Cong., July 5, 1994, revised Aug. 30, 2007, effective Aug. 30, 2007), art. 6 (China) (clarifying that the government can expropriate land but that it must pay compensation; the insertion of this new article required the renumbering of all subsequent articles in the law).

54 CHEN, *supra* note 23, at 117–18.

principle of state ownership."[55] At the same time this mechanism placed local governments in a position in which they could raise enormous amounts of money by selling land use rights. This new revenue source was particularly important after 1994, when national tax reform reduced the resources that had previously been available to local governments, forcing them to search elsewhere for funds.[56] In addition, this structure created an opportunity for a private real estate market to flourish, with the constitutional change presumably designed to afford investors confidence that their real estate investments would enjoy greater legal protection than they had in the past.[57] Post-1988 changes to the Chinese Constitution reflect this tense dichotomy between private ownership and Marxist doctrine. For example, Article 6 was amended in 1999 by the addition of the following sentence:

> During the primary stage of socialism, the State adheres to the basic economic system with the public ownership remaining dominant and diverse sectors of the economy developing side by side, and to the distribution system with the distribution according to work remaining dominant and the coexistence of a variety of modes of distribution.[58]

In fact, this discord between China's socialist past and its desire to become a part of the world economic regime extends beyond constitutional provisions that specifically address property rights.[59] The 1982 Chinese Constitution states that the "basic task of the nation ... is to concentrate its efforts on socialist modernisation."[60] The 1993 constitutional revisions added that this task must be

---

55 LUBMAN, *supra* note 13, at 184; *see also* Chengri Ding & Gerrit Knaap, *Urban Land Policy Reform in China's Transitional Economy*, in EMERGING LAND AND HOUSING MARKETS IN CHINA, *supra* note 11, at 9, 14 ("As a milestone in the evolution of the Chinese Constitution, the 1988 amendment is significant, because it allowed the state to maintain ownership and at the same time promoted land market development without provoking political turmoil.").

56 *See* Joyce Yanyun Man, Siqi Zheng & Rongrong Ren, *Housing Policy and Housing Markets: Trends, Patterns, and Affordability*, in CHINA'S HOUSING REFORM AND OUTCOMES 3, 5 (Joyce Yanyun Man ed., 2011).

57 For a discussion of the extent to which increased security of land tenure may lead to sustainable economic growth, see Joyce Palomar, *Contributions Legal Scholars Can Make to Development Economics: Examples from China*, 45 WM. & MARY L. REV. 1011 (2004); *cf.* Donald C. Clarke, *Economic Development and the Rights Hypothesis: The China Problem*, 51 AM. J. COMP. L. 89 (2003) (discussing the relative importance of security of property and enforcement of contract rights).

58 XIANFA art. 6 (2004).

59 *See, e.g.*, MARTIN HART-LANDSBERG & PAUL BURKETT, CHINA AND SOCIALISM: MARKET REFORMS AND CLASS STRUGGLE 61 (2005) (observing that "the Chinese Communist Party launched a process of economic transformation that has created an economy that has little to do with socialism").

60 XIANFA pmbl. (1982).

accomplished "in accordance with the theory of building socialism with Chinese characteristics."[61] This last phrase was dropped in 2004, in favor of the term "Chinese-style socialism."[62] The clause "socialist market economy" first appeared in this paragraph in 1999.[63] Phrasing of this type is not limited to legal documents emanating from Beijing. For example, the 2004 edition of the *Pudong Yearbook*, an annual publication touting recent accomplishments in the development of the Pudong New Area in Shanghai, states that "Pudong will take [the] lead in basic socialist modernization."[64]

The Property Rights Law, which became effective in 2007, continues to reflect this discord. For example, Article 3 of this law states, "The State shall consolidate and develop unswervingly the public sector of the economy and at the same time encourage, support and guide the development of the non-public sectors of the economy."[65] The Property Rights Law also restates the fact that all land is owned by either the government or agricultural collectives.[66]

Even prior to the law's adoption, the National People's Congress debates over the proposed law exposed serious ideological splits within the Chinese Communist Party, with some arguing for continued rapid development and others responding that this trend is contrary to socialist principles.[67] One noted Chinese

---

61 *Id.* (1993).
62 *Id.* (2004).
63 *Id.* (1999).
64 PUDONG NIAN JIAN 2004 [PUDONG YEARBOOK 2004] 18 (2004).
65 Wuquan Fa [Property Rights Law], art. 3.
66 *Id.* art. 47 (stating, in somewhat circular fashion, "The urban lands are owned by the State. Such rural land and the land on the outskirt of the city as belonging to the State according to law shall be owned by the State."); *see also* McKinnell & Walker, *supra* note 7, at 31 ("According to Marxist theory, land is singled out as incapable of being regarded as a commodity, since it is not a product of man's labour—land exists by itself.").

Other articles in the same chapter confirm state ownership of "mineral resources, waters, [and] sea areas," Wuquan Fa [Property Rights Law], art. 46, most "natural resources," *id.* art. 48, certain "wild animals and plants," *id.* art. 49, "[t]he radio spectrum," *id.* art. 50, certain "cultural relics," *id.* art. 51, "national defence resource[s]," *id.* art. 52, and certain "[p]ublic facilities like railways, roads, electric power, communications and gas pipes," *id.* The new statute clarifies that land "owned by the State" is owned "by the whole people." *Id.* art. 45. Collective-owned property is addressed in numerous places in the new statute. *See, e.g., id.* art. 43 (addressing transfer of agricultural property to construction uses). Note as well that the law prohibits the mortgaging of "[o]wnership of the land." *Id.* art. 184.

The new statute clarifies that certain natural resources are not owned by the state, but rather "are collectively-owned." *Id.* art. 48; *see also id.* arts. 58–63 (elaborating on the types of property that are collectively owned and discussing some attributes of collectively owned property); *id.* art. 184(ii) (generally prohibiting mortgaging of land use rights owned by collectives, even if occupied by "house sites, private plots and private hills").

67 *See* Joseph Kahn, *A Sharp Debate Erupts in China over Ideologies*, N.Y. TIMES, Mar. 12, 2006, at A1 (noting "calls to make 'social equity' the focus of economic policy, replacing the earlier leadership's emphasis on rapid growth and wealth creation"); *see also*

scholar objected strenuously to an earlier draft of the law, stating that its provisions "go against the fundamental stance and principles of Marxism, [and] the CPC's [Communist Party of China's] orientation and principles of socialist legislation."[68] Even the Chinese government's own English-language website refers to the final version of the statute as "the most controversial law since the Communist Party came to power in 1949" and notes that it passed only after an unprecedented seven readings.[69]

Attributes of the Land Use Right

While the 1988 constitutional amendment authorized the granting of land use rights, the State Council established the durational limits by regulation.[70] The government may transfer land use rights to residential property for a term of up to seventy years. For commercial property, the maximum term is forty years. Industrial and other types of land use rights may not be granted for terms in excess of fifty years.

The initial holder of a granted land use right technically is required to develop the land within two years. One statutory section imposes a penalty of up to 20 percent of the fee paid for the land use right if the land is not developed within one year and allows for forfeiture of the land use right if the land is not

---

LUBMAN, *supra* note 13, at 2 ("[G]iven the novelty of the legal institutions created or revived since the late 1970s, it is no wonder that their development has been limited, hesitant, and uncertain.").

68 Gong Xiantian, *A Property Law (Draft) that Violates the Constitution and Basic Principles of Socialism*, EUROPE SOLIDAIRE SANS FRONTIÈRES, Sept. 2006, http://www.europe-solidaire.org/spip.php?article4161. Edward Steinfeld argues that in situations of conflict such as this one, the Chinese government routinely favors "the side of progress" over "hold[ing] the line politically." EDWARD S. STEINFELD, PLAYING OUR GAME: WHY CHINA'S ECONOMIC RISE DOESN'T THREATEN THE WEST 45 (2010).

69 *NPC's Approval of Key Laws Seen As Promotion of Social Justice by Chinese Academics*, GOV.CN CHINESE GOVERNMENT'S OFFICIAL WEB PORTAL, Mar. 16, 2007, http://english.gov.cn/2007-03/16/content_553062.htm; *see also* Jianfu Chen, *China's Civil and Commercial Law Reforms: Context and Transformation*, *in* LAW, WEALTH AND POWER IN CHINA: COMMERCIAL LAW REFORMS IN CONTEXT 109, 128 (John Garrick ed., 2011) (describing the law as "a revolution in legal thought and legal development").

70 Zhonghua Renmin Gongheguo Chengzhen Guoyou Tudi Shiyongquan Churang He Zhuanrang Zanxing Tiaoli [Provisional Regulations on Assigning and Transferring the Urban State-Owned Land-Use Right] (promulgated by the State Council, May 19, 1990, effective May 19, 1990), art. 12 (China); RANDOLPH & LOU, *supra* note 30, at 127–28 (observing that the constitutional amendment authorized the granting of land use rights but that the State Council established the actual durational limits by regulation); *see also* Chengshi Fangdichan Guanli Fa [Law on the Administration of Urban Real Estate], art. 8 (authorizing the granting of land use rights for a fixed number of years).

developed within two years.[71] Many people, however, indicated to me that this rule is frequently ignored; in one expert's straightforward opinion, "Every policy in China, you can change!" Rights holders may pay an additional fee to extend the term beyond two years, may initiate minimal construction before the two-year period expires as a means of formally meeting the use-it-or-lose-it requirement, or may seek extensions of this two-year term, which generally have been readily available. However, several experts did confirm that this rule actually is enforced in practice at least some of the time. In at least some of these cases in which the right has been forfeited, the purchaser of the right did not receive a refund of the purchase price.

One person noted that the Shanghai government has hinted that it may begin to enforce the two-year rule more strictly, as a means of slowing the overheated real estate market and reducing the ability of investors to speculate on land use rights in undeveloped land. In the short run, stricter enforcement of this rule might lead to more intensive development, as rights holders whose two-year terms are nearing expiration begin construction they might otherwise have deferred. But in the long run, those who are considering acquiring land use rights for future construction might be inclined to wait if they fear that the rights they wish to purchase will expire before they are ready to use them. If demand for land use rights began to dry up, prices presumably would drop.

The initial and subsequent non-government holders of land use rights may further transfer them.[72] However, there are limits on this transferability. For example, in an apparent effort to head off speculation in undeveloped land, the law prevents the initial holder of a residential land use right from transferring the right to a third party until it has constructed at least 25 percent of the proposed structure.[73] However, one scholar who mentioned this requirement to me also noted that this rule is frequently disregarded, in part because of uncertainty as to exactly how much construction has been completed on any given project. In addition, developers can circumvent the rule easily by transferring all of the stock in the entity that owns the land use right rather than by transferring the land use right itself. Some real estate professionals also advised me that in parts of China, the purchaser is prohibited from using borrowed funds for the acquisition of a

---

71 Chengshi Fangdichan Guanli Fa [Law on the Administration of Urban Real Estate], art. 26.

72 Wuquan Fa [Property Rights Law], art. 143 ("Except as otherwise provided for by law, the owner of the right to the use of land for construction use shall have the right to transfer, exchange, make as capital contribution, donate or mortgage the right to the use of land for construction use."); *see also* RANDOLPH & LOU, *supra* note 30, at 131–32 (discussing the transferability of granted land use rights).

73 *See, e.g.*, Chengshi Fangdichan Guanli Fa [Law on the Administration of Urban Real Estate], art. 39 (prohibiting a grantee from further transferring a land use right before, "for housing construction projects, 25 percent of the total investment has gone through").

land use right, but they were unable to clarify whether this is a legal restriction, a limitation imposed by lenders, or simply common practice.[74]

The issue of registration of land use rights merits further attention, in light of the 2007 Property Rights Law.[75] The new law makes it clear that registration is necessary to establish an owner's right to use land. Article 9 states, "Unless otherwise provided by law, the establishment, modification, transfer and lapse of the right in real property shall only take effect upon registration pursuant to laws," and Article 139 provides that "[t]he right to the use of land for construction use shall be set upon registration."[76]

It is widely believed that the grantee of a land use right may not register that right until the grantee has paid the entire acquisition fee, although at least one of the experts I interviewed disputed this assertion and no statute appears to require advance payment explicitly.[77] One Chinese lawyer indicated to me that the requirement of full payment in advance has recently been modified in some instances, and that some owners have been permitted to pay the fee on a periodic schedule that is similar to regular rent payments. This approach allows the government to pace its receipt of the income from the sale of the land use right.

The provisions of the Property Rights Law also appear to mandate registration of mortgages in all cases.[78] These provisions of the new Property Rights Law take

---

74 *See supra* notes 190–91 and accompanying text.

75 The Property Rights Law addresses registration in numerous sections. Wuquan Fa [Property Rights Law], arts. 9–22, 139.

76 *Id.* arts. 9, 39; *see also* Tudi Guanli Fa [Land Administration Law], art. 12 ("Any change to be lawfully made in land ownership, in the right to the use of land or in the purpose of use of land shall be registered."); Chengshi Fangdichan Guanli Fa [Law on the Administration of Urban Real Estate], art. 36 (requiring registration of the ownership of real estate when it is transferred or mortgaged).

77 Several of the professionals I interviewed made the claim that the entire fee must be paid in advance, as do some published secondary sources. *See, e.g.*, RANDOLPH & LOU, *supra* note 30, at 152 (stating that the fee must be paid in full prior to registration); CAO PEI, REAL ESTATE LAW IN CHINA 72 (1998) (noting that the entire fee for the granting of the land is due when the land use right is granted). However, the only statutory support I could find for this proposition is equivocal. Article 39 of the Law on the Administration of Urban Real Estate provides, "The transfer of real estate with the right of land use shall comply with the following conditions: (1) All the fees in concern with the lease of the right of land use have been paid in accordance with provisions prescribed by the contract for the lease and the certificate of the right to use the land has been obtained." Chengshi Fangdichan Guanli Fa [Law on the Administration of Urban Real Estate], art. 39. This statutory language implies that the contract might provide for payments over time.

78 Wuquan Fa [Property Rights Law], art. 187 ("Where a party mortgages assets [including houses and land use rights], he shall register the mortgaged property, and the mortgage contract shall become effective as of the date of registration."). *But see id.* art. 199(iii) (referring to claims secured by unregistered mortgages).

precedence over any contradictory portions of the earlier Guaranty Law.[79] The Guaranty Law also seemed to mandate recordation of mortgages, if somewhat more obliquely.[80]

Distinctions Between the Chinese Land Use Right and the Western Ground Lease

The Chinese granted land use right should not be confused with the ground lease familiar to Western real estate lawyers.[81] As the previous discussion has illustrated, the two devices present considerable differences. The land to which use rights are granted must be developed within a fixed amount of time or the right is forfeited. There are official limits on the transferability of land use rights. In at least some parts of China, the purchaser evidently may not use borrowed funds for the acquisition of a land use right. The price for the land use right apparently must be paid entirely in advance, which is rarely the case with a ground lease. Moreover, landlord–tenant law generally does not apply to land use rights.[82]

The Property Rights Law makes it clear that the holder of the land use right also must own the improvements constructed on that land. Article 142 of the Property Rights Law states, "The ownership of the building, structure and their accessory facilities built by the owner of the right to the use of land for construction use shall belong to such owner, unless there is evidence to the contrary sufficient to

---

79 *Id.* art. 178 ("In case of any discrepancy between the Guarantee Law [sic] of the People's Republic of China and this Law, this Law shall prevail."); *cf. id.* art. 8 ("Where there are laws stipulated otherwise in respect of property rights, such laws shall be observed.").

80 *See* Danbao Fa [Guaranty Law] (promulgated by the Standing Comm. Nat'l People's Cong., June 30, 1995, effective Oct. 1, 1995), art. 41 (China) ("Where a party mortgages [certain types of] property ..., he shall register the mortgaged property, and the mortgage contract shall become effective as of the date of registration."); *id.* art. 43 ("Where a party mortgages other [types of] property, he may of his own will, register the mortgaged property, and the mortgage contract shall become effective as of the date of execution."). There are strong incentives to register mortgages even when registration seems to be optional under Article 43 of the Guaranty Law. *See id.* ("If a party does not register the mortgaged property, he may not defend against the claims of third party [sic].").

81 *See* Stein, *supra* note 46, at 42–43 (noting similarities and differences between the Chinese land use right and the Western long-term ground lease); Whitman, *supra* note 31, at 38 (same); *see also* RANDOLPH & LOU, *supra* note 30, at 18–19 (expressing the belief that the Chinese land use right is derived from German civil law concepts and not from the common law ground lease).

82 RANDOLPH & LOU, *supra* note 30, at 125–26 (emphasizing that most of Chinese landlord–tenant law does not apply to holders of granted land use rights); *cf.* INVESTMENT IN GREATER CHINA: OPPORTUNITIES & CHALLENGES FOR INVESTORS 105 (CCH Asia eds., 2003) (observing that the Chinese land use right displays elements of both a leasehold interest and a contract right).

invalidate that."[83] Similarly, Article 146 provides, "Where the right to the use of land for construction use is transferred, exchanged, made as a capital contribution or donated, the buildings, structures and their accessory facilities affiliated with such land shall be disposed of accordingly."[84] Conversely, Article 147 states, "Where the buildings, structures and their accessory facilities affiliated with a land for construction use is transferred ..., the right to the use of such land for construction use as being occupied by such buildings, structure and their accessory facilities shall be disposed of accordingly."[85] And Article 182 clarifies, "Where houses are mortgaged, the land use right to the construction lot occupied by the houses shall be mortgaged at the same time. Where the land use right to the construction lot is mortgaged, the houses fixed on the land shall be mortgaged at the same time."[86]

As this discussion demonstrates, the Chinese land use right is both similar to and different from the Western ground lease. Because Chinese land can be owned only by the government or agricultural collectives and because ownership of a land use right carries with it ownership of the improvements on that land, the granting of a land use right by definition severs ownership of the land from ownership of the building constructed on that land, just as the Western ground lease does. But because the owner of the improvements on Chinese land is required to hold the underlying land use rights, and because those rights most likely have to be paid for in full at the outset, the developer must incur the capital expense of acquiring the land use right in its entirety at the beginning of the construction process. The ground lease structure, by contrast, allows the developer to avoid all or most up-front land acquisition costs. The Chinese land use right, in short, is not a financing device.

Government Sale of Land Use Rights

The process for the government's sale of a land use right, like so many other procedures in Chinese law, derives from a combination of written law and actual practice.[87] Shanghai's procedure for the granting of land use rights on state-owned land serves as a useful illustration of these practices. The government initiates

---

83   Wuquan Fa [Property Rights Law], art. 142.
84   *Id.* art. 146.
85   *Id.* art. 147.
86   *Id.* art. 182; *see also* Chengshi Fangdichan Guanli Fa [Law on the Administration of Urban Real Estate], art. 32 (same); *see generally* 2 JAMES M. ZIMMERMAN, CHINA LAW DESKBOOK 842 (3d ed. 2010) (discussing this issue in the context of registration of real estate transfers).
87   *See* Chengshi Fangdichan Guanli Fa [Law on the Administration of Urban Real Estate], arts. 12–13 (describing the procedures for the granting of land use rights); *see also* CHEN, *supra* note 23, at 252–53 (discussing the recent historical development of these procedures).

the sale process by deciding on requirements and specifications for a tract. It asks the Department of Land Administration to evaluate the property's value, and this office establishes a minimum price for the land use right. The government publicizes these requirements and specifications and makes the relevant documents available to prospective bidders. Bidders then submit sealed bids. Each bid from a developer is solely a price bid, as the government has already established all of the specifications in advance. Note that Shanghai permits open auctions as well, but these are rarely employed.[88]

Shanghai's government is not required to select the highest bidder, a fact that leads unsuccessful bidders to wonder whether they have been outflanked by corrupt competitors and opens the government up to more generalized charges of cronyism and graft. The government's position, publicized regularly and somewhat defensively, is that it wishes to consider the reputation, experience, skill, and financial strength of each bidder and not just the amount it has bid, as a means of ensuring that the winning bidder is capable of completing the project successfully. While it might appear to the public that the government would benefit the most by selecting the highest bidder and receiving the greatest amount of money for the land use right, the government maintains that a project that is less financially remunerative in the short run but more likely to be completed successfully may end up being more beneficial to the community in the long run.

Despite the municipal government's protestations, prospective bidders who have good personal relationships with highly placed government officials are widely perceived as enjoying an edge; whether they truly do or not is almost immaterial to these popular notions. These perceptions are further enhanced by a belief that the specifications themselves sometimes seem to have been drafted with particular prospective bidders in mind. Similar concerns are raised by the foreclosure process, which is often seen as providing advantages to favored bidders. In many of the discussions I had with Chinese real estate professionals, concerns that bureaucrats with unfettered discretion favor developers with *guanxi* permeated the conversation. As one lawyer put it, even in Shanghai, it never hurts to know someone.

Whatever its lingering flaws, Shanghai's method of auctioning land use rights has improved dramatically and is generally recognized as having improved. While government officials still enjoy substantial discretion, Shanghai's current approach

---

88 More generally, land use rights in China may be sold by negotiated agreement, by invitation of tenders by the government, or by auction. 2 ZIMMERMAN, *supra* note 86, at 833. For a discussion of regulations promulgated in 2002 that affect the acquisition of land use rights, see T. Oliver Yee, *A Bid for a New Future: What Are the Effects and Challenges of the New National Public Bidding Regulations on Land Use Rights Assignment in China?*, 4 WASH. U. GLOBAL STUD. L. REV. 447, 449–51, 455–57 (2005) (noting that new national regulations, modeled on those already in effect in Shanghai, will no longer permit negotiated agreements for transfers of land use rights for business operations, but also observing that there have been difficulties in implementing these regulations).

is a significant advance over the mechanism employed before 2002, under which the municipality would approach several reputable developers and negotiate with them privately before selecting one. Some of the less commercialized provinces apparently still negotiate sales of land use rights in this less transparent manner. Imperfect though they may be, Shanghai's present procedures are widely viewed as among the most impartial in China.[89]

The calculation of the minimum price that the Department of Land Administration undertakes can be a complex one. As a starting point, the floor price should reflect some base value for the land use right itself. But if the government plans to undertake the additional costly tasks of relocating current residents and demolishing existing structures, it will pass the expenses it incurs in undertaking these activities along to the bidders in the form of a higher minimum price.[90] Demolition and resettlement can be controversial, time-consuming, and exceedingly expensive. As a result, many Chinese developers prefer to acquire land that is already vacant. This preference may lead to development on the urban fringe rather than in more heavily populated central locations.

In some cases, the government also factors a third component into the minimum price, reflecting certain infrastructure costs that the redevelopment of the land will necessitate. For example, the bidder may have to foot the bill for facilities specific to the lot, such as utility connections, or for more general social demands, such as a new school or hospital that might now be needed as a result of increased construction in the area that includes the new development. Sometimes, the government adds the cost of these necessary improvements to the minimum price and then uses these funds to develop this infrastructure itself. If it does so, then this last component of the minimum price is loosely analogous to the impact fees that some American jurisdictions impose. In other cases, the government simply requires the purchaser of the land use right to construct this infrastructure on its own, as one of the conditions to acquiring the land use right. In these instances, the requirements imposed on the developer resemble those seen in many American subdivision control laws.

Expiration of Land Use Rights

One obvious question about China's current system of land use rights is what happens to the right and the structures on the land when the term of the right expires. The new Property Rights Law appears to require the government

---

89 See DALI L. YANG, REMAKING THE CHINESE LEVIATHAN: MARKET TRANSITION AND THE POLITICS OF GOVERNANCE IN CHINA 208–13 (2004) (discussing the trend toward the use of auctions in the granting of land use rights). *But see id.* at 211 (describing Shanghai and other municipal governments as "hooked on land revenue"); *supra* note 118 (noting the recent scrutiny of corruption in Shanghai).

90 See *infra* Chapter 6.

to renew the land use right, at least for residential property. Article 149 of the Property Rights Law states, "The term of the right to the use of land for building houses shall automatically renewed [sic] upon expiration," while noting that for other uses, the right "shall be renewed according to laws and regulations upon expiration."[91] This provision does not address the duration of the renewal term, the question of whether the holder of the right must pay an additional fee, or the issue of how any such fee will be calculated. Numerous experts confirmed that the questions of whether rights holders may renew their rights at the end of their terms and the charge for any such renewals are great mysteries that the Property Rights Law leaves unresolved and are a source of considerable consternation to many investors.

Since the system of land use rights dates back to 1988 while most land use rights are granted for periods of forty or more years, China's legal system and real estate market have had few occasions to address these issues so far. One Chinese lawyer told me that he was aware of a handful of instances in which shorter-term land use rights, granted originally for less than the legal maximum term, had been approaching their expiration dates. While the lawyer stated that the government legally could have recovered possession of the land and the improvements now on the land, he personally knew of cases in which the government either had been willing to negotiate an extension of the land use right or had retaken possession but provided compensation for the improvements.

Article 22 of the Law on the Administration of Urban Real Estate appears to state that, if certain conditions are met, an application for the extension of a land use right "shall be approved" by the government and the holder of the right must pay an extension fee.[92] This Article does not clarify what the terms or price of the extension shall be. Professors Randolph and Lou argue that the government must renew, essentially giving the holder of the land use right a right of first refusal,[93] but Article 22 may be more equivocal than they suggest. One expert suggested to me that a more accurate translation of Article 22 is that these applications "*should* be approved," not "*shall* be approved," which implies a greater level of government discretion. It is also worth noting that Article 58 of the Land Administration Law states that the government may re-take land formerly subject to land use rights if the holder of the right fails to seek an extension "or, if he has, [and] the application is not approved."[94]

---

91 Wuquan Fa [Property Rights Law], art. 149.
92 Chengshi Fangdichan Guanli Fa [Law on the Administration of Urban Real Estate], art. 22 (providing that (i) the holder of a land use right that wishes to extend it must apply for such an extension no later than one year before the right expires; (ii) such applications "shall be approved"; and (iii) the user of the land shall execute a new contract "and pay fees for the granting in accordance with the regulations").
93 RANDOLPH & LOU, *supra* note 30, at 128–29.
94 Tudi Guanli Fa [Land Administration Law], art. 58(3).

Even if Chinese government entities are not required to renew land use rights that are nearing their expiration dates, it is reasonable to assume that they will be willing to negotiate extensions of these rights in exchange for the payment of a periodic or one-time fee. Public pressure to implement such a policy is likely to increase exponentially as the first wave of land use rights begins to approach its expiration date and the holders of those rights discover that lenders have become unwilling to finance construction or renovation on the land. This pressure will increase still further as the land on which tens of millions of residential units are constructed approaches the date on which that land and those improvements are scheduled to revert to the government.[95] Given the absence of *ad valorem* property taxes in China and given the fact that government at all levels will someday run out of desirable land on which to grant new land use rights, government entities will be searching desperately for new sources of revenue in the coming years.[96] China has recently approved a trial of an *ad valorem* property tax in Shanghai and Chongqing municipalities.[97] One of the experts I interviewed argued, however, that these trials are designed more as a signal to the property market to slow down and less as a test of an actual property tax.

The amount of this renewal fee could fall anywhere within a wide range. At the high extreme, the fee could amount to an annual payment equal to the fair market rental value of the land at the time of the renegotiation, perhaps with periodic increases built in. Land use rights renewed under such a system would resemble Western ground leases to a somewhat greater extent than current Chinese land use rights do, with the government serving as ground lessor to all. Alternatively, the charge could be established as a one-time fee that is equal to the discounted present value of this rental stream over the duration of the extension period. This second method more closely parallels the current approach of charging a party that acquires a land use right the entire fee for the right at the outset.

At the low extreme, the government might seek only a small percentage of the value of the land each year. If this occurs, China will have adopted a real property revenue-generation system not unlike that followed in much of the United States.

---

95 *See* Stein, *supra* note 46, at 46–47 (discussing several possible options for addressing this problem); Whitman, *supra* note 31, at 38 (noting the "general expectation that granted land use rights will be renewed upon their expiration").

96 *See, e.g.*, Weiping Wu, *Fiscal Decentralization, Infrastructure Financing, and Regional Disparity*, *in* CHINA'S LOCAL PUBLIC FINANCE IN TRANSITION 41, 47 (Joyce Yanyun Man & Yu-Hung Hong eds., 2011) ("It is unlikely that cities can count on revenue from asset sales as a major, lasting source of funding to expand infrastructure construction and maintenance."). While there is no general *ad valorem* property tax, other taxes are levied on those who use land. Government revenues from these taxes appear to be small. *See* Ding & Knaap, *supra* note 55, at 16 (describing the proceeds of one of these taxes as "so minimal that they barely reflected land ownership").

97 *China Approves Property Tax Trials to Curb Prices*, BLOOMBERG NEWS, Jan. 28, 2011, http://www.bloomberg.com/news/2011-01-28/china-approves-property-tax-trials-in-shanghai-chongqing-to-curb-prices.html.

Under this regime, holders of land use rights could maintain their occupancy for the duration of the renewal term on the condition that they make regular payments to the government in an amount that is far lower than the rental value of the property. The fee a Chinese right-holder would pay to maintain its land use right would be loosely analogous to *ad valorem* real property tax payments in the United States. If these rights were renewable indefinitely, the holding of a land use right would be tantamount to fee simple ownership. The government could also adopt any number of intermediate, hybrid methods of calculating the renewal fee.

One fairly senior real estate professional stated his belief that, at the end of the first seventy years, Chinese land would begin to be privatized, with the government selling it to the owner of the expiring land use right. Other experts agreed and suggested that these permanent transfers might even be free. I asked the first professional how the government would be able to square sales of this type with Communist doctrine. He replied, "We are making progress gradually, step by step. That is beyond me." He also observed that some of the compromises set forth in China's current Property Rights Law constitute progress toward this same outcome.

Several real estate professionals suggested to me that when the government must decide whether to renew land use rights and at what cost, land should be divided into two categories. For residential property, the right should be renewable at little or no cost. In effect, the holder of the land use right would end up owning an interest that is similar to fee simple title in common law countries. By contrast, for commercial property, the government would retain the right to recover the land and any improvements when the initial term expires. This would place the government in a position in which it could negotiate with the holder of the expiring right, which would presumably be willing to pay fair market value in exchange for renewal rights.

Amusingly, one government official recently attempted to quell concerns about the renewability of land use rights by suggesting publicly that holders of these rights should not worry about losing their property when the terms expire because construction quality is so poor that most buildings will have little value after thirty years anyway. This statement immediately caused property values to drop. The government official then backed off somewhat, suggesting that buildings might maintain their value for forty, or even fifty, years. The consensus among the people with whom I spoke, however, is that the fast pace of construction today, coupled with the fact that contractors often hire rural migrants who have little experience working in the construction industry, leads to buildings of extremely poor quality, and that the thirty-year estimate might not be far off the mark.[98]

---

98 Some buildings do not even survive until their first day. A partially completed 13-story residential building in the Minhang District of Shanghai recently toppled onto its side during construction, nearly unblemished. Fortunately, the building was not yet occupied and the accident occurred in the early morning on a Saturday, so only one worker was killed. Cao Li, *Building Collapse Kills One Worker in Shanghai*, CHINA DAILY, June 27,

Land Use Rights, Land Use Controls, and Financial Pressure on the Government

The Chinese land use right system also ends up functioning as an informal zoning arrangement. When the government announces the availability of land, it places limits on the uses it will permit for that land, and it restates these limits in the written document that it executes with the eventual purchaser of the land use right.[99] The government thereby achieves by contract what American jurisdictions accomplish under a variety of land use control laws. The establishment and transfer of land use rights is not the only method of land use control in China—and land that is not subject to land use rights is not restricted by these types of controls—but the land use right is one component of an overall land use system.[100]

The government can, if it chooses, be fairly heavy-handed in the way in which it uses the land use right system to control patterns of land use. If the government wishes for one area to become, say, a center of international banking, it can decide that it will grant land use rights to international banks only in that area. This approach may be a step less intrusive than forcing existing banks to relocate, but it guarantees that when a bank chooses to move, it will have to move into the designated area. Similarly, when the Shanghai government wanted to encourage foreigners to relocate to the Jinqiao section of Pudong, it increased the likelihood of this happening by letting the proprietors of several international schools know that their desire to acquire land use rights would most likely be met should they select locations in Jinqiao.[101]

The division of land into government-owned land and land owned by agricultural collectives also serves as a basic land use control. The government may not transfer land use rights on collective-owned land, which means that this land

---

2009, http://www. chinadaily.com.cn/bizchina/2009-06/27/content_8330265.htm (news account with photos).

99 *See, e.g.*, SOMMERS & PHILLIPS, *supra* note 11, at 61–80 (describing the process of acquiring land use rights from the government for the development of a mixed-use project); RANDOLPH & LOU, *supra* note 30, at 391–92 (setting forth the provisions regulating land use contained in one of the official forms of contract for granting land use rights on state-owned land).

100 For more on the regulation of the use of land in China, see generally Tudi Guanli Fa [Land Administration Law]. For instance, Article 17 of the Land Administration Law requires that governments at all levels "draw up overall plans for land utilization ... for national economic and social development, the need for improvement of national land and for protection of the natural resources and the environment, the capacity of land supply, and the demand for land by various construction projects." *Id.* art. 17.

101 *See* Peter T.Y. Cheung, *Guangzhou and Tianjin: The Struggle for Development in Two Chinese Cities*, *in* CITIES IN CHINA: RECIPES FOR ECONOMIC DEVELOPMENT IN THE REFORM ERA 18, 46–47 (Jae Ho Chung ed., 1999) (noting that "foreign banks have to set up their branches or headquarters in Pudong first if they would like to be given the authority to carry out renminbi business in the future"); *infra* notes 126, 311 and accompanying text.

must be converted to government-owned land before the government can grant land use rights on it. One expert observed to me, however, that some agricultural collectives own land that has been converted to commercial uses. This land is typically located in suburban areas into which the neighboring city has sprawled, raising the value of a collective's agricultural land and making it more attractive to commercial developers. Some of these collectives have received permission to build commercial structures on their land. This places them in a position in which they can retain the profits resulting from the increased intensity of land use and pass them along to the members of the collective in the form of dividends.[102] Note, however, that collective-owned land may not be mortgaged.[103]

The price of a land use right is a function of the area of the improvements that can be constructed on the land. If that area changes as the building evolves, the price is adjusted accordingly. This fact provides a stark illustration of the tension that local governments face between regulating land uses and maximizing revenues: a bigger building may be undesirable for land use planning reasons, but it will generate more revenue.

The possibility of profiting from the sale of land use rights creates enormous conflicts for local governments, and not only on the lot-by-lot basis just mentioned. Municipal planning bodies may have devised long-term land use programs that restrict certain types of developments in specified areas. At the same time, these municipal governments must glimpse enormous revenue-raising possibilities from the sale of prime, restricted land to a developer that wishes to use it in a way that might not comport with the overall land use plan. Internal and external pressures are growing to place greater emphasis on environmental considerations, and Shanghai officials frequently stress the increasing amount of green space that is available to residents of that city. But if land that is slated for a downtown park proves to be considerably more valuable to its owner—the municipality—than anticipated, the incentive to sell the land use right to a developer will grow correspondingly.

Nearly every expert with whom I met concurred that provincial and municipal governments employ the sale of land use rights as an essential means of keeping themselves afloat financially. Rapid appreciation in the price of land has made these rights quite valuable in some parts of the country, and government bodies in these regions appear to treat land use rights as cash cows to be milked as the need arises. Of course, these government entities must recognize that if they dispose of this land too rapidly, they will damage both their own ongoing financial viability and the overall real estate market.[104] Short-term needs, however, tend to trump longer term ideals. There is a great deal of discord between the proclivity

---

102   *See* RANDOLPH & LOU, *supra* note 30, at 61 n.8 (discussing this phenomenon).

103   Wuquan Fa [Property Rights Law], art. 184(ii); Danbao Fa [Guaranty Law], art. 37(2).

104   *Cf. infra* note 177 and accompanying text (comparing China's approach with that employed by Russia following the disintegration of the Soviet Union).

of municipalities and provinces to raise needed funds by selling off land use rights and the primary objective of the central government, which is to maintain overall social stability on a nationwide basis. Beijing perceives far greater reasons to slow the real estate market down and suffers far less when it succeeds in doing so.

Chapter 4
Ownership Entities: Who Owns Land, and How Do They Own It?

The Structure of the Ownership Entity

Most real estate projects in Shanghai are domestically owned, primarily by limited liability companies. Limited liability companies are formed in accordance with the Company Law, which was adopted in 1993 and has been amended three times since then.[105] In addition to allowing for the creation of limited liability companies, the Company Law also provides for the establishment of joint stock limited companies.[106] The minimum registered capital requirements for joint stock limited companies are much higher than the parallel requirements for limited liability companies, which probably explains why real estate entities generally are formed as limited liability companies.[107]

Acquisition of Land Use Rights by the Ownership Entity

One of the first tasks for a newly formed limited liability company that intends to develop real estate is to acquire the necessary land use rights. In many cases, the limited liability company that obtains the land use right is itself partly owned by a private developer-manager and partly owned by a local government entity. This structure often results from the fact that a local government entity controls the land that the private developer needs and provides the land use right to the ownership entity as its contribution to that entity.[108] In other words, the local government

---

105   Gongsi Fa [Company Law] (promulgated by the Standing Comm. Nat'l People's Cong., Dec. 29, 1993, revised Dec. 25, 1999, Aug. 28, 2004, and Oct. 27, 2005, effective Jan. 1, 2006), arts. 23–76 (China) (addressing limited liability companies); *see generally* CHEN, *supra* note 23, at 245 (discussing an earlier version of this law).

106   Gongsi Fa [Company Law], arts. 77–146 (addressing joint stock limited companies); 1 ZIMMERMAN, *supra* note 86, at 135–36 (translating the name of this entity as "company limited by shares").

107   *Compare* Gongsi Fa [Company Law], art. 26 (listing requirements for forming limited liability companies, including a minimum registered capital of 30,000 yuan), *with id.* art. 81 (listing requirements for forming joint stock limited companies, including a minimum registered capital of five million yuan).

108   *See* Gongsi Fa [Company Law], art. 27 (stating that a shareholder of a limited liability company may make its capital contribution by "contributing such non-currency

controls an essential ingredient of the development—the land—and uses its control of that asset as a means of gaining an ownership interest in the entity that will develop that land. As Kenneth Lieberthal notes, "In China the state is always at least your silent partner."[109]

By making an in-kind contribution to the ownership entity, the local government becomes a partial owner of the project. This ownership interest allows the government both to retain some control over the development and to profit from it. One pair of commentators indicates that political units have theoretically been prohibited from profiting from real estate development in this manner since 1990.[110] However, several of the experts I interviewed referred rather matter-of-factly to the current existence of these types of public–private real estate joint ventures.

The other co-owner of the limited liability company, a private entity, provides the professional know-how and much of the cash. It appears that the size of the fractional interest in the ownership entity that local governments demand has been dropping over time—one expert suggested that the percentage of a typical project owned by the government partner has decreased from 60 percent to 40 percent, while another suggested that government entities today might not hold any equity stake at all—and that many of these joint ventures are now controlled by the private party. Similarly, a state-owned enterprise (SOE) might receive a land use right from a local government at little or no cost, or might already own the right. The SOE can then contribute its land use right to a development entity that it jointly owns with a local developer or, occasionally, a foreign partner.

Government Participation in Real Estate Ventures

This government participation in real estate ventures is not surprising. In the earliest days of the modern Chinese real estate market, SOEs or the government itself were the only entities in a position to jump-start the real estate development industry, as there simply was no one else with any expertise or capital. This pattern differs somewhat from that exhibited by manufacturing ventures, where foreign investors played a larger role from the outset. Foreign companies felt more comfortable forming joint ventures with Chinese manufacturing enterprises and entering the Chinese market even in the late 1980s and early 1990s. Perhaps foreign companies believed that manufacturing goods in China would not be terribly dissimilar from manufacturing goods elsewhere, while developing real estate in China would be dramatically different from developing real estate in other locales. Or perhaps

---

property as ... land-use rights" and requiring that these rights be appraised).

109 KENNETH LIEBERTHAL, MANAGING THE CHINA CHALLENGE: HOW TO ACHIEVE CORPORATE SUCCESS IN THE PEOPLE'S REPUBLIC xv (2011).

110 RANDOLPH & LOU, *supra* note 30, at 132–34.

foreign investors were uncomfortable with the lack of certainty about property rights that Chinese law then provided.

Even as China's real estate industry has matured and private entities have acquired the experience, confidence, and financial wherewithal necessary to take more prominent roles in the development process, there are still sound reasons for the government to continue to invest. China's real estate market is booming, particularly in the larger cities in the eastern part of the country, and government entities wish to benefit from the huge profits available from investing in real estate. The government also participates in the real estate market in less direct ways. Most of the major banks operating in China are government-owned or -controlled. As a result, approval of real estate loans may be motivated as much by a lender's aim of advancing more generalized societal goals as by its desire to be repaid with interest.[111]

SOEs, which generally are less efficient than privately owned businesses, have recently been attempting to diversify into the successful real estate industry to improve their overall performance. Since SOEs historically have comprised part of the "iron rice bowl" social service network, often providing workers with a guaranteed job, housing, schools, and health care, the government wants these entities to survive. "Because the large SOEs are responsible for many aspects of the lives of their workers, reforming them presents social and political as well as economic challenges. Dismantling them would threaten to throw huge numbers of workers into unemployment, and a nationwide safety net does not exist."[112] The responsibility that SOEs previously undertook for housing their workers reflects the belief, now discredited in China, that housing for workers is not a commodity but rather is a necessary cost of manufacturing a product.[113] While the government may want SOEs to continue to provide other social benefits to their workers, the cost of furnishing these services renders SOEs uncompetitive in global markets.[114]

---

111   For a more detailed discussion of the Chinese lending industry, see *infra* Chapter 7.

112   LUBMAN, *supra* note 13, at 107.

113   Man, Zheng & Ren, *supra* note 56, at 3 (noting, in 2011, "The housing reform in 1998 totally abandoned the old system of linking housing distribution with employment units."); Jean Jinghan Chen & David Wills, *Pioneer Urban Housing Reform in China*, in THE IMPACT OF CHINA'S ECONOMIC REFORMS UPON LAND, PROPERTY AND CONSTRUCTION, *supra* note 7, at 122, 123 (noting, in 1999, "Traditionally, housing in China has been viewed as a non-useful cost of production that must be borne to produce the truly valued output which consists of manufactured goods."); *see generally* CAO, *supra* note 77, at 3 (observing, in 1998, that under Marxist doctrine, "land and property were not commodities, and therefore must not be the objects of private investment and trade"). Note, however, that even though work units no longer provide housing to their workers, they may provide cash subsidies to them.

114   Chen & Wills, *supra* note 113, at 125 (observing, in 1999, "The housing burden of the SOEs has been one of the fundamental reasons for their inefficiency and their incurred production losses.").

SOEs, then, are seeking profits in areas such as real estate to offset the losses they must bear in other parts of their overall operations.

If an SOE fails, either the government must step in and provide these benefits directly or the SOE's former employees will suffer the type of reduction in comfort and security that can lead to more generalized social unrest.[115] Nonetheless, the increase in the number of private businesses and the growth in foreign trade have caused some SOEs to fail, which places the government in the position of having to sell off a bankrupt enterprise's assets. To the extent those assets include desirable real estate, the government may wish to profit from this newly available investment opportunity, thereby increasing the SOE's salvage value. Once again, this places the government in the role of co-owner of a real estate development entity. Moreover, if the government has already established a restrictive land use plan covering this land, it now has both a financial incentive and the legal capacity to ignore this plan. One expert suggested to me that a major reason for the failure of land use planning in so many parts of China is the conflicting stimuli affecting government entities in this situation. Faced with contradictory desires to implement a much-needed land use plan and to profit from the flourishing real estate market, Chinese government entities often choose the latter.

By a variety of different paths, then, a government entity may end up as an investor in a real estate entity. By co-owning the limited liability company that invests in real estate, the government is also able to exert significant control over the construction process and the ultimate product. One real estate professional even suggested to me that most of the residential real estate developers in Shanghai are entirely state-owned: the local government forms entities that it owns or controls and then directs prime land to them. Naturally, all of this government participation in the real estate industry makes it more difficult for private companies to compete.

Much like the SOEs, private companies with a primary emphasis in industries other than real estate are seeking to diversify their portfolios, and real estate has proved to be one of the most successful investment sectors during the last several years. The government, reluctant to allow competition from these well-off private entities, has begun to limit the ability of these companies to operate in the real estate arena. It even has taken steps to encourage these companies to sell their real estate assets to state-owned real estate holding companies, so that the government rather than the private owner can enjoy the future profits from the real estate.

---

115 "The one indignity the Chinese people will not tolerate is the destruction of their savings. The population's unspoken truce with the country's autocratic leaders has long been that they must continue to deliver improved living standards in return for maintaining power." JOE STUDWELL, THE CHINA DREAM: THE ELUSIVE QUEST FOR THE GREATEST UNTAPPED MARKET ON EARTH 278 (2002).

The Importance of Personal Connections

The concept of land's "worth" is a sticky one in a nation in which the real estate market is just beginning to emerge. It is hard to place a value on much of China's land, and it was harder still when the market in land use rights first started to develop. Land use rights, which are already time delimited, have been available for only a brief time, and the land that the government is offering has not been privately held in recent years. Uncertainty about land values is compounded further by the overall volatility of China's young real estate markets.

Whatever the market decides a given parcel of land is worth, local governments sometimes convey a land use right to a public–private joint venture for less than this perceived value. The entity then can quickly resell a portion of the land use right at a higher price per square meter and recoup some or all of its total cash investment in the project before it begins construction. The end result of this two-step transaction is that the entity can obtain the right to develop the land it retains for free or at a steep discount. This process suggests that the private co-owner of the entity often is someone with close connections to the government, such as a former government official, or that the private partner has otherwise induced the government entity to sell the land initially at a bargain price.

Land has become the hottest of commodities in many parts of China, and government units that wish to profit from developing land may lack the necessary expertise. Those professionals who possess this know-how and are willing to share the spoils with the government—or certain workers within the government—are more likely to obtain coveted land use rights. Even in cases in which there is no outright corruption, developers and lawyers who master the nuances of an ever-changing legal and administrative system and maintain cordial relations with the bureaucrat whose approval is essential hold a huge advantage over their competitors. Given how rapidly China's business laws are developing and how variably they are applied, *guanxi* is likely to remain an important factor in these business dealings for the foreseeable future. As one developer bluntly told me, in perfect idiomatic English, "A new developer needs good connections with the local government. Otherwise, he's screwed."

In recent years, fair public auctions have become far more common, as various levels of Chinese government endeavor to fend off charges of corruption. I was regularly told by different players in the Shanghai real estate market that that city runs one of the cleanest operations in China.[116] Auctions of land use rights in

---

116 *See, e.g.*, Jamie P. Horsley, *Shanghai Advances the Cause of Open Government Information in China*, CHINA LAW CENTER, YALE LAW SCHOOL, Apr. 15, 2004, *available at* http://www.law.yale.edu/documents/pdf/Shanghai_Advances.pdf, at 3 (noting some ways in which Shanghai has been making its urban planning and redevelopment processes more transparent); *see also* YATSKO, *supra* note 6, at 216 ("Western investors ... often comment that Shanghai authorities follow the rules compared with Chinese officials in the provinces,

Shanghai have become fairly transparent and open during the past several years.[117] Even so, progress against corruption has been somewhat halting.[118]

Some of the early developers—beneficiaries of a system that rewarded *guanxi* more overtly—may have built up a huge competitive edge. By constructing their projects at a time when the market was difficult to enter without connections, they became the market leaders. Their connections afforded them the opportunity to obtain the experience and skills that they and others lacked. This newfound expertise complements their personal contacts and allows these industry leaders to maintain their head start to a degree that later market entrants have had difficulty reducing.

Some of these early developers, having benefited from the Wild West real estate environment of the 1990s, may even have encouraged the adoption of legal changes to make the rules more fair: having established a huge lead, they now wished to lock in their advantage by ensuring that no one else can ever do what they succeeded in doing when the rules were more lax. Interestingly, one of the Chinese people I interviewed compared the edge enjoyed by these early entrants with *guanxi* to the one he perceives the United States as enjoying under the World Trade Organization. He suggested that those who are "in the lead" are prone to cement their benefits by encouraging the enactment of ostensibly neutral rules that serve to institutionalize their advantage.

Many high-end real estate transactions today are limited to those developers with demonstrated success and the proven capacity to finance and construct major projects, a group that largely consists of those who could acquire land use rights under the more opaque procedures prevalent in the initial days of the current boom. And even if *guanxi* is not as essential as it once was, it surely does not hurt even now. These realities help to explain why most successful real estate developers in China are Chinese.

Foreign and Domestic Investors

To the extent there is foreign investment in real estate ownership entities, it overwhelmingly comes from ethnic Chinese who live outside mainland China. Multinational corporations have also entered the market recently. Morgan Stanley,

---

particularly in southern China.... They also find Shanghai to be a relatively ethical place to do business, particularly compared with southern China.").

117 For a discussion of how Shanghai has modified its procedures for transferring land use rights, see *supra* notes 87–90 and accompanying text.

118 *See, e.g.*, James T. Areddy, *Corruption Crackdown Targets Shanghai Inc.: Beijing Sends Signal, Stalling Glitzy Projects of City's Ousted Chief*, WALL ST. J., Feb. 6, 2007, at A1 (discussing firing and detention of Chen Liangyu, Shanghai's Communist Party Secretary, following allegations of "mismanagement and theft ..., influence peddling and other misdeeds").

Merrill Lynch, and Citigroup are among the well-known overseas entities that have made significant investments in Shanghai real estate during the past few years, often in high profile locations such as the Lujiazui Trade and Finance Zone of Shanghai's Pudong New Area. But the government still restricts the ability of foreigners to invest in real estate, especially in commercial and luxury residential projects. The experts I spoke with disagreed about whether the government has permitted any of these top-tier projects to be wholly foreign-owned. One developer told me that these internationally known foreign entities insist on owning their projects, while a real estate agent insisted that the first-class office buildings in Pudong remain state-owned, as the government continues to require public ownership as a means of controlling the development process and enjoying the resulting investment gains.

Moreover, in some areas that had not been developed intensively before the current real estate surge, such as portions of Pudong, the municipal government established first-level developers and conveyed the empty or nearly empty land to these state-owned entities. These entities installed basic infrastructure, subdivided the land, and conveyed land use rights in the smaller subdivided parcels to the parties that ultimately developed them or will do so. This approach ensured that the government would profit from the increased value brought about by the installation of the infrastructure, the intensification of the permitted uses that it decided to allow, and the more general appreciation in land values. At the same time, this monopolistic process limited competition among sellers, thereby maintaining the high prices that the government would receive. It also served to keep the profits from the appreciation of this land within China, as foreign entities would have lacked the ability to obtain land use rights in the first instance. The municipal government played a role similar to that of a subdivider in an American residential development, but with the added advantages of being able to control most or all of the land from the beginning and determine the uses to which it could be put.

General contractors sometimes serve as joint owners of real estate entities as well. This may sound like good investment foresight by builders that hope to profit from partial ownership of the project and not solely from the construction process itself, and in some cases it may be precisely that. More often, though, this appears to be a form of developer financing.[119] In the earlier days of the modern Chinese real estate market—which is to say, a few years ago—cash-strapped developers often would pay their contractors very slowly. In effect, they were forcing these contractors to extend interest-free loans to them, by having them contribute materials and labor for which they would not receive payment for months. And if the project failed, the contractors would become unwilling partners in the risk, as they would be unlikely to receive payment at all.

---

119 *See infra* Chapter 7 for a discussion of the general contractor as an involuntary lender; *infra* Chapter 9 for a discussion of the contractor's role in the overall construction process.

The government, in one of many efforts to slow what it fears is becoming a real estate bubble, has placed restrictions on the ability of owner entities to pay their contractors slowly. The intent is to ensure that developers have access to the necessary cash before incurring legal obligations to their contractors. In theory, this policy should lead to developers that are more financially stable and contractors that are more likely to be paid for their work. Developers, however, have quickly learned to evade the effect of these restrictions by bringing their contractors in as minority co-owners of the project. The contractor's provision of materials and labor presumably is viewed now as its contribution to the limited liability company, for which it has already received consideration in the form of its minority interest in the entity, rather than as its performance under a construction contract, for which it is entitled to prompt payment.

This discussion of ownership entities cannot be considered complete without a brief discussion of the Wenzhounese. In the early days of China's new real estate market, most citizens gave little thought to investing in land and buildings. The concept was simply an alien one to the hundreds of millions of people emerging from nearly half a century of strict Communist rule and collective ownership of property. Residents of Wenzhou, in Zhejiang Province on the nation's east coast, were ahead of the real estate investment curve and were among the first Chinese citizens to begin investing in the new real estate market.[120] Wenzhounese would collect money via "the tin plate," effectively passing the hat to amass sufficient funds to buy a project together. These rudimentary joint ventures helped to spark the real estate market at a time when most other investors chose to hold back or never dreamed of investing in real estate in the first place. They also established a disproportionate number of Wenzhounese as leaders in the real estate industry. When other Chinese saw how well Wenzhounese investors were faring and knowledge of this broad social change began to diffuse throughout China, the real estate market began to take off more broadly.[121]

---

120 *See* STUDWELL, *supra* note 115, at 34–37 (describing Wenzhou's economic rise since the 1980s and attributing it to a combination of individual resourcefulness and geographic isolation).

121 *See generally* EVERETT M. ROGERS, DIFFUSION OF INNOVATIONS 6 (5th ed. 2003) ("Diffusion is a kind of *social change*, defined as the process by which alteration occurs in the structure and function of a social system. When new ideas are invented, diffused, and adopted or rejected, leading to certain consequences, social change occurs.") (emphasis in original).

Chapter 5

Choosing Where to Build: The Private Market and Government Pressure

The Private Profit Motive and Government Control

In China's socialist market economy, the decision about where to build is resolved, not surprisingly, by a combination of private profit motive and government inducement or compulsion. Developers seek to buy land use rights and then build structures on that land in locations that will be profitable. The government simultaneously uses its power—including both its ownership of the underlying land and its position as an equity holder in many developer entities—as a means of channeling development where it wishes. To the extent that the government hopes to force development of areas that are sparsely populated, it also benefits from the business reality that it is far more advantageous for private developers to build on land that does not need to be cleared of current occupants and structures, a process that can be both controversial and expensive.

The profit motive of real estate developers requires no explanation and seems to cross international cultural barriers with little need for translation. The developers I interviewed generally wish to make money and seemed a bit surprised that an American would see any need to ask a Chinese developer about this. These professionals also recognize that they are working in an environment that is heavily regulated. Thus, I sought to understand the goals and mechanisms of China's formal and informal land use controls.

Government Planning and Public Input

Chinese government entities do engage in land use planning and zoning. While China's methods of regulating land use are not my principal topic here, it is fair to summarize these processes by stating that the government's land use plans are developed in a top-down manner, with little or no citizen input. For example, China's City Planning Law does not appear to require public input at any point during the planning process.[122] In nearly every conversation I had, I asked my

---

122 *See, e.g.*, Chengshi Guihua Fa [City Planning Law] (promulgated by the Standing Comm. Nat'l People's Cong., Dec. 26, 1989, effective Apr. 1, 1990), art. 4 (China) ("The state shall guide itself by the principle of strictly controlling the size of large cities and developing medium-sized and small cities to an appropriate extent in the interest of a rational

Chinese counterparts if they could provide me with an example of citizen input into any aspect of land use planning. In my months of interviews, they provided me with only one concrete illustration: the dramatic 360-degree circular exit ramp on the Puxi side of Shanghai's new Nanpu Bridge was suggested to planners by a twelve-year-old girl. As one Western lawyer succinctly explained to me, the Chinese government has much more power to force things than that of the United States.

One Chinese real estate consultant told me that "people in China don't like to give suggestions. They think the government will do everything. So the people don't have the motivation." Another possible explanation for the lack of public participation is that citizen input has been devalued for so many years that China's people are simply unfamiliar with the concept. Numerous conversations with my own students—who seemed baffled by the idea of citizen input into government decisions of any type—have persuaded me that this may be an important factor in the lack of citizen involvement in the land use planning process. Shanghai's residents may still be gun-shy, as well. In the past, those who offered suggestions that contradicted the plans of government officials often came to regret it, so local residents may have decided that the best course is to remain unobtrusive.[123]

One expert advised me that some government entities do invite public comment, but that citizens' suggestions are followed only rarely. Discouraging or rejecting input from the very people who will be most affected by land use regulations surely must hamper effective government planning. Nonetheless, the government has become more keenly attuned to the need for better land use planning and environmental control in recent years. Even a government-mandated plan may be preferable to haphazard and aimless construction; even a government that is indisposed to follow citizen input will get it right sometimes. A Chinese lawyer suggested to me that citizen input may have more of an impact regarding changes to existing land use plans than initial plans. This implies that the government does not listen to its citizens until after it has blundered once on its own and needs advice on how to correct course.

Recently, the land use planning process has become more transparent, though hardly more citizen-based. Shanghai, for instance, engages in multiple levels of planning. The first step is "Open Planning," in which Shanghai's municipal government makes a proposal that must be approved by both the Shanghai Municipal People's Congress and the State Council. Following successful completion of this step, the Shanghai Municipal People's Government (or, for less significant

---

distribution of productive forces and of the population."); *id.* art. 6 ("The compilation of the plan for a city shall be based on the plan for national economic and social development"); *id.* art. 11 (describing "the compilation of hierarchical urban plan[s] for the whole nation").

123   *Cf.* Jamie P. Horsley, *Village Elections: Training Ground for Democratization*, CHINA BUS. REV., Mar.–Apr. 2001, at 44, 51 (tracing increases in citizen participation since the early 1980s and describing the process as "the world's largest grassroots democratic education process," but also noting the continuing need for "nurturing a society that understands the rights and responsibilities of citizens in a modern state").

projects, the Shanghai Urban Planning Administration, an administrative arm of the municipal government) specifies requirements for individual blocks of land. After this step has been completed, re-zonings, while occasionally available, are difficult to obtain. Then, in the third step, technical specifications are proposed for individual buildings. Steps four and five consist of inviting bids on the transfer of specific land use rights and executing a contract with the successful bidder. These steps appear to mirror to some degree the land use process in the United States, although the Chinese process offers virtually no opportunity for input from outside the government, even by those considering bidding.

In the first days of Shanghai's modern real estate market, potential real estate developers could become involved in the planning process even earlier. Back in the 1990s, the government would ask developers to find a block and propose a real estate development for that block. Developers thus could locate land they wished to develop and pitch their proposals to the government. This method is rarely used today. Rather, the government makes its planning decisions in the manner described above and invites proposals from developers who must comply with these detailed specifications. Alternatively, the government may invite proposals for specific blocks that it has designated but not yet planned in great detail so that the developer can participate in the later stages of the planning process. By relying on these latter methods today, the government maintains a high degree of control over land use policy and also retains some ability to slow down the real estate market if it is threatening to overheat.

Population Dispersal

Shanghai also has sought recently to reduce population density in its urban core and promote new development in outlying areas of the vast municipality. Shanghai Municipality covers 6,340.5 square kilometers,[124] but much of this area is not urbanized. The outlying portions of the municipality are used in a variety of ways, including as agricultural land and forests. Population density in Shanghai ranges from 43,425 persons per square kilometer in the downtown Huangpu district to only 567 persons per square kilometer in outlying Chongming County.[125] I observed small farms interspersed with heavily developed urban areas along the road connecting downtown Shanghai and the outlying Minhang District.

The Shanghai government previously had established satellite communities as commuter towns in remote and more thinly populated portions of the municipality. As the populations of these outlying townships have swelled and automobile

---

124 OFFICE OF SHANGHAI CHRONICLES: A GENERAL SURVEY OF SHANGHAI, http://www.shtong.gov.cn/node2/node82288/node82289/node82299/userobject1ai111106.html (last visited July 19, 2011).
125 SHANGHAI: POPULATION AND EMPLOYMENT, http://www.shanghai.gov.cn/shanghai/node17256/node17432/node17435/userobject22ai17.html (last visited July 19, 2011).

traffic downtown has become a huge problem, the government has accelerated the dispersal process still further by trying to relocate selected industries to these satellite towns. The municipal government's hope is that these satellite towns will become larger and more self-sustaining, with residents working in the local industry rather than commuting downtown. Vehicular traffic may continue to increase, but at least commutes will be shorter and traffic will be more decentralized.

The Songjiang area of Shanghai, for example, has been designated as a base for the electronics industry. As a result of this policy, Songjiang is expected to house one million people in just a few years. The Shanghai Planning Museum, a fascinating combination of historical exhibits and chamber-of-commerce-style boosterism, has displayed detailed plans for the development of outlying Chongming Island—the third largest island in China and a portion of Shanghai Municipality—as an environmentally friendly planned community.

Government compulsion sometimes is more direct. In the early years of the Pudong development, the municipal government aimed to transform the Lujiazui area into a center of banking and finance. At the "Pudong 15" exhibit at Pudong Exhibition Hall in 2005, celebrating the fifteenth anniversary of the opening up of Pudong, I saw a 1984 academic article on display entitled, "Where is Shanghai's Manhattan?" This same exhibit also noted that, in the years leading up to the announcement of the new Pudong project, the government had encouraged the publication of more than 100,000 articles on the topic, to create a "good environment of public opinion." Similarly, and as noted earlier, Shanghai wanted the nearby Jinqiao area of Pudong to become a residential nucleus for expatriates living in Shanghai. To these ends, the government informed foreign banks that they could obtain business licenses only if their offices were physically located in Lujiazui. International schools received similar directives and were instructed to operate in Jinqiao.[126]

These rather heavy-handed efforts to control land use largely succeeded in accomplishing their goals. Today, Lujiazui has evolved into Shanghai's financial district, and the Jinqiao area of Pudong now is home to approximately twenty international schools, which in turn serve as a magnet for foreigners. Similarly, the government indirectly financed Pudong's pioneer urban residents by selling land use rights to them at relative bargain prices. Not only was the government paying the huge cost of the massive infrastructure development needed in this previously rural region's early days, it also was subsidizing those considering moving to the area.

Government Use of Incentives

Developers sometimes need even stronger coercion because some projects simply are not economically feasible standing on their own. Two professionals separately

---

126 *See supra* note 101 and accompanying text; *infra* note 311 and accompanying text.

explained to me how an overseas Chinese developer was induced to spearhead the redevelopment of the older Shanghai neighborhood that is now the upscale Xintiandi shopping area. At the time the idea was first hatched, the developer believed the project to be infeasible. Shanghai's government sweetened the pot by offering this company additional prime land elsewhere in the city; the value of this extra property apparently was sufficient to change the developer's mind. Once again, the municipal government provided an indirect subsidy, and the market—goosed by these government incentives—got the job done from there.

Just as it may increase its inducements when it wants an area to blossom, the government also can reduce its incentives or coercion if it wishes for development in an area to cool. After fifteen years of encouraging or forcing development in Pudong, the Shanghai government began to recognize that at least some sections of this area's real estate economy may have overheated. The district government of Pudong, which had been permitted to retain money raised from the sale of land use rights within the district for construction of infrastructure projects there, was told that it would thereafter have to remit this money to the Shanghai municipal government. The Pudong district government thus will have fewer resources available to encourage further development within the district. Meanwhile, Shanghai's municipal government will increase its ability to use profits from the sale of land use rights in prosperous Pudong to target neighborhoods elsewhere in the municipality that are growing more slowly. The central and municipal governments have also used tax policy and interest rate adjustments as a means of controlling the level of expansion of the real estate market more broadly.

Conflicts Between the Central Government and the Provinces

The previous example illustrates the potential for conflict between the government of a municipality and the government of a district within that municipality. But an even larger problem is the possibility of disagreements between the central government and a province or municipality. Many of the provinces and municipalities profit significantly from the granting of land use rights. These lower-level governments retain 70 percent of the proceeds from sales of land use rights, remitting the other 30 percent to Beijing.[127] Since there is no general system of *ad valorem* property taxation in China, provinces and municipalities fund a significant portion of their ongoing operations and capital expenditures from the sale of land use rights. These government entities also benefit from the increased income taxes they can collect down the road if the land is ultimately used in a productive way. So it is greatly to the benefit of these lower-level government entities to keep the real estate market expanding for as long as possible: the more land that developers want to buy and the higher the prevailing price, the more

---

127 Tudi Guanli Fa [Land Administration Law], art. 55.

money these government entities will collect to fund their ongoing operations and their massive capital expenditures.[128]

Although the central government receives its portion of the sale proceeds, it has its own reasons to fear unremitting land price appreciation. As urban residential prices continue to increase at a rate faster than that at which urban salaries are rising, there is growing concern that fewer and fewer of the urban residents who do not already own their homes will be able to afford to buy units, leading to unhappiness among those priced out of the residential real estate market.[129] Meanwhile, if the urban real estate bubble ever bursts, those who have succeeded in buying their own homes and riding the residential real estate wave may not like where it deposits them.[130] Whichever way the real estate market ends up moving, the government in Beijing is enjoying only a small portion of the benefit of current real estate growth but will likely bear the brunt of any citizen unrest that might materialize from it.

The central government seems to be particularly concerned about the preservation of agricultural land.[131] The continued upswing in urban real estate prices threatens to dislocate peasants, and not just poorer urbanites, as cities expand inexorably into neighboring agricultural property. The central government may be anxious about shortages of food in modern China, although the nation currently seems quite capable of feeding itself and exporting surplus food.[132] But the government's larger worry seems to be the enormous potential for upheaval in rural areas if peasants continue to lose land without having alternative economic opportunities available to them. As Professor Peerenboom notes, "Land disputes

---

128 *See* Ding & Knaap, *supra* note 55, at 21–22 (noting that as much as half of some cities' revenues comes from the sale of land use rights).

129 *See, e.g.*, Man, Zheng & Ren, *supra* note 56, at 11–12 (estimating that housing in major cities in China has become markedly less affordable than in major cities in the United States, Canada, and several other Western nations).

130 *See, e.g.*, Bob Davis, *China Risks Being Next Property-Bubble Blow Up*, WALL ST. J., June 27, 2011, http://online.wsj.com/article/SB10001424052702304569504576403 793565756986.html (noting how recent stimulus spending by the Chinese government has driven property prices to unsustainable highs). *But see* Gregory C. Chow & Linlin Niu, *Residential Housing in Urban China: Demand and Supply*, *in* CHINA'S HOUSING REFORM AND OUTCOMES, *supra* note 56, at 47, 47 (disputing whether there is a real estate bubble in China, and arguing that recent increases in housing costs reflect increases in income and construction costs rather than speculation).

131 *See, e.g.*, Tudi Guanli Fa [Land Administration Law], arts. 4, 22, 24, 31, 33–34 (limiting the conversion of agricultural land for construction purposes).

132 *Cf.* George C.S. Lin & Samuel P.S. Ho, *China's Land Resources and Land Use Change*, *in* EMERGING LAND AND HOUSING MARKETS IN CHINA, *supra* note 11, at 89, 94 & n.11 (quoting a study finding that China's cultivated land provides 88 percent of China's food needs while acknowledging that figures such as this one are unreliable; the authors note that changes in dietary habits and farming technology might allow greater food production from less and less agricultural land); *id.* at 116 & n.28 (same).

have become a major source of unrest in rural China and indeed throughout China. The Land Bureau is the leading defendant in administrative litigation suits, accounting for some 15 percent of all such cases."[133]

For rural residents, the land they cultivate is not just their livelihood, but also their social security. They generally do not qualify for the same social services as urban residents, under the assumption that the land they farm will continue to provide them with economic benefits throughout their lives. If these residents lose the use of the land they have been farming, the compensation they receive may allow them to afford a newer and more modern urban dwelling but probably will not be large enough to provide them with an income during or after their working life. The ability of these former farmers, who generally have lived in rural areas all their lives, to replace this income in an urban setting is likely to be limited. One person I interviewed stated that compensation in these instances will include a lifetime income benefit, but others were more equivocal on this point. Some people indicated that former rural residents may be able to qualify as urban residents after relocation, which would allow them to obtain certain social welfare benefits for which they were previously ineligible.

Several different people—including one lifelong inhabitant of Pudong—suggested to me that long-time residents of the formerly rural areas of Pudong are generally satisfied with the benefits that recent urbanization has brought. However, this does not seem to be the case throughout China's rural areas more broadly.[134] Beijing, understandably intent on squelching the next peasant revolution before it begins, has imposed strict limits on the reduction in land that is available for cultivation.[135]

In a nation that abhors chaos more than it cares about the protection of individual liberties, this concern about social turmoil may be the most important reason why the central government is trying to tamp down the real estate market. But the government's ability to restrain the market forces it has unleashed is limited. In fact, the real problem may not be that large numbers of peasants are being displaced, but rather that the compensation they are receiving for the loss of their farmland does not accurately reflect the true market value of their land for development purposes. Peasants might readily accept payment for their land

---

133   PEERENBOOM, *supra* note 2, at 482 (footnote omitted).

134   *See, e.g.*, Howard W. French, *Villagers Tell of Lethal Attack by Chinese Forces on Protesters*, N.Y. TIMES, Dec. 11, 2005, § 1, at 3 (describing a dispute over compensation for the use of residents' land in which security forces killed as many as 20 residents of the village of Dongzhou in "the deadliest use of force by Chinese forces against citizens since the Tiananmen massacre in 1989"; the article notes that residents compared the behavior of police to that of "Japanese occupiers of the last century" and the "Chinese Nationalist Army of Chiang Kai-shek").

135   Wuquan Fa [Property Rights Law], art. 43 ("The State adopts special protection with regard to the agriculture land, strictly limiting the transfer of agriculture land to construction land so as to control the total quantity of the construction land"); RANDOLPH & LOU, *supra* note 30, at 25–28.

if they did not feel that they were being undercompensated by a government that then profits enormously from transferring that same land to developers for a far greater price.[136]

One expert informed me that the central government has placed quotas on sales of land use rights on a province-by-province basis. Provinces with thriving real estate markets, however, have been permitted to purchase unused quota from other areas. This overall process does serve to spread the wealth somewhat, with prosperous locales such as Shanghai having to send some money to provinces with less dynamic markets in exchange for additional development quota. But it probably does not succeed in reducing development in the more successful provinces to the extent the central government may have hoped. Nor does it adequately address the argument that much of the urban development in relatively wealthy locales such as Shanghai has actually been financially supported by the rest of China.[137]

Interestingly, another expert, from another part of China, questioned whether transfers of quota were permissible. This second expert concurred, however, that the entire effort at limiting real estate development is difficult for the central government to police. One professional informed me that the central government has been taking satellite photos of agricultural areas on a regular basis and comparing them over time, to confirm that cultivable land is being employed for agricultural purposes throughout the growing season and is not being used in other ways without the knowledge of the central government.

Although Beijing theoretically controls the nation's land market, lower levels of government have economic incentives to see that market continue to blossom. These municipal and provincial governments profit greatly from the initial transfer of land use rights and continue to benefit by imposing taxes on subsequent property transfers and income taxes on businesses that operate on this land. Lower levels of government have their reasons for wanting to see the surge continue, and they use their substantial control over local real estate markets to encourage continued growth.

---

136 *See, e.g.*, Chengri Ding, *Consequences of Land Policy in China: Deciphering Several Emerging Urban Forms*, *in* SMART URBAN GROWTH FOR CHINA 109, 114 (Yan Song & Chengri Ding eds., 2009) (describing 1992 transactions in which agricultural land in Pudong was taken from farmers, converted to state-owned land, then resold to developers at a price that was 150 times the compensation the farmers had received, with the total loss of value to farmers in Pudong estimated at nearly $11 billion); Eva Pils, *Waste No Land: Property, Dignity and Growth in Urbanizing China*, 11 ASIAN-PAC. L. & POL'Y J. 1 (2010) (rejecting the claim that property rights are desirable because they lead to economic growth in light of the mistreatment of Chinese peasants under the current system of compensation); *How to Make China Even Richer*, THE ECONOMIST, Mar. 25, 2006, at 11 (suggesting that "it is the absence of reform that is proving destabilising, as peasants protest violently against land seizures by local governments keen to exploit the land themselves.").

137 YASHENG HUANG, CAPITALISM WITH CHINESE CHARACTERISTICS: ENTREPRENEURSHIP AND THE STATE 178, 228–31 (2008) (describing ways in which rural residents have unwittingly financed recent urban development in China).

Chapter 6

Demolishing Existing Structures, Relocating Current Residents

China's Shortage of Developable Land

The land mass of China is almost exactly the same size as that of the United States, but China has more than four times the population.[138] A much larger proportion of China's land area consists of deserts and rugged mountains that are thinly populated and likely to remain that way. China has an ocean coastline along only its eastern edge, which makes its interior areas much less accessible by ship or rail than are those in America. "More than 20 percent of [China's] land (e.g., deserts and land covered by glaciers and/or snow) is unusable for any purpose; mountainous areas comprise another 30 percent of China's territory."[139] As a result, "China feeds more than 20 percent of the world's population on less than 7 percent of the world's farmland."[140]

It is no wonder that the eastern part of China is thickly inhabited and that there is little or no unused land in that portion of the country—even rural areas are densely packed by American standards.[141] As a result, it is difficult to find a

---

138 The CIA website lists China's area at 9,596,961 square kilometers (fourth largest in the world) and its estimated population as of July 2011 at 1,336,718,015. CIA, THE WORLD FACTBOOK – CHINA, https://www.cia.gov/library/publications/the-world-factbook/geos/ch.html (last visited July 19, 2011). Comparable numbers for the United States, including the 50 states and the District of Columbia, are 9,826,675 square kilometers (third largest in the world) and 312,232,044 people. CIA, THE WORLD FACTBOOK – UNITED STATES, https://www.cia.gov/library/publications/the-world-factbook/geos/us.html (last visited July 19, 2011). The area figures for the two nations include both land and water; if only land is included, China is slightly larger than the United States.

139 Ding & Knaap, *supra* note 55, at 13 (2005).

140 *Id.* Note, though, that statistics about the Chinese economy tend to be extremely unreliable, particularly when they are furnished by Chinese government agencies. *See, e.g.*, Lin & Ho, *supra* note 132, at 89 & n.1 (quoting three different recent estimates of the amount of cultivated land in China that vary from 94.97 to 160 million hectares).

141 *See, e.g.*, Jean Jinghan Chen & David Wills, *Introduction, in* THE IMPACT OF CHINA'S ECONOMIC REFORMS UPON LAND, PROPERTY AND CONSTRUCTION, *supra* note 7, at 1, 5 (estimating that over 90 percent of China's population lives in the eastern third of its land mass); Lin & Ho, *supra* note 132, at 92 (estimating that "more than 40 percent of the Chinese people live[] in East China on less than 14 percent of the country's total land area").

desirable site for any new project in or near China's eastern cities that will not require the relocation of existing residents, sometimes in large numbers. If the land is to be redeveloped, either the government or the developer must relocate these residents, some of whom are likely to object strenuously. Real estate developers naturally prefer to work with vacant land whenever possible, but vacant land is hard to come by.

The amount of housing that is being developed or redeveloped in China today is astonishing. According to one Chinese publication, "Housing construction in urban and rural areas averaged 860 million square meters a year between 1985 and 1992. The peak year of 1988 saw more than 1 billion square meters of housing completed."[142] This same publication lists the average living space per person in 1992 as 18.9 square meters for rural residents and 6.9 square meters for urban residents, which suggests that in excess of 350 million Chinese are living in housing built during that single eight-year period.[143] These staggering numbers are consonant with China's laudable goal of improving housing conditions for all Chinese citizens.[144] Of course, much of this construction is on urban land that was not previously vacant, which means that many or all of its former occupants have had to relocate.

Demolishing Structures and Resettling Residents

The process of relocating current occupants of property and demolishing existing structures is a complex and expensive one. It has changed over time. And like everything else in China, it arises from a combination of a small measure of written law and a larger portion of interpretation by government officials who hold much discretion. The topic of demolition and resettlement is exceedingly complex and raises sensitive social and political issues that are far beyond the scope of this book. However, a brief summary of this process itself is necessary here, because demolition and resettlement comprises such an important piece of so many real estate transactions in China today.[145]

---

142   THE CHINESE ECONOMY INTO THE 21ST CENTURY: FORECASTS AND POLICIES 137 (Li Jingwen ed., 2000).

143   *Id.* at 182–83.

144   *See, e.g.*, Chengshi Fangdichan Guanli Fa [Law on the Administration of Urban Real Estate], art. 4 ("The State shall ... support the development of construction of residential houses so as to gradually improve the housing conditions of residents.").

145   Expropriation of private property for the public interest is authorized by both the Chinese Constitution and China's Property Rights Law, provided that the owner is compensated. XIANFA art. 10 (2004) ("The state may in the public interest expropriate or take over land for its use in accordance with the law and provide compensation."); Wuquan Fa [Property Rights Law], arts. 42, 148 (including similar provisions that provide greater detail). The definition of "public interest" is no less controversial in China than it is in the United States. Kelo v. City of New London, 545 U.S. 469 (2005). For an excellent

As previously noted, all land in China is owned either by the state or by agricultural collectives. However, because the state has the power to expropriate land from agricultural collectives, the collectives own their land at the mercy of the state. The state has repeatedly demonstrated that it is willing to requisition agricultural land if it believes the property can be put to uses that are more economically productive.[146] The Chinese government thus effectively owns or controls all domestic land. Individuals or business entities may acquire land use rights from the government for terms ranging up to seventy years and then may own a structure or unit on that land.

In urban areas, many of the residents living in older units may not own either the units themselves or the underlying land use rights. Chinese law appears to recognize "homestead" rights in free-standing houses. However, the legal status of these homestead rights is somewhat murky, and homestead rights are not applicable to units in multiple-dwelling buildings, which is where most urban Chinese live.[147] More likely, older housing units occupied by urban residents have been provided to them by the government, their work unit, or, occasionally, an agricultural collective that owns some land that has become urbanized. Alternatively, some of these older units are now being sold or rented by work units to their employee-occupants rather than being provided as a benefit to their workers. Either way, these units are likely to be extremely run-down and not terribly valuable or desirable. The occupants are entitled to compensation if the government forces them to relocate. But as expert after expert emphasized to me, the amount they will receive, reflecting both the poor condition of the building and the occupants' likely lack of ownership of either the structure or the land use right, will be minimal.

By contrast, those urban occupants who have purchased residential units during the past two decades are likely to own newer and more modern units that were constructed after land use rights became marketable. These units, which are more valuable and more recently constructed, are far less likely to be redeveloped—for the second time in the last ten or twenty years—than are older and shabbier units that usually are not owned by their occupants. They would also be considerably more expensive for the government to acquire. The owners of these newer units thus are less likely to face relocation.

If the overall value of a housing unit is defined to include both the value of the land use right to the underlying land and the value of the unit located on that land, one expert estimated for me that in a typical requisition of this sort, the land use right represents 20 percent of this overall value while the structure represents the other 80 percent. So a resident who is displaced from an older housing unit that she does not own may receive 80 percent or less of the overall value of an

---

treatment of some of the problems that the current process of demolition and relocation creates in China, see Chenglin Liu, *Informal Rules, Transaction Costs, and the Failure of the "Takings" Law in China*, 29 HASTINGS INT'L & COMP. L. REV. 1 (2005).

146 *See* RANDOLPH & LOU, *supra* note 30, at 59 & nn.1–2, 73–74 & n.47.
147 *Id.* at 107–10.

old unit and then have to purchase 100 percent of the value of a newer and more expensive unit, with the percentage increase reflecting the fact that the buyer must now purchase the land use right as well as the unit built on it.[148]

Given the poor quality of much of the older housing stock in urban areas, residents may be all too happy to take this money, either negotiated with a developer or forced on them by the government, and move to a more inviting dwelling. In some cases, occupants who settle quickly and amicably with the government receive compensation bonuses of as much as 20 percent. By providing these incentives, the government hopes to induce potential holdouts to take the larger sum early and relocate without a fight, while putting peer pressure on their neighbors to do the same. But even with any settlement bonus, the amount of compensation the owners of older units are likely to receive will seem modest in today's competitive real estate market and probably will require them to relocate to less expensive outlying areas of their city.[149] Moreover, as a result of rapid price appreciation, the longer these buyers wait to buy their new unit, the less they will be able to afford.

In the earlier days of China's new housing market, which is to say a decade ago, the government typically paid compensation in kind, providing relocatees with new apartments. Today, with a more mature residential real estate market, a citizenry that has quickly become sophisticated about investing in residential real estate, and a wider range of apartments available, these relocatees are almost certain to receive cash compensation, which allows them greater personal choice as to where to live. Either way, the overall result of the relocation process in urban areas seems to be the gradual displacement of poorer, long-time urban residents to more modern housing on the outer fringes of the city, and their replacement downtown by more affluent purchasers who can afford the rapidly increasing prices of homes in the urban center. One journalist has described, "[a]midst the dazzling skyscrapers of modern China, ... thousands upon thousands of dissatisfied, disenfranchised people ... the flotsam and jetsam of China's rising tide of prosperity."[150] In short, Chinese metropolitan areas seem to display characteristics that are the exact opposite of those of many of their American counterparts, in which more affluent

---

148 For a discussion of the grievances of those who lose older housing but do not receive compensation for the value of the underlying land use right, see You-tien Hsing, The Great Urban Transformation: Politics of Land and Property in China 73–74 (2011).

149 "'It's very good. Now I have five rooms. I have a kitchen and a toilet—before we just used a chamber pot .... It's a little far, but I like it.'" Yatsko, *supra* note 6, at 33 (quoting a former downtown resident forced to relocate to a Shanghai suburb after her original neighborhood was redeveloped). The author continues by noting that this resident's feelings are not universally shared by relocatees. *Id.* at 34–36.

150 *China's Rise: Inward-Looking or Expansionist?* (NPR radio broadcast June 30, 2011), *available at* http://www.npr.org/templates/transcript/transcript.php?storyId=137460232 (last visited July 19, 2011) (quoting correspondent Rob Gifford; while the quote concerns relocations in more recent years, the report focuses on displacement for large public projects).

residents have tended to move to the suburbs, abandoning the urban core to the poor.

More than one expert, however, suggested that in recent years this trend has reversed to a considerable degree. Developers have become so desperate to acquire rights to land in downtown areas that they are forced to pay prices much closer to fair market value to existing residents whom they wish to displace. At the same time, these incumbent residents have become far savvier and have learned to hold out for much larger amounts. With their sizable cash settlements, these relocatees are in a position in which they can actually afford to remain close to their old downtown neighborhoods. They typically cannot afford new construction, which, by definition, must cost considerably more than the amounts they received to relinquish their old units. However, they often can purchase relatively new second-hand units nearby. These long-time residents of the neighborhood can replace their run-down older units with decent and more modern housing in the same general vicinity, while the developer acquires the land it covets and can redevelop it into expensive new units.

The trend of developers paying huge relocation payments to city dwellers who occupy older units has also led to increasing resentment among some urban residents. Those who are paid large sums to relocate benefit greatly, while neighbors whose land has not yet been purchased by a developer may be left with a very old apartment that they do not own and no cash. The randomness with which some people become dramatically wealthier from real estate is causing social tension within downtown urban districts. This is yet another illustration of how the Chinese government will need to address the strains created by growing inequality of wealth within the new China.

Transferring Cleared Land to Developers

Once the government has removed the existing occupants from the land, it is in a position to transfer the land to a developer. The price the government can charge for land use rights on this newly vacated land will reflect its, and the market's, assessment of what can now be built on the land. In addition, the government has succeeded in driving the price higher by going to the trouble, expense, and inconvenience of demolition and resettlement. As one expert stated to me, "[The] land price is higher for clean land."

It is important to emphasize here that the government typically profits greatly by taking the land at a price that reflects its less intensive original use and then conveying land use rights for more intensive uses at current market rates to developers who plan to construct higher-end housing or commercial projects. By exercising its powers to requisition land, remove the current users of the property, assemble large development parcels, and allow more intensive uses and densities, the government can enrich itself enormously. Many observers, along with some displaced residents, find this fact extremely troubling. But note that while most of the experts with whom I raised this issue either stated or implied that this is the case, one Chinese lawyer strenuously disagreed with this assertion.

Of course, there is the possibility that the government will lose money if property values decrease during the time when the land is being requisitioned, cleared, and conveyed to a developer. However, land prices in China seem to have increased relentlessly during the past two decades. Besides, real estate values would have to drop precipitously before the decrease would offset the government's built-in advantage in buying out occupants of run-down homes (many of whom do not hold land use rights) and assembling large development parcels that can thereafter be repurposed for more intensive uses by commercial developers (all of whom will hold land use rights in this same property).

In the earlier days of the modern Chinese real estate market, the government occasionally was willing to bear much of the business risk of a relocation and demolition project on its own. For example, if a high-profile foreign company wanted to invest in specific land to build a manufacturing facility, it might contract with the government for that parcel, to be delivered vacant at a specified date in the future. The government would then approach the occupants and seek to relocate them at a negotiated price. This process obviously entailed great risk to the government, as it would have already committed to a sales price before knowing the actual cost of buying out the existing occupants. The government presumably believed it would benefit in the long run, in the form of higher tax revenues and increased economic development in the area, even if it lost money on the specific real estate transaction. This sequence of events has become far less common as the Chinese real estate market has matured, the government has gained experience, and outside buyers have become more anxious to acquire rights to develop land in China.

Several speakers emphasized that the government has become considerably more reluctant during the past few years to requisition older dwellings for private commercial development, whether before or after identifying the eventual developer for the land. This hesitancy reflects the government's concerns about both business risk and public perception. Existing residents have become more sophisticated and have learned to hold out for higher compensation. The government has been compelling would-be developers to deal with these holdouts directly, especially when the number of holdouts is non-trivial. This shift places the financial hazard of ever-more-expensive buyouts on the developer rather than on the government. If the deal balloons in price or falls through completely, it is no longer the government's problem.

I observed a number of blocks in Shanghai that were obviously on their way to being redeveloped, but with an occasional old building still standing, presumably occupied by a resident who had not yet reached final agreement with the block's developer. Private developers, meanwhile, sometimes acting through intermediary relocation companies, have occasionally resorted to intimidation and violence as a means of encouraging these remaining residents to reduce their demands and leave quickly. In one recent Shanghai incident described for me by several different interviewees, a couple was killed when their apartment was set on fire in an apparent attempt to intimidate them into leaving.[151]

Moreover, while the government still technically holds the right to requisition this land, public pressure has made these requisitions more and more unpopular. At a time of increasing real estate prices and widespread worry about housing costs, the government does not wish to be perceived as assisting real estate developers in enriching themselves by depriving poorer residents of their long-time homes in exchange for minimal compensation. Some of the older buildings slated to be razed may have historical value as well, and there is growing, if still slight, support in China for historic preservation of significant structures.

Several of the experts who shared their views on this topic with me expressed sympathy for the plight of these poorer urban residents, along with concerns that overall social instability might increase if these controversial land requisitions continue. In fact, even when the purpose of a land requisition is unquestionably public, the removal of a resident from their home is controversial. Chinese citizens have protested publicly in front of government ministries and there have been cases of self-immolation in Beijing.[152] Requisitions for purposes that are less obviously public raise even greater worries for the government. This distinction mirrors the outcry over takings for economic development in the United States.[153] Nonetheless, many who are knowledgeable about the Shanghai real estate market believe that the government continues to assist real estate developers actively, sometimes employing illegal methods to do so.

---

151 Liu, *supra* note 145, at 1–2 & n.5.

152 *See, e.g.*, Stanley Lubman, *China's Critical Disconnect*, WALL ST. J. CHINA REAL TIME REPORT, June 21, 2011, http://blogs.wsj.com/chinarealtime/2011/06/21/chinas-critical-disconnect (describing a murder-suicide by a businessman who unsuccessfully sought reasonable compensation for the taking of his home for a highway that was never constructed; the blog post places some of the blame on central government policies that have decentralized political power and thereby reduced accountability); *Farmer Sets Self on Fire at Tian'anmen Square*, CHINA DAILY, Sept. 15, 2003, http://www.chinadaily.com.cn/en/doc/2003-09/15/content_264285.htm (describing the farmer as dissatisfied with a relocation decision; the article does not address the legitimacy of the farmer's claim); *see also* Liu Li, *City Denies Reports on Large-Scale Evictions*, CHINA DAILY, Mar. 11, 2004, http://www.chinadaily.com.cn/english/doc/2004-03/11/content_313666.htm (claiming that controversial evictions "are in tune with the capital city's long-term development, and are not merely for the Beijing 2008 Olympic Games").

153 *See* Kelo v. City of New London, 545 U.S. 469 (2005) (holding that takings for purposes of economic development do not violate the "public use" requirement of the Fifth Amendment). I was in Shanghai both before and after the Supreme Court decided *Kelo*, and my faculty colleagues were following the case with great interest. Several of the experts I interviewed asked me extremely knowledgeable questions about *Kelo*, with which they were quite familiar. Of course, elected and appointed officials in the United States who make unpopular decisions of this type are more accountable to the public, particularly at the city and county level.

Shanghai's government instituted a land reserve system several years ago. Under this system, the government will relocate urban residents from a desirable block before a developer has been identified and will stockpile this urban land. When the government later chooses to release this land from its reserves, it will allow developers to bid for it competitively. The government establishes a minimum price that allows it to recoup its earlier demolition and relocation costs, although market-driven bids are likely to exceed this minimum by a substantial amount, particularly if some time has elapsed between the acquisition and the sale. The land reserve method allows the government, rather than the developer, to take the initiative on land use planning. It also divorces the process of requisitioning older housing stock from the subsequent conveyance of the vacant land to a particular developer, a separation that may help to insulate the government from the charge that residents are being relocated at the behest of a specific developer.

Agricultural Collective Land

Agricultural collective land poses a knottier problem, since neither the agricultural collective itself nor the government may grant land use rights to developers or homeowners on this land. The government first must requisition it and convert it to state-owned land before the government can grant land use rights on it.[154] In this sense, China's dual land market differs significantly from that of the United States and other Western nations, in which there is a unitary market.

The agricultural collective is generally entitled to compensation for its land when it is converted into state-owned land. However, it is difficult to determine what rural land is truly worth since there has been no viable market in agricultural land in China for more than half a century. Agricultural collective land also can be requisitioned by the government and then granted back to the collective in the form of a granted land use right. This process allows the collective either to use the land for non-agricultural purposes itself or to re-transfer the granted land use right to a third party and enjoy the profit from its increased value for development purposes.[155]

Granted land use rights are also to be contrasted with allocated land use rights. After Chinese law began to recognize granted land use rights, allocated land use rights were distinguished as land use rights that a user obtained free of charge.[156] Allocated land use rights ordinarily have an indefinite term as long as the stated

---

154 Chengshi Fangdichan Guanli Fa [Law on the Administration of Urban Real Estate], art. 9 ("The land-use right for the collective-owned land within a planned urban district may be granted with payment only after it is requisitioned in accordance with the law and turned into State-owned land").

155 RANDOLPH & LOU, *supra* note 30, at 134–35, 145–46.

156 *Id.* at 86.

use for which the right was granted continues.[157] The indefinite term and lack of required consideration characteristic of an allocated land use right reflect its origin as part of the socialist planned economy.[158] They also make allocated land unsuitable for commercial development.

Many of the people I spoke with believe that the government is paying unfairly low amounts to the collectives for their farmland, by which they mean that the government is calculating fair market value on the assumption that the highest and best use still is agricultural. To a great extent, the government appears to be limited by the provisions of the Land Administration Law. Article 47 of the Land Administration Law provides that compensation for requisitioned agricultural collective land shall be equal to six to ten times the average annual crop output during the preceding three years, plus additional amounts for resettlement, fixtures, and crops not yet harvested.[159] Provincial and lower-level governments may increase these totals to maintain living standards, but the adjusted total for land compensation and resettlement expenses may not exceed thirty times the average annual crop output during the preceding three years unless the State Council raises the rates due to special circumstances.[160]

These statutory valuation options all reflect what the land is worth as farmland and not the current fair market value as might be determined by a negotiated transfer between willing participants. If the prospective buyer expects to develop the land more intensively, the land almost certainly is worth considerably more to this buyer than its agricultural value as determined by Article 47. After the collective receives the compensation award from the government, it typically provides the displaced farmers with either cash or in-kind compensation; in some cases, the farmers may be relocated to other collectives. Once the land has been transferred from the collective to the state, the government can then grant land use rights on it to developers at much higher prices—values reflecting the fact that residential or commercial development has become the new highest and best use.

In short, the government is profiting, at the expense of agricultural peasants, from changing patterns of land use and its own exclusive legal power to transform undevelopable farmland into developable urban land.[161] This process roughly

---

157 Chengshi Fangdichan Guanli Fa [Law on the Administration of Urban Real Estate], art. 23; RANDOLPH & LOU, *supra* note 30, at 91.

158 RANDOLPH & LOU, *supra* note 30, at 89.

159 Tudi Guanli Fa [Land Administration Law], art. 47.

160 *Id.*

161 *See, e.g.,* Anthony Gar-on Yeh, *The Dual Land Market and Urban Development in China, in* EMERGING LAND AND HOUSING MARKETS IN CHINA, *supra* note 11, at 39, 43 ("Because the municipality monopolizes the supply of this type of land, it can acquire rural land from farmers at a monopolistic price and sell it to developers at market price. A municipality can make a considerable profit because of the great difference between land-acquisition and land-lease prices."); William Valletta, *The Land Administration Law of 1998 and its Impact on Urban Development, in* EMERGING LAND AND HOUSING MARKETS IN CHINA, *supra,* at 59, 67 ("In many requisition deals a large windfall of new value resulted from the

mirrors the method described above for clearing urban land that is occupied by older housing, with the added complication that the displaced residents are farmers and thus are losing their livelihood as well as their home. Keep in mind that in the United States, 0.7 percent of the labor force is engaged in "farming, forestry, and fishing,"[162] while in China, the percentage of the labor force engaged in "agriculture" is 38.1 percent.[163] Even if these categories are not defined in precisely the same way, it is clear that a vastly higher proportion of the Chinese population leads a life that revolves around agricultural production. And the education, literacy, and social gaps between urban and rural dwellers are much greater in China than in the United States and other Western nations. In short, a very large number of poor farmers are being deprived of their homes and their jobs in exchange for relatively paltry amounts of money.

Over the next two decades, as many as 300 million Chinese may move from rural areas to cities.[164] And "in less than thirty years following 1992, the number of migrants from the countryside to China's cities will considerably exceed the entire present population of the United States."[165] These estimates were confirmed for me by numerous real estate professionals with whom I spoke. One of these experts noted to me that while greater freedom of movement is likely to reduce disparities of wealth among different regions of China, it also is likely to create massive social disorder along the way, and for many decades to come.

General concerns about the upheaval that might be caused by the loss of agricultural land to real estate development appear to have led to the amendments to the Land Administration Law that became effective in 1999.[166] These changes require comprehensive land use planning at all levels of government and make it more difficult for lower-level government entities to modify permitted land uses.[167] These statutory changes obviously were not up to the task. Several different experts advised me that disagreement over how to handle the continuing problem of compensating farmers fairly for lost land was one of the primary reasons for

---

reclassification of the land [from rural to urban]. The requisition procedure was designed to capture all of this value for the state or municipality."); Valerie Jaffee Washburn, *Regular Takings or Regulatory Takings? Land Expropriation in Rural China*, 20 PAC. RIM L. & POL'Y J. 71 (2011) (discussing this expropriation surplus).

162 CIA – THE WORLD FACTBOOK – UNITED STATES, https://www.cia.gov/library/publications/the-world-factbook/geos/us.html (last visited July 19, 2011).

163 CIA – THE WORLD FACTBOOK – CHINA, https://www.cia.gov/library/publications/the-world-factbook/geos/ch.html (last visited July 19, 2011).

164 Ding & Knaap, *supra* note 55, at 32.

165 LIEBERTHAL, *supra* note 109, at 12 (suggesting that 12 million rural residents migrate to cities each year). Citing similar numbers, You-tien Hsing notes that similar increases in the level of urbanization took 120 years in Britain and 40 years in the United States. HSING, *supra* note 148, at 2.

166 Valletta, *supra* note 161, at 69.

167 Tudi Guanli Fa [Land Administration Law], arts. 8, 12, 17–20, 24 (2004); RANDOLPH & LOU, *supra* note 30, at 136–38.

the delay in the adoption of China's property law, which was under discussion for years before its ultimate adoption in 2007.[168]

Even more worrisome to those concerned about the unfairness of these relocation policies is the fact that the profits the government extracts from the agricultural collectives often are used to fund government operations that primarily benefit the urban core. Some professionals bluntly view this process as a transfer of wealth from poor peasants living in outlying collectives to wealthy downtown city dwellers.[169] Furthermore, agricultural workers, who are not considered urban residents and therefore do not qualify for certain social welfare benefits, typically depend on the regular production from their agricultural collective land as their retirement fund.[170]

One lawyer advised me that some of these peasants actually receive income for life in exchange for the loss of their land; another expert explained that these farmers are given jobs as a form of supplementary non-cash compensation. Still another expert indicated that if an entire agricultural collective is converted to state-owned land, the displaced farmers become urban residents, which makes them eligible for retirement benefits, health care, and unemployment insurance. The Chinese government has also been experimenting in certain provinces by abolishing the legal distinction between urban residents and peasants.[171] Nonetheless, the central government continues to worry that perceptions of unfairness about the process of converting land from agricultural to more intensive uses will combine with the growing income disparity between the booming eastern cities and the lagging rural areas to increase the level of peasant unrest.

One expert suggested that more and more developers today are being forced to negotiate directly with agricultural collectives rather than acquiring land from the government after the government has obtained the land from the collectives. The government, while still nominally required to serve as intermediary, plays a far more passive role than it formerly did. This process bears some similarities to the approach the government has begun to take when resettling poor residents of urban areas, as discussed earlier. Another knowledgeable person advised me that

---

168 *See, e.g.*, Kahn, *supra* note 67 (describing the 2006 shelving of the proposed property law by the National People's Congress because some scholars and advisers feared "China's rising income gap and increasing social unrest" and noting that some Chinese economists view peasants as "economically disenfranchised"); *supra* notes 67–69 and accompanying text.

169 *See supra* note 137 and accompanying text.

170 *Cf. supra* notes 111–15 and accompanying text (discussing similar concerns with respect to state-owned enterprises).

171 *See, e.g.*, Keith B. Richburg, *In China, Chafing under Ancient Permits; Access to City Services; Critics Say "Hukous" Are Outdated and Discriminatory*, WASH. POST, Aug. 15, 2010, at A8 (describing the household registration system and recent attempts at reforming it); Joseph Kahn, *China to Drop Urbanite–Peasant Legal Differences*, N.Y. TIMES, Nov. 3, 2005, at A8 (emphasizing the government's efforts to "slow the country's surging wealth gap and reduce social unrest").

Shanghai is undertaking a pilot study that would allow agricultural collectives to trade land use rights in certain urban zones. This would establish a transaction structure that places the collective in a position to retain more of the gains from the transfer of rights to developable land.

In these evolving settings, developers will have to reach their own accords with collectives, which presumably have learned to hold out for prices that more accurately reflect the highest and best use for their land. Developers then will pass these increased costs along to the ultimate purchasers, who now will have to pay a price that factors in the true worth of the land they are occupying. The premium attributable to the enhanced value of the land for construction purposes will thereby indirectly benefit the rural residents of the collective who have been displaced.

In an effort to cool down the real estate market while reducing the number of peasants who end up without land to cultivate, the central government has recently enforced land preservation plans that place strict limits on the amount of arable land that can be converted to more intensive uses.[172] Developers must either replace the land themselves or contribute to a fund that is used to replace the land or reclaim previously unusable land. One expert referred to this reclamation process as "turning mud into agricultural land." It turns out that he really meant it: one method of providing replacement land is to shore up muddy areas in the ever-growing Yangtze River Delta, not far from Shanghai. He expressed concern that the Three Gorges Dam, which has reduced the amount of silt that flows downstream and collects in the delta, may diminish the amount of mud available for reclamation. Another expert expressed inordinate faith in the ability of the Yangtze Delta to continue to grow, predicting that "one day China will reach the United States."

Other experts question the effectiveness of land reclamation. They note that reclaimed land often is less fertile than the corresponding land lost to agriculture and that reclamation of marginally fertile land may have negative environmental effects.[173] The central government, which is extremely concerned with maintaining overall social stability, once again finds itself directly at odds with provincial and municipal governments, which rely on habitual sales of land use rights to fund their ongoing operations and capital improvement budgets.

The Continuing Need for Developable Land

China's cities are growing physically larger at a shocking rate. The average amount of space per resident is on the rise, cities are increasing the amount of public space

---

172 *See* Tudi Guanli Fa [Land Administration Law], arts. 31–42 (2004) (requiring conservation of agricultural land, preservation of topsoil, re-use of "wasteland," and other similar preservation measures).

173 Lin & Ho, *supra* note 132, at 118.

such as parks, and tens of millions of rural residents are migrating to the cities—often without work permits—in search of jobs. An exhibit I viewed at the Shanghai Planning Museum stated that in the prior twenty years, Shanghai had razed 4.281 million square meters of blighted housing holding 900,000 households. The city replaced these outdated units with 16.2 million square meters of new housing for the displaced families and for many newcomers. This new construction constituted 53 percent of the gross area covered by housing in Shanghai.

The same exhibit stated that Shanghai's average per capita green space grew from 2.41 square meters to 9.15 square meters between 1997 and 2003. During this time period, the official population had been relatively stable and the unofficial population had been growing steadily. This museum also touted the advantages of some specific new low-density suburban developments that are being built along the city's urban boundary. With more people and more space per person than ever, Shanghai is expanding both upward and outward, devouring land along the way.

Development thus is proceeding rapidly and will continue to do so. The obvious conclusion that any observer reaches is that a sensible developer would rather build on land that is already thinly populated than obtain rights to land which it will have to persuade numerous residents to leave. This conclusion helps to explain the popularity and success of locales such as Shanghai's Pudong New Area, where the few prior residents could be relocated at relatively low expense. Pudong's development also was hastened by tax incentives, excellent new infrastructure, and some rather heavy-handed government pressure.[174] The Chinese government at all levels was anxious to see this project succeed, as were the real estate developers involved. Demolition and resettlement costs are far lower in sparsely populated areas such as Pudong used to be, which translates into greater profits and greater ease for the developer and lower prices for the end user.

Several of the experts I interviewed argued that China's vast stock of government- and collective-owned land ensures that the Chinese economy will not collapse any time soon, as some Western experts have nervously predicted.[175] The government can simply keep transferring land use rights on the ever-expanding urban fringe—land that it either owns already or can easily acquire from agricultural collectives—at hefty prices that reflect the land's increasing value for urban residential or commercial use.[176] These experts argue that as long as the

---

174 *See supra* notes 101, 126 and accompanying text; *infra* note 311 and accompanying text.

175 "Confronted with an insolvent banking system, a rising budget deficit and unfunded welfare liabilities, the reaction of ministers is to claim that the state owns all kinds of valuable assets [including land] that it can sell to cover its expenditures." STUDWELL, *supra* note 115, at 260. Studwell continues by disagreeing with this argument, but most of the Chinese professionals I met do not share his skepticism.

176 "Given that cities generate more than 70 percent of the country's economic output, China's economic success inevitably fuels demand for land at the urban fringes, where economic development activity is most intense." Xiaochen Meng & Yanru Li, *Urban*

government has land use rights that it can sell, it will never run out of cash. One of the Chinese experts I met favorably contrasted China's slow and smooth approach with that employed after the disintegration of the Soviet Union by Russia, which disposed of state-owned assets at a much more rapid rate. By selling off state-owned assets—including the right to use land—at a more measured speed, China not only preserved its assets for future use or sale but also retained greater control over the ultimate use of these assets for a longer period of time.[177]

Land Supply in the Chinese Transitional Economy: Case Studies in Beijing and Shenzhen, *in* EMERGING LAND AND HOUSING MARKETS IN CHINA, *supra* note 11, at 125, 125.

177 *See also* Bo-Sin Tang & Sing-Cheong Liu, *Property Developers and Speculative Development in China*, *in* EMERGING LAND AND HOUSING MARKETS IN CHINA, *supra* note 11, at 199, 201 ("In contrast with many Eastern European countries, China did not pursue full-prong privatization or 'shock therapy' in its reform process. Instead, it pursued incremental changes, thereby decreasing the likelihood of major social instability."); *cf.* PEERENBOOM, *supra* note 2, at 460 (arguing that Russia's poor experience with privatization reflects the fact that it sought to privatize in the absence of the rule of law and at a time when its institutions were weak).

Chapter 7
Lenders and Loans: Where Does All the Money Come From?

An Introduction to Chinese Mortgages

As a first approximation, it is accurate to say that Chinese legal usage of the term "mortgage" is similar to common law usage.[178] Article 180 of the Property Rights Law lists seven different types of property that may be mortgaged, including houses and land use rights, while Article 34 of the Guaranty Law lists six different types, with much overlap between the two groupings.[179] The 2007 Property Rights Law provides that it controls in the event of any inconsistency between that law and the earlier Guaranty Law.[180]

Other types of property that are mortgageable include items that would be considered personalty in the United States and thus not subject to mortgage

---

178 Article 179 of the Property Rights Law states, "Where a debtor or a third party, for performance of the mortgaged debt, secures the creditor's rights with property without transference of its possession, if the debtor defaults, the creditor shall have priority in satisfying his claim from such property." Wuquan Fa [Property Rights Law], art. 179. Similarly, Article 33 of China's Guaranty Law states:
> Mortgage as used in this Law means that the debtor or a third party secures the creditor's rights with property listed in Article 34 of this Law without transference of its possession. If the debtor defaults, the creditor shall be entitled to convert the property into money to offset the debts or have priority in satisfying his claim from the proceeds of auction or sale of the property ....

Danbao Fa [Guaranty Law], art. 33. Both of these statutory provisions define the terms "mortgagor," "mortgagee," and "mortgaged property." *See also* Wuquan Fa [Property Rights Law], art. 143 ("Except as otherwise provided for by law, the owner of the right to the use of land for construction use shall have the right to transfer, exchange, make as capital contribution, donate or mortgage the right to the use of land for construction use."); *id.* art. 170 ("Unless otherwise stipulated by laws, holder [sic] of security interest shall have priority in satisfying its claim if a debtor defaults in its obligations."); *see generally* Guanghua Yu, *The Role of Mortgages: A Case for Formal Law*, in THE DEVELOPMENT OF THE CHINESE LEGAL SYSTEM: CHANGES AND CHALLENGES 113, 131 (Guanghua Yu ed., 2011) (arguing that the gradual clarification of Chinese mortgage law in recent years has led to an expansion of bank lending).

179 Wuquan Fa [Property Rights Law], art. 180; Danbao Fa [Guaranty Law], art. 34.

180 Wuquan Fa [Property Rights Law], art. 178.

law.[181] But note as well that separate chapters of the Property Rights Law and the Guaranty Law address pledges, indicating that realty and personalty are treated differently.[182] Leaseholds are not specifically enumerated as mortgageable in either statute's list and apparently may not be mortgaged.[183]

Project Loans and Cash-Flow Loans

Commercial loans in China, much like those in the United States, come in two varieties and serve two different objectives.[184] A developer may seek a project loan, which is analogous to an American construction loan, and may also seek a cash-flow loan to be used to support the daily operation of the completed building, which parallels the American permanent loan.[185] Project loans usually are issued for a term of twelve to eighteen months, reflecting the fact that construction schedules in China are considerably faster than in the United States. Any visitor to China can witness how quickly developers erect buildings. Construction sites often operate—noisily—twenty-four hours per day, seven days per week, with plenty of willing laborers from the provinces to keep projects moving ahead relentlessly.

Project loans are disbursed in periodic installments,[186] but borrowers sometimes can negotiate for a modest amount to be advanced initially in a lump sum. Although project loans are available for terms of more than twelve months, one developer explained that his company prefers loans with a term of no more than twelve months because the loan is then considered a short-term loan. Short-term loans require the borrower to meet fewer application formalities and are less closely supervised. If construction ends up taking longer than the projected

---

181 See, e.g., Danbao Fa [Guaranty Law], art. 34(2), (4) (listing such items as "machines" and "means of transport").

182 Wuquan Fa [Property Rights Law], arts. 208–22 (addressing pledges of "movables"); Danbao Fa [Guaranty Law], arts. 63–74 (same); Wuquan Fa [Property Rights Law], arts. 223–29 (addressing pledges of "rights," including commercial paper, securities, and intellectual property); Danbao Fa [Guaranty Law], arts. 75–81 (same).

183 See RANDOLPH & LOU, supra note 30, at 244–46 (discussing the desirability of permitting leasehold mortgages).

184 See generally Gregory M. Stein, Mortgage Law in China: Comparing Theory and Practice, 72 MO. L. REV. 1315, 1326–29 (2007) (distinguishing between project loans and cash-flow loans).

185 This chapter examines the relationship between borrowers and lenders, while Chapter 9, infra, discusses the construction process in China, including construction lending.

186 See Danbao Fa [Guaranty Law], art. 59 (defining "[a] mortgage of maximum amount" as a mortgage of property "to secure the creditor's claims which occur successively during a given period of time and to the extent of the total amount of the claims"); see also Wuquan Fa [Property Rights Law, arts. 203–07 (addressing, but not defining, mortgages of maximum amount).

twelve months, it is a relatively straightforward process for the borrower to obtain an extension of the term of the project loan, thereby avoiding the stricter regulations that would have applied had the developer sought a longer-term loan from the outset. Building permits in some jurisdictions are also valid for a term of only twelve months, which provides an additional incentive for meeting such a condensed construction schedule.

Cash-flow loans are generally not relevant to the construction of residential buildings, as the developer conveys the residential units upon completion of the building and the individual residential buyers secure their own financing. For commercial buildings that are to be rented out, cash-flow loans with a term of three to five years are common, and the same lender that provided the project loan for the building will frequently extend the subsequent cash-flow loan to the developer. These loan durations are considerably shorter than is typically seen in the United States. As foreign lenders have entered this market, however, the terms for cash-flow loans have begun to increase. One foreign lender is reportedly extending cash-flow loans with twelve-year terms. Interest rates tend to be lower for cash-flow loans than for project loans. This difference presumably reflects the fact that a completed building constitutes more dependable security for the repayment of a loan than does a building that is still under construction.

Despite the availability of cash-flow loans, one developer explained, developers would prefer to sell units, even in commercial buildings, rather than retain them. This preference may reflect a belief that the market is near its peak now and there is nothing to be gained by waiting to sell. Whether the developer plans to sell the completed units or retain them, defaults on project and cash-flow loans are rare, because property values have been increasing steadily. Property owners thus have both the incentive and the ability to keep their loan payments current.

The experts I met all agreed that commercial real estate lenders are almost exclusively domestic mainland Chinese banks. Other loan funds come from lenders in Taiwan and Hong Kong. Lenders that are based in nations with large expatriate Chinese populations, such as Australia, Canada, and the United States, also serve as significant sources of mortgage loan funds.

Residential loans pose particularly thorny issues, as I address in considerably more detail in the next chapter. By all accounts, prices for residential real estate in Shanghai far exceed what the typical buyer ought to be able to afford. Yet buyers keep buying and lenders keep lending, while the default rate has remained low. Nearly every person I spoke with confirmed that lenders require verification of official income before they will lend to a residential buyer, and nearly all of these people agreed that the income statements employers supply to lenders often overstate the typical applicant's income significantly. One Chinese expert vehemently disagreed, insisting that a typical bank analysis is more rigorous than this. While most lenders recognize that these statements probably are unreliable, they make these residential loans anyway and merely demand the untrustworthy documentation for their files.

Lenders, in short, routinely extend credit fully aware that the actual official income of the average residential borrower to whom they are lending will be insufficient to cover the monthly loan payment. In addition, there are no national credit reporting agencies in China, which means that lenders have no dependable means of assessing the overall financial reliability of their loan applicants. Interestingly, I was told that this problem exists to an even greater degree in the growing automobile loan industry, leaving lenders with the problem of tracking down this mobile collateral after a borrower defaults.

So how do residential buyers make their payments? To begin with, authorized income is only part of the story for most Chinese. In addition to the income reported from their official—and therefore taxable—jobs, many workers earn "gray" income from various sources. As I heard repeatedly, this income is usually in cash, some of it may not be legal, and nearly all of it goes untaxed by the government. Lenders assume, and perhaps receive informal assurances, that their borrowers have other sources of income that cannot be officially verified. In addition, borrowers frequently obtain short-term loans from family members to help them make their regular payments on their acquisition loans. Thus, the purchase of a residential unit becomes a family affair, and several generations may be contributing to the purchase and living in the unit. Family contributions such as these are likely to give considerable comfort to lenders that might otherwise worry about the borrower's dedication to repaying the loan.

With home prices appreciating as rapidly as they have in the past several years, many buyers are making their purchases largely for investment purposes. If their loan payments become more than they can handle, they can sell their apartments quickly and at a significant profit; if they do not sell their units voluntarily and repay their debts, their lenders can foreclose with little risk of loss. In fact, I heard over and over of investors who buy multiple residential units with the idea of selling them within a few months. These buyers do not anticipate renting the apartments out, and many units have unfinished interiors. The owners hold these apartments empty and wait a few months while the property appreciates. As a result, many of the new residential units in Shanghai have never actually been occupied. These apartments are commodities, not residences.

The murkiness and unreliability of lending standards, particularly for residential loans, probably goes a long way toward explaining why a secondary market in real estate loans has not yet developed in China.[187] Some Chinese real estate experts were simply unfamiliar with the concept of a secondary mortgage market, and several sophisticated experts greeted my inquiries about such a market with a puzzled "*mei you*,"[188] signifying "we don't have this." Other experts seemed

---

187 *See generally* Whitman, *supra* note 31, at 57–58 (describing the beneficial features of a secondary mortgage market).

188 This universal response translates literally as "don't have," but a foreign visitor to China quickly grasps that this multi-purpose rejoinder can signify anything from "I don't understand" to "don't bother me."

keenly aware of the absence of and need for a market in which residential mortgage loans can be securitized, with one professor explaining that the government had previously prohibited the securitization of mortgage loans but that it authorized a pilot project in 2005.

This professor implied that the government wants each major lender's percentage of nonperforming loans to go no higher than it currently is. By compelling banks to retain residential loans, which are extremely likely to be repaid, the government helps to ensure that the banks maintain or improve the overall quality of their portfolios. Several experts stated that there have been securitizations in China, but upon further questioning, it appeared that they were actually speaking of participations: in every such case, the speaker was referring to the sale of fractional interests in a single large mortgage affecting just one parcel rather than the issuance of securities backed by a pool of smaller mortgages.

Given the low rate of residential loan defaults during the past decade—an era in which the number of homeowners has mushroomed—banks simply may not see any reason to reduce or spread the risk of holding a portfolio of individual mortgage loans. A small group of lenders controls a huge share of the residential market, and these lenders may see little need to sell loans to raise cash when they already hold enormous reserves of depositors' savings. Nonetheless, the government appears to recognize the potential value of securitization and the ways in which the availability of securitization could ease overall access to credit and help smooth out regional disparities in the availability of funds.[189] Several speakers referred to new tax and accounting policies dating back to 2005 that are designed to encourage the growth of a secondary mortgage market, and one spoke of an increase in the number of domestic ratings agencies.

China may one day see the growth of a secondary mortgage market. This seems to be an area in which foreign participants in the Chinese real estate market will have many skills and much experience to offer. So far, though, the Chinese real estate industry has been able to flourish without a secondary market in residential real estate mortgages. And recent experiences in the United States may persuade China that its domestic residential markets are doing just fine without any input or interference from the West.

How Does the Developer Finance Construction?

Developers in China, like those in the West, would prefer to limit their personal risk and maximize their leverage by borrowing funds. They may take advantage of several direct and indirect sources of loans. To a certain extent, they may be able to mortgage their undeveloped land use right to a lender in exchange for funds to be

---

189 Zhou Xin & Koh Gui Qing, *China C. Banker Eyes Explosive Growth in Securitisation*, REUTERS, Apr. 27, 2011, http://www.reuters.com/article/2011/04/28/china-economy-securitisation-idUSL3E7FS09S20110428.

used for the acquisition of that right or the development of a structure to be built on the land. They can mortgage the partially completed building to a lender. The developer can presell units—in particular, residential apartments—and require that each buyer pay a deposit to reserve a unit and then make additional payments as construction progresses. These payments are, in essence, a loan from the buyer to the developer to be used to finance construction. And developers frequently delay payments to contractors, forcing these contractors to finance construction involuntarily.

Mortgaging the Unimproved Land Use Right

Different experts provided different answers to the question of whether banks would lend in return for receiving a mortgage on an unimproved land use right.[190] One Chinese lawyer stated that lenders will not lend funds to developers to pay for the granted land use right itself. The buyer must pay the government in full with its own cash when the buyer acquires the right. Lenders simply are unwilling to lend until they know that the borrower already has acquired the land use right. A Chinese developer confirmed this point with respect to Shanghai, but indicated that the practice differs in Shenzhen, another explosive real estate market.

One law professor disagreed with the lawyer, stating that developers are permitted to mortgage an unimproved land use right in order to obtain a loan for the development of the structure to be built on that land. Perhaps that professor was recognizing that such loans are legally permissible, without commenting on whether banks routinely grant them. Or perhaps he was observing that banks are willing to lend against a land use right if the funds are to be used for construction, which means that the value of the security will be increasing, but not if they are to be used for acquisition, where the value of the security remains constant. In the latter of these two cases, of course, the lender presumably would wish to receive a mortgage on the improvements and not just on the naked land use right.

These potentially inconsistent responses collectively suggest not only that each professional's experience with the application of these rules and policies is different, but also that bank policies and government regulations continue to evolve over time and vary from place to place within China. Frequent changes in the rules may reflect the degree to which the government wishes to encourage or discourage development as the market matures, as well as the accrual of experience over a relatively brief span of time. I was told by two different developers that it was possible several years back for a developer to function by mortgaging a land use right as security for the loan used to purchase that right, without contributing

---

190 Land use rights may legally be mortgaged. Wuquan Fa [Property Rights Law], art. 180 ("The following property ... may be mortgaged: ... (ii) Land use right to building lot ...."). But while this provision clearly permits the mortgaging of a land use right, it does not clarify whether a right can be mortgaged as security for a loan when the loan proceeds are used to acquire that same land use right.

any of its own money. This suggests either that banks were willing to live with 100 percent loan-to-value ratios at the time because the government was struggling to encourage private development or, perhaps, that government entities were selling land use rights for less than their true fair market value.

Note as well that under the Property Rights Law and other Chinese statutes, a mortgage on a construction lot does not provide the mortgagee with a security interest in improvements that are subsequently built on that lot. The land lender may foreclose on the lot after it is developed and the improvements will be sold along with the land, but the land lender is not entitled to any of the foreclosure proceeds attributable to the improvements.[191] Chinese law thus contemplates that lenders can obtain mortgages on undeveloped land.

In the current, overheated climate, mortgage loans that may once have been available for developers to acquire land use rights appear to have become scarce and possibly nonexistent, as state-controlled lenders try to cool the market gradually. Banks may also have come to realize that they have been shouldering too much development risk and may now be seeking to place more of this risk on their borrowers. Note also that government entities that are selling land use rights may impose their own requirements as a means of slowing down the pace of development, on top of any applicable lender limitations. To illustrate, one expert advised me that interested bidders must now deposit 30 percent of the estimated value of the land use right with the government before they even qualify to bid on it.

The fact that a developer must raise the cash it needs to acquire a land use right with little or no access to borrowed funds provides further evidence that the Chinese land use right and the Western ground lease function in quite distinct ways, despite some apparent similarities, as already discussed above. The ground lease allows the Western developer to operate without the need to acquire fee title to the underlying land. Thus, the ground lease functions as a financing device. By contrast, the Chinese developer must purchase the underlying land use right at the outset and, as just noted, may be unable to finance this purchase. This distinction serves as a reminder that the principal purpose of the Chinese land use right is to allow the Chinese government to sever official state ownership of the land from the private right to develop it. It also reminds the Western observer yet again of the uneasy tension in China today between the private right to develop property and the socialist conception of common ownership of land.

---

191 Wuquan Fa [Property Rights Law], art. 200; *see also* Chengshi Fangdichan Guanli Fa [Law on the Administration of Urban Real Estate], art. 52 (permitting mortgages on lots that will be improved by housing but clarifying that the mortgagee of the land does not have priority with respect to the portion of the foreclosure proceeds that derive from these improvements); Danbao Fa [Guaranty Law], art. 55 (same).

Mortgaging the Improvements

Whether or not banks will extend acquisition loans secured by mortgages on undeveloped land use rights, they will lend for the construction of the building itself and will insist on receiving a mortgage on the improvements.[192] Improvements are mortgageable, and a mortgage on an existing building automatically creates a mortgage on the underlying land use right.[193] When banks are considering whether to extend a project loan, they require the applicant to submit four documents:[194] (1) the land use right certificate from the government, evidencing that the borrower is the holder of the land use right; (2) the zone certificate, indicating that the height and bulk of the proposed building comply with the requirements of the applicable architecture zone;[195] (3) the land zone certificate, demonstrating that the proposed use is permissible in that land zone; and (4) the construction permit, which authorizes construction. These documents are analogous to an American developer demonstrating that they hold title to the property, that their plans comply with all applicable zoning laws, and that they have received a building permit. Although banks do technically require the submission of these four documents, the first of these four—evidence of the land use right—is the most important one to the lender. It is the land use right that will serve as security for the repayment of the loan. In fact, some years ago, this submission was the only one that banks required.

---

192 *See supra* notes 184–89 and accompanying text (discussing project loans); *infra* notes 263–71 and accompanying text (same); RANDOLPH & LOU, *supra* note 30, at 247–48, 253–54 (discussing how mortgages operate when securing future advances used to construct improvements).

193 *See, e.g.*, Danbao Fa [Guaranty Law], art. 36 (stating that a mortgage on either a land use right or the residential improvements on that land automatically creates a mortgage on both). *But see* Wuquan Fa [Property Rights Law], art. 200 (noting that a mortgage on land that is subsequently improved does not create a security interest in the improvements and that, upon foreclosure, the land and the improvements may be sold together but that the mortgagee of the land shall receive none of the proceeds attributable to the improvements); Danbao Fa [Guaranty Law], art. 55 (same); Chengshi Fangdichan Guanli Fa [Law on the Administration of Urban Real Estate], art. 52 (stating that a mortgage on an undeveloped land use right does not encumber a home that is subsequently built on that land). *See generally* ZHONGZHI GAO, INVEST IN CHINA: A PRACTICAL GUIDE TO REAL ESTATE LAW 147 (2005) ("It is of practical use to distinguish mortgage of land from mortgage of land and buildings on the land.").

194 For more detailed discussion of these required submissions, see *infra* notes 263–71 and accompanying text. Note also that different experts translated the names of these documents into English in slightly different ways.

195 Interestingly, one experienced real estate developer told me that the obtaining of this certificate in Shanghai requires the developer to demonstrate, among other things, that the building contains defense facilities, such as underground tunnels, to be used in the event of war. In the alternative, the developer may pay a fee in lieu of providing these facilities.

Obtaining these four certificates, which are prerequisites for the receipt of a project loan, requires significant cash outlays from the prospective borrower. One developer estimated that obtaining these four documents consumes roughly 30 percent of the typical development budget, with most of that expense attributable to the cost of purchasing the land use right. The charge for obtaining a land use right is even higher if the seller had to bear demolition and relocation expenses. Since all or a significant part of this money must be laid out before the developer is eligible for a mortgage loan, it appears that current policies limit development to entities that are both well-capitalized and well-connected. Smaller entities will probably have tremendous difficulty raising the funds for these initial outlays, and commercial lenders may not be willing or allowed to advance any portion of these amounts.

One expert indicated that project lenders may also insist that a new building be at least partially constructed before they will lend and accept a mortgage in exchange. Developers that are subjected to this additional burden must be in a position not just to acquire the land use right and obtain the other necessary documentation, but also to commence construction with their own funds. They will not be able to borrow any funds until the project is partly completed. The incomplete structure then will serve as security for a loan of the funds needed to complete construction. This requirement increases still further the amount of equity the developer must raise before it is in a position to borrow any construction funds.

The loan-to-value ratio is an additional topic for discussion between developers and their lenders. Developers and lawyers suggested to me that loan-to-value ratios fall in the 50–80 percent range, with 60 percent being typical. This is a term the two parties may negotiate heavily, with more experienced and reliable developers receiving relatively larger loans than their fledgling counterparts.[196]

One small developer bemoaned her complete inability to procure bank loans, because banks will not deal with a company so small. This developer must finance construction entirely via equity, raising funds by selling shares in her company. Even large developers, who are more likely to obtain conventional loans, decry the bureaucratic squabbles they must endure before being able to proceed. One developer noted to me that in a typical project, the developer must obtain 120 government "chops" (official seals), down somewhat from 160 in earlier years. These government requirements are applied unevenly, however, and a lack of *guanxi* on the part of the developer may lead to stricter-than-normal application of these rules to its project.

---

196 *See also* INVESTMENT IN GREATER CHINA: OPPORTUNITIES & CHALLENGES FOR INVESTORS, *supra* note 82, at 309 (describing additional regulatory limits that apply in Shanghai).

Presales as a Form of Financing

Developers are also able to obtain significant financing from the eventual purchasers of the residential and commercial units that they plan to build. They often presell units before the units are completed, and sometimes before construction even begins. These presales typically require large downpayments, along with significant progress payments as construction moves forward. Thus, the buyer is providing an interest-free loan to its builder before the buyer can occupy the unit or mortgage the unit to the buyer's own lender. The preselling of residential units is an extremely important topic in China and is addressed in considerable detail in the next chapter.

Involuntary Financing by Contractors

Contractors serve as another source of funds for developers. It is common practice for contractors to undertake significant amounts of construction and to pay for the building materials they have used long before the developer pays them for their labor and reimburses them for their cash outlays. Contractors will frequently not receive their first payment until they have completed roughly one-third of the work. One expert observed that the competition for construction jobs is sufficiently intense that if a contractor wants a particular job, it will have to advance funds to the developer in this manner. Given that much of the labor for urban construction projects is furnished by migrant workers from rural China who lack permits to serve as urban construction workers, it would not be surprising if contractors are passing these delays along to their workers, slow-paying undocumented peasants who often do not speak the local dialect and who are in no legal position to complain.

If a project fails, the contractor may never receive payment at all. Similarly, late payments from developers to contractors do not always bear interest. It is at least plausible to assume that contractors factor these risks and costs into their bids. Whether or not this is the case, contractors who are paid slowly end up serving as another source of construction financing for the developer. By way of contrast, in a typical American construction project, the developer pays the contractor on a monthly basis, one month in arrears, and often holds back 5–10 percent of the amount due as a retainage. The developer borrows the bulk of these funds from its construction lender. Interest on the ever-growing construction loan balance accrues on a monthly basis and compounds.

In an effort to slow the real estate market and protect contractors, the Chinese government has recently prohibited the practice of using contractors as reluctant lenders. To the extent that these new rules have been effective, developers must either begin the project with more money of their own or borrow funds from other sources so they can pay their contractors more promptly. As previously noted, however, developers have found ways to circumvent these limitations, and contractors have grudgingly gone along. For example, the developer may sell an interest in the ownership entity to the contractor.[197] Such a sale transforms the contractor from a creditor entitled to prompt payment into a minority co-owner that must contribute labor and materials to the entity in exchange for its ownership stake.

Interestingly, several different experts confirmed that there is no legal mechanism in place in China for a lender to perfect a security interest in tenant rents. Borrowers may pledge the income stream from tenant rentals to their lenders, but lenders have no way to perfect their security interest in this collateral. On new residential and commercial construction projects that will be sold upon completion, this legal shortcoming is unlikely to have much relevance, since there are no rent-paying tenants in possession and there never will be. Nonetheless, these experts expressed frustration with this gap in Chinese real estate practice. It seems likely that China will have to permit the perfection of security interests in tenant rents at some future time.

Lending Standards

Although banks do require the submission of the legal documents described above before they will extend credit, few of the experts I met expressed much confidence in lenders' internal financial lending requirements. Banks appear to make the decision to lend based solely on the legality of the project and the government's wish to see the project proceed and are far less concerned with the financial viability of the completed development. When I asked one Western expert who works in China whether Chinese developers gathered market data or prepared feasibility studies for proposed new projects, he laughingly replied, "A lot of these buildings were just built."[198] He did concede that this approach has changed recently, with some banks adopting lending standards more familiar to Westerners.

This lack of concern with "the numbers" of a given project may reflect inexperience relative to Western institutions, though one would think that lenders would have developed that sort of expertise by now. More likely, it is a reminder that nearly all banks in China are state-owned or state-controlled, unlike typical Western lenders. The government uses the banking system as one tool of social policy, subsidizing construction of politically desirable projects even if those ventures are not otherwise financially viable.

Many Westerners today view the modern Chinese economy as moving quickly toward capitalism, but one Westerner with significant experience in China's real

---

197 *See supra* Chapter 4 for a discussion of the contractor as the potential holder of an equity interest in the project; *infra* Chapter 9 for a discussion of the overall construction process.

198 *See also infra* notes 475–76 and accompanying text (describing the construction of a huge shopping mall that was built with no advance market analysis and that has been dramatically unsuccessful).

estate market described China's economy to me as "the farthest thing from a free market you can get without being centrally planned."[199] This odd combination of lenders that are charged with advancing specific government ends and developers that seek to maximize profits and returns while minimizing risks leads to outcomes that differ in important ways from those seen in Western real estate markets.

One expert suggested that developers actually prepare two feasibility studies at the outset of their projects, a bare-bones form for the lender, providing evidence that all legal hurdles have been cleared and that the project is viewed as politically necessary, and a more realistic one for internal consumption only, demonstrating that the development actually will be profitable. A second speaker, who was extremely knowledgeable about China's banking system, advised me that the banks themselves also have two different sets of standards. As a starting point, all banks must comply with guidelines imposed by government agencies charged with bank oversight. In addition, each bank's board of directors sets internal credit policies for that bank, and these internal policies are likely to be more stringent than the bare minimum levels established by banking regulators. One real estate developer argued that banks actually take the decision whether to lend quite seriously, hiring experts to analyze the property, having the land surveyed, and undertaking research as to the strength of the market. Yet another expert suggested that private developers have great difficulty obtaining financing today, with banks far more willing to lend to state-owned developers. This is because the leading banks either are publicly traded already or hope to be in the near future, and thus are subject to greater oversight and supervision than in the past.

Another real estate specialist, discussing the rapid early development of the Pudong New Area in Shanghai, commented that for publicly desirable projects in that zone, banks were required to lend. Private projects that the government saw as having significant public benefit could always count on receiving a green light from their state-supported lender. By contrast, for projects offering largely private benefit, developers had to negotiate with banks individually to obtain loans. This approach presumably enhances the municipal bottom line for jurisdictions that are attempting to upgrade and modernize quickly, since ostensibly private projects with significant public benefit will not look as if they were built with any direct outlay of government money. The solvency of the government-controlled bank, which has been forced to underwrite a quasi-public improvement that is

---

199 See also Yingjie Guo, *In Search of Wealth and Power: The Character of the Chinese State and Limits to Change*, in LAW, WEALTH AND POWER IN CHINA: COMMERCIAL LAW REFORMS IN CONTEXT, *supra* note 69, at 53, 69 (describing the many ways in which the state participates in, and benefits from, market activities); John E. Anderson, *The Path to Property Taxation*, in CHINA'S LOCAL PUBLIC FINANCE IN TRANSITION, *supra* note 96, at 145, 148 ("China's emerging real estate market is not a robust free market in which the invisible hand allocates resources. Rather, it is an emerging market situation where at present ambiguities in the definition and enforcement of property rights limit the full development of markets.").

unlikely to produce cash flow that is adequate to repay the loan, is another story. The government similarly uses its control over the transfer of land use rights as a means of directing specific uses toward or away from specific districts.

There is a more benign explanation for the fact that real estate loans do not seem to be evaluated on the basis of the economic viability of the project. The short history of the post-Mao real estate market has been one of steadily appreciating real estate values, and most real estate loans have been successfully repaid. Under this explanation, the banks initially adopted a rather short-sighted view of the lending process, and their over-optimism has been repeatedly rewarded ever since. To the extent that banks are assessing projects at all, they may be willing to make risky loans in the belief—supported by all of their recent experience—that the project will appreciate rapidly and the borrower will repay the loan. Several speakers acknowledged that China's banks face serious problems arising from nonperforming loans but argued that most of those loans were made to enterprises engaged in businesses other than real estate. Some obsolete state-owned manufacturing enterprises possess few assets of value that an unpaid lender can pursue. Real estate borrowers, by contrast, have pledged to their lenders an asset that is both valuable and appreciating.

If this explanation is accurate, developers will be sure to keep paying their loans even if their debts currently exceed the market value of their assets, because they have faith that the project soon will increase in value and have positive equity. Stated more accurately, these developers believe that the market currently undervalues their property by failing to factor in adequately its anticipated appreciation. Beliefs such as these are bolstered by most of China's recent history, which for the Chinese real estate market is the only history that matters. We can expect China to learn from tough experience at some point in the future, when the inevitable pullback occurs.

Note as well that many of the experts I met focused their discussions on the thriving residential markets. Since residential units are generally sold upon completion, if not sooner, developers recoup their investments quickly, pay off their loans, and move on to the next project. The purchasers of these new residential units have so much on the line—including, often, the residence and life savings of themselves, their parents, and their grandparents—that they will find some way to pay off their acquisition loans. Commercial developments may fare differently. In these settings, the developer may choose to hold the project for investment income for a period of time after the project is complete, and the owner's ability to repay a mortgage loan depends on the receipt of a reliable flow of tenant rents.

One real estate expert provided a more worrisome explanation for the lack of connection between creditworthiness and credit availability. In this speaker's view, the government and its banks help favored candidates invest in real estate. This speaker's implication—not stated outright—is that a successful project will indirectly redound to the benefit of the bank officials who agreed to fund it. Banks lend to favored developers, who surreptitiously reward the decision-makers at those banks. While this expert did not directly accuse bank officers of corruption, another real estate professional did tell me, "Law is for the honest people. Like you and me. They restrict people like you and me." The first real estate expert was more optimistic about the future, however, noting that behavior of this type is becoming less common as the market matures and grows more internationalized, as key lenders consider public offerings of their shares, as the government struggles to slow down a very hot real estate market, and as the government and the public become more attuned to the difficulties that institutionalized government graft can cause.

More generally, lending officers at state-owned banks face institutional incentives that do not always lead to the maximization of profits. In Western nations, bank profitability may translate into generous bonuses for key loan officers while bank losses may send these same officers to the unemployment line. The individuals who make credit decisions have a personal interest in the success or failure of their employers' projects. But Chinese banks are state-owned and must satisfy government policymakers rather than shareholders who demand transparency and profits.

One real estate consultant explained to me that Chinese banks assign a lending quota to each of their lending officers and that the officers' bonuses depend solely on meeting these targets. Employees are not rewarded for making good lending decisions or penalized for making poor ones. The pressure simply is to lend, and there is little linkage between the fortunes of the bank and the fortunes of those who work for the bank. If loans become troubled as the project progresses, similar incentives come into play. There is no reason for a state-owned bank to concede that an earlier lending decision was a poor one; rather, the bank is likely to lend still more money to keep the project afloat. It is easy to avoid the negative publicity of acknowledging a bad loan when the bank's money supply is essentially unlimited and no one ever gets to see the books.

Opaque procedures that encourage speedy development may have been exactly what China needed in the 1980s and 1990s, as a rapidly changing government nurtured a new market in real estate. Even unsuccessful projects can help to jump-start an economy, by providing jobs for workers and helping real estate professionals gain experience. But the government has become concerned that today's markets are dangerously overheated and has taken steps to slow the market as gently as possible. For example, governments at various levels regularly adjust interest rates, minimum downpayments, and the rates of various taxes to encourage or discourage development as market conditions warrant, and have also enacted policies to discourage investment in dwellings that will not be owner-occupied.[200] In addition, some units of government have become more inclined to enforce the requirement that the initial holder of a land use right build on the property within two years, which until recently had been routinely ignored. While not all of these recent changes have a direct effect on the relationship between

---

200 For a discussion of taxes applicable to residential units, see *infra* note 260 and accompanying text.

borrower and lender, all of them are manifestations of the government's desire to keep appreciation of real estate prices in check and all suggest that there will be further tightening in lending standards.

The government also seems worried that ordinary citizens who invest their nest eggs in real estate could suffer dramatic losses if real estate prices drop precipitously. The individual right to invest is explicitly protected by the Property Rights Law.[201] Chinese citizens, however, have generally not experienced the types of down markets that might make them more circumspect in their investments. Many might assume that recent years are typical and might be underestimating the longer-term risks of investing in an unsettled and rapidly developing real estate market. Chinese law provides lenders with the right to foreclosure, which means that a real estate recession might cause many new homeowners to lose their recently purchased dwellings.

Article 195 of the Property Rights Law, for example, provides that an unpaid lender "may, through agreement with the mortgagor, be paid out of the proceeds from the conversion of the mortgaged property or from the auction or sale of the mortgaged property," or else the lender may bring suit.[202] Article 198 states that a foreclosed mortgagor retains the excess of the sale proceeds over the balance of the debt but remains responsible for paying any shortfalls, and the following Article clarifies the rights of junior lenders.[203] Despite the government's concerns about excessive investments in residential units, one banker informed me that the default rate by homebuyers is still only about 1.5 percent, a fact that likely reflects the ever-increasing value of residential real estate.[204] Note as well that the Supreme People's Court ruled in 2004 that a lender may not sell a home when

---

201 Wuquan Fa [Property Rights Law], art. 65 ("The legal savings, investment and returns of individuals shall be protected by law.").

202 *Id.* art. 195.

203 *Id.* arts. 198–99.

204 By contrast, in the first quarter of 2011, default and delinquency numbers improved slightly in the United States but still continued to show the effects of the ongoing real estate crisis. On a seasonally adjusted basis, 8.32 percent of all mortgage loans on one- to four-unit residential properties were delinquent, and 4.52 percent of all such loans were in foreclosure. "Seriously delinquent" loans, including all loans that are in foreclosure or at least 90 days overdue, constituted 8.10 percent of all loans. More than half the mortgage loans in foreclosure in the United States are secured by real property located in just five states. *Significant Declines in 90+ Day Delinquencies and Foreclosures in Latest MBA National Delinquency Survey*, PRESS RELEASE—NDS, MORTGAGE BANKERS ASSOCIATION (May 19, 2011), http://www.mortgagebankers.org/NewsandMedia/PressCenter/76676.htm. Fannie Mae, which uses different definitions and calculates the rates somewhat differently, offers numbers that are only moderately less worrisome. *Monthly Summary*, FANNIE MAE (APRIL 2011), http://www.fanniemae.com/ir/pdf/monthly/2011/043011.pdf;jsessionid=NYGI2ZC4NOQZPJ2FECISFGQ.

the borrower is in default if it is the borrower's sole residence.[205] A commercial developer indicated that the default rate on commercial property held for rental income is also very low.

Sources of Funds: Lenders and the Government

The amount of construction in China is shocking and is one of the first things a Western visitor notices. China is seeking to meet a half-century of pent-up demand in a decade or two, and Chinese citizens wish to improve their living standard while also making their presence known to the world. To some extent, this requires large outlays of government funds, particularly for the building of infrastructure. Nonetheless, many new projects are being built and financed privately.[206] This raises a key question: where do the banks in a rapidly developing but still poor nation come up with the funds their borrower clients are demanding? Or, stated more directly, where is all this money coming from?

Much of the money seems to come from the savings of China's nearly 1.4 billion citizens. Along with its huge population, China has a very high savings rate, estimated to be in the range of 40 percent. A recent Brookings Institution Commentary suggests that gross domestic savings in China, including savings by enterprises, exceeds 50 percent, and that the average savings rate for urban households in 2009 was 29 percent.[207] By contrast, the personal savings rate in the United States rose to 6.4 percent in June 2010,[208] after bottoming out at

---

205 *See, e.g.*, Yongheng Deng & Peng Fei, *Housing Finance in China, in* CHINA'S HOUSING REFORM AND OUTCOMES, *supra* note 56, at 121, 132 (discussing this ruling and its effect on the residential lending market). Recall that many residential properties in urban areas are investment properties that are not occupied by their owners and thus do not fall within the scope of this decision.

206 Keep in mind that the term "private" can have a very different meaning in China. Entities that are developing real estate may be wholly or partially state-owned or state-controlled, and the same is true for the lenders that finance their projects. My use of the term "private" covers the range from truly private entities, including those owned at least in part by non-Chinese individuals or entities, to government-influenced entities—both developers and lenders—that are attempting to operate somewhat like private businesses. For a more detailed discussion of the distinction between public and private in China, see *infra* Chapter 10.

207 Eswar Prasad, Kai Liu & Marcos Chamon, *The Puzzle of China's Rising Household Savings Rate*, BROOKINGS INSTITUTION, Jan. 18, 2011, http://www.brookings.edu/articles/2011/0118_china_savings_prasad.aspx; *see also Economists Defend China's High Savings Rate*, CHINA DAILY, Jan. 7, 2009, http://www.chinadaily.com.cn/bizchina/2009-01/07/content_7375620.htm (estimating China's household savings rate at 30–40 percent and noting the low debt level of Chinese households as compared to American and European households).

208 Yian Q. Mui, *As Wages Stall, Savings Rate Rises: Unease about U.S. Economy Data Suggest Recovery Not Yet Self-Sustaining*, WASH. POST, Aug. 4, 2010, at A12.

−2.3 percent in 2009.[209] Comparisons of this type can be somewhat misleading. Americans are more likely than Chinese to be able to rely on income sources that may not be reflected in the savings rate, including future social security benefits; pre-tax savings accounts such as 401(k) plans and Individual Retirement Accounts; capital gains; and home appreciation.[210] Nonetheless, it is clear that China's citizens are sitting on a huge pool of savings. This trend may slowly be starting to shift toward increased consumerism, however. One real estate expert explained to me that children of the 1970s believe one should "earn more, spend less"; children of the 1980s believe one should "earn more, spend more"; and children of the 1990s believe one should "earn less, spend more."

Until recently, there were few consumer goods on which Chinese citizens could spend their disposable income, and even now many Chinese appear to be saving as much as they can in case the future is not as bright as the present. Chinese parents generally may have only one child. Families, and thus child-rearing expenses, are relatively small, although some families may be supporting aging parents as well. The lack of a comprehensive social security system combined with the knowledge that a child without siblings may end up supporting two parents and four grandparents has encouraged some fairly frenzied savings. Meanwhile, the average family in China, particularly in urban areas in the eastern part of the nation, is quickly becoming much wealthier. So the amount of private savings potentially available for lending continues to grow.

Families that wish to invest for the future have limited choices about where to place their savings, and bank accounts seem to be one of the few safe alternatives. Banks, however, pay a low interest rate of 0.50 percent on savings accounts, which means that Chinese savers will not get rich placing their savings in the bank.[211] The nation's nascent stock markets in Shenzhen and Shanghai have been plagued by volatility, and many people still view these stock markets with great apprehension. Many of the listed companies are state-owned enterprises that retain control of one class of shares and offer a second class to the public. I asked one expert what, exactly,

---

209 David Wilson, *U.S. Savings Rate Falls to Depression-Era Levels: Chart of Day*, BLOOMBERG NEWS, Jan. 6, 2010, http://www.bloomberg.com/apps/news?pid=newsarchive&sid=aexjnfkHISt0.

210 *See, e.g.*, Milt Marquis, *What's Behind the Low U.S. Personal Saving Rate?*, FRBSF ECONOMIC LETTER (FEDERAL RESERVE BANK OF SAN FRANCISCO), No. 2002-09 (Mar. 29, 2002), at 1, http://www.frbsf.org/publications/economics/letter/2002/el2002-09.pdf (noting the complexity of calculating an accurate savings rate for the United States, while also observing that households save more when they perceive that they need to accumulate more wealth for future consumption).

211 Bank of China currently pays 0.50 percent interest on renminbi demand deposits, with somewhat higher rates available for lump-sum deposits committed for fixed time periods. BANK OF CHINA, RMB DEPOSIT RATES 2011-04-06, http://www.boc.cn/en/bocinfo/bi4/201104/t20110405_1347157.html. One consultant advised me that a typical Chinese bank earns 60 percent of its income from the spread between the interest rate the bank receives from its borrowers and the much lower interest rate the bank pays to its depositors.

an investor could expect when buying the shares available to the public, and he responded, "It is like a casino," while also noting that he never buys stock himself. This expert also confirmed that insider trading is rampant and, though illegal, is rarely prosecuted. Overseas investment opportunities are virtually nonexistent in a nation with strict currency controls.[212]

So for the typical Chinese investor, real estate and low-rate interest-bearing savings accounts appear to be the most viable options.[213] Many invest in both. Chinese banks are amply stocked with funds to lend, and Chinese citizens have been competing aggressively to find real estate to purchase. This shortage of investment opportunities also helps to explain the high rate of ownership of second homes, many of which are being held for investment purposes. By 2007, 15 percent of urban households owned more than one home.[214]

In fact, one of the reasons supplied to me most regularly for the success of residential real estate markets in certain Chinese cities is the lack of alternative investment options available to the typical citizen. Savings accounts pay minimal interest, the erratic stock exchanges are viewed with intense suspicion, and apartments are appreciating at an enormous, if unsustainable, rate. So every Chinese saver wants to buy an apartment now and sell it quickly, in the hope that any market plunge will not occur until later. Many of the people I spoke with, having never experienced a prolonged price drop in a relatively free market, do not appear to believe that a real estate crash will ever occur, or they acknowledge the possibility without seeming to recognize the practical effects it would have on them and on their nation.

One real estate developer claimed that the government simply prints money and supplies it to the banks as needed. Elementary macroeconomic theory suggests that this approach, if followed to any material extent, would lead to significant inflation. While prices in China have undoubtedly been on the rise, inflation does not appear to have been a widespread problem in China during the past several years. However, it is difficult to know exactly how much inflation there truly is in a nation in which the market remains so heavily controlled by the government.

---

212 *See* Janet Ong, *China May Ease Rules on Investing Overseas*, INT'L HERALD TRIB., Sept. 22, 2004, http://www.iht.com/articles/2004/09/22/bloomberg/sxchina.php (noting that "China bans its citizens from buying stocks abroad to prevent an exodus of foreign reserves," while also recognizing that China must comply with World Trade Organization rules and must provide its citizens with adequate investment options).

213 *See, e.g.*, Dwight H. Perkins, *China's Land System: Past, Present, and Future, in* PROPERTY RIGHTS AND LAND POLICIES 70, 82 (Gregory K. Ingram & Yu-Hong Hong eds., 2009) ("Housing has afforded better returns than the banks, at least during the past decade, and has been less volatile than the stock market."); *cf.* Iris Kuo, *Of All the Tea in China, "Puer" Is the Hottest*, WALL ST. J., Oct. 2, 2007, at 1 (describing a recent sevenfold increase in the price of puer tea followed by a 60 percent backslide, all fueled by speculative investments and sales).

214 *See* Youqin Huang & Chengdong Yi, *Patterns of Second-Home Ownership in Chinese Cities, in* CHINA'S HOUSING REFORM AND OUTCOMES, *supra* note 56, at 89, 89.

Even if we assume that the government is not increasing the money supply as a means of meeting borrowers' demands or supporting insolvent financial institutions, it may well be using existing government revenues for those purposes. If this is the case—a plausible theory in a nation with numerous state-owned banks that are rumored to be insolvent—then the government is simply serving as an indirect lender. Instead of spending its tax receipts and other revenues directly on infrastructure or other development, the Chinese government might be using some of those same revenues to support banks that lend for these same purposes without any realistic prospect of being repaid.[215] Chinese citizens thus may be supporting China's banks indirectly, by paying taxes to a government that dispenses some of these revenues to banks for risky loans to government entities and real estate developers, and directly, by placing significant private savings in those same banks.

Another possible explanation is that China's favorable trade imbalance with Western nations, particularly the United States, provides indirect funding to China's lending institutions. Manufacturing facilities earn huge amounts of cash by selling their wares to Western consumers. These manufacturers may be saving some of their money in China's banks, where the funds are available to be lent to real estate developers. And since many of these manufacturers are owned at least in part by the same Chinese state that controls these banks, the government is essentially a huge entrepreneur. This giant manufacturing company, with hundreds of millions of employees, is diversifying its portfolio by reinvesting profits from its primary manufacturing business into real estate loans in Shanghai, some of which it knows and expects will never be repaid.[216]

The Ultimate Source of Funds: The Chinese People, Past, Present, and Future

The question of where the banks get their money is inseparable from the question of where the Chinese government obtains its money, because the banks are government-owned and the government is supporting the nation's real estate growth. Moreover, both Chinese lenders and China's government ultimately obtain their assets from the Chinese people. Perhaps the best and most complete answer

---

215 *See, e.g.*, David Barboza, *China's Cities Piling Up Debt To Fuel Boom*, N.Y. TIMES, July 6, 2011, at A1 ("A recent report ... predicted that local government investment corporations could generate up to $460 billion in loan defaults over the next few years. As a percentage of China's G.D.P., that would be far bigger than the $700 billion troubled-asset bailout program in the United States.").

216 For a discussion of China's plans for investing its "immense reserves of foreign currency," see Jim Yardley & David Barboza, *China to Open Fund to Invest Currency Reserves*, N.Y. TIMES, Mar. 9, 2007, at C3; *see also* Keith Bradsher, *Dollars to Spare in China's Trove*, N.Y. TIMES, Mar. 6, 2007, at C1 (addressing China's foreign investments).

to the question of where all the money is coming from was the one supplied to me by a thoughtful and forthright government official. I asked this man the more general question of how the Chinese real estate market has been able to perform so well so rapidly, particularly when compared to corresponding markets in other developing nations. He supplied three cogent answers, with the first of the three being the most notable.

"Our Ancestors"

As this gentleman delicately stated, the primary source of financial support for China's government, and thus for its lending institutions, is "our ancestors," by which he meant prior generations of Chinese. Other experts with whom I spoke concurred in this view. The Chinese government currently owns all the land in the nation aside from land owned by agricultural collectives, and the government retains the power to requisition agricultural land whenever it chooses. It nationalized the land it owns or controls over the course of roughly three decades, usually paying the prior owners of the land little or nothing in the way of compensation.[217] In the early rounds of these condemnations, rural landlords were the principal targets, but by the 1970s, the government was taking the remaining private urban land.

Today, the Chinese government supports its operations in large part by selling off land use rights in this same land, often to the same types of real estate professionals who were the primary targets of uncompensated nationalization during Mao's time. China is only just beginning to experiment with the imposition of *ad valorem* property taxes, so unlike American cities and counties, Chinese government entities cannot depend on a steady stream of revenues flowing regularly from a stable real property tax base. China relies instead on income taxes,[218] real property transfer taxes, user fees, and, most significantly, proceeds from the sale of long-term rights to use the same land that the government requisitioned between 1949 and 1982.

Structural Issues: The Central Government Versus Local Governments

Stated more directly, the Chinese government is funding its operations in significant part by selling to private parties land that it previously seized from other private parties—including, perhaps, their grandparents. Putting aside the irony that the Chinese government came to power promising to reduce the harmful influence of

---

217 *See generally* RANDOLPH & LOU, *supra* note 30, at 9–11 (discussing the history of land nationalization in China since 1949 and noting disagreements among Chinese scholars as to when this process was completed).

218 Collection of income taxes appears to be problematic in an economy so heavily reliant on cash and in which so many people seem to have gray-market income. I witnessed a large public rally, complete with a uniformed brass band, encouraging citizens to pay their income taxes.

landlords and now is supporting itself by selling these landlords' former holdings to real estate developers, this method of raising funds creates ongoing structural problems for government operations.

To begin with, different levels of government in China have become participants in and beneficiaries of the current real estate boom, and not just referees or superintendents of it. The urban population is growing and China's citizens are demanding higher living standards, so municipal governments must ensure that housing and infrastructure continue to improve in both quality and quantity. Municipal governments such as Shanghai depend on the revenues from the regular sale of land use rights and are in the best position to fund continued growth and modernization if real estate values keep appreciating. One expert estimated that local governments receive 50–70 percent of their revenues today from the sale of land use rights. Another suggested that the national average was closer to 20 percent, but with rates as high as 50 percent in Beijing and Shanghai. The participatory role of these government entities in the real estate market places them in direct conflict with the central government, which wants to maintain social order by ensuring that residential real estate remains affordable and that the gap between the haves and the have-nots does not grow too large.

The central government, in other words, must ensure that Shanghai, Inc., which holds huge tracts of very valuable real estate, does not act in a way that is harmful to the nation as a whole. For example, the central government has established limits on the amount of land that can be converted from agricultural-collective ownership to government ownership, which is a prerequisite to the sale of land use rights in this land by municipal governments. These limits, as previously noted, both slow real estate development on the outskirts of urban areas and reduce the amount of land that is lost to agricultural use.

Agricultural Land Loss

The central government appears to be particularly concerned about the loss of farmland for two distinct reasons. First, it wants to ensure that China remains capable of feeding itself.[219] Second, it wants to avoid the social upheaval that would be associated with a massive and rapid relocation of tens or hundreds of millions of peasants who migrate to urban areas because they have lost their land, along with

---

219   *See* Lin & Ho, *supra* note 132, at 116 (suggesting that China's land resources will not remain adequate for its growing population). *But see* Shlomo Angel, Midori Valdivia & Rebecca M. Lutzy, *Urban Expansion, Land Conversion, and Affordable Housing: The Case of Zhengzhou, in* CHINA'S HOUSING REFORM AND OUTCOMES, *supra* note 56, at 137, 152–53 (arguing that eliminating land conversion quotas will not have a negative effect on China's ability to provide sufficient food for its citizens). *See generally supra* notes 131–37 and accompanying text (discussing concerns about China's ability to provide adequate food for its population).

the dignity—and retirement security—that farming provides.[220] So, for example, the Land Administration Law states, "Overall plans for land utilization shall be drawn up in accordance with the following principles: (1) strictly protecting the capital farmland and keeping land for agriculture under control lest it should be occupied and used for non-agricultural construction."[221] Further, when planning what land is to be used for urban construction, "[a]ttention shall be paid to making full use of the existing land earmarked for construction and using little or no land earmarked for agriculture."[222] The new Property Rights Law states, "The State adopts special protection with regard to the agriculture land, strictly limiting the transfer of agriculture land to construction land so as to control the total quantity of the construction land."[223] Expropriation of "basic farmland" requires approval by the State Council.[224] Note also that those who illegally convert cultivated land to other uses are subject to criminal prosecution.[225]

Lower-level governmental units, by contrast, have great incentives to sell the most desirable land first, and to sell off land at a rate that is too rapid to be sustainable over the long term. These governments wish to convert agricultural-collective land to government-owned land so they can sell it off, and they also wish to redevelop urban parcels that are occupied by dilapidated older structures. Downtown property is being cleared of run-down residential and commercial buildings, some of which have not seen any maintenance in more than half a century. It is hard to argue that some of these marginally habitable structures merit preservation. But the occupants of these structures receive compensation that reflects the low value of these units. This guarantees that there will continue to be massive residential relocation within major metropolitan areas, as poorer downtown residents use their meager compensation to purchase newer units in less costly outlying areas, while middle-class Chinese spend their newfound wealth on downtown apartments. This process guarantees the destruction of many older urban communities, along with their vibrant street life. It also may create political stresses in a rapidly changing China, and "the change of mainstream urban residents from proletarians and socialist workers into petty bourgeois and property owners may weaken the base of the communist administrative socialist system."[226]

---

220 *See* PEERENBOOM, *supra* note 2, at 482 (noting prevalence of land disputes).
221 Tudi Guanli Fa [Land Administration Law], art. 19.
222 *Id.* art. 22.
223 Wuquan Fa [Property Rights Law], art. 43.
224 Tudi Guanli Fa [Land Administration Law], art. 45; *see generally id.* arts. 31–42 (addressing the protection of cultivated land).
225 Xing Fa [Criminal Law] (promulgated by the Standing Comm. Nat'l People's Cong., July 1, 1979, revised Mar. 14, 1997, Dec. 25, 1999, Aug. 31, 2001, Dec. 29, 2001, Dec. 28, 2002, Feb. 28, 2005 & June 29, 2006, effective June 29, 2006), art. 342 (China) (authorizing punishments for violations that include imprisonment, detention, and fines).
226 Ya Ping Wang, *Recent Housing Reform Practice in Chinese Cities: Social and Spatial Implications*, *in* CHINA'S HOUSING REFORM AND OUTCOMES, *supra* note 56, at 19, 42.

Will the Government Run Out of Land?

Downtown land commands the highest price in the market for land use rights, suggesting that sales of less central land in future years will generate lower prices on an inflation-adjusted, per-square-meter basis. The government will thus have to sell larger and larger tracts faster and faster if it hopes to continue to feed its habit of operating off the proceeds of sales of land use rights. Governments that maintain their solvency by selling off a finite natural resource tend to mine the most accessible and desirable ore first. Their remaining assets are less valuable and may run out altogether.

Land use rights last for forty, fifty, or seventy years, depending on the purpose for which they are conveyed, and the government receives the entire fee for the sale of the land use right at the time of the initial conveyance. It is entirely possible that the government will dispose of the right to use all of the most desirable land well before the first round of land use rights begins to expire. Recall that the current system of transferable land use rights has existed only since the late 1980s and that sales of land use rights did not begin in earnest until a few years later, which means that most existing land use rights still have many years to run. This suggests that the government will have to wean itself from its addiction to these sale proceeds at some point before the first round of land use rights begins to expire. The problem is not just that the land that is left in ten or twenty years will be less desirable, it is also that there may not be any marketable land left by then at all.

Once the government discovers that it has run out of marketable land before a substantial number of land use rights expire, its only alternative will be to locate new funding sources, such as additional taxes, an approach that is likely to be as unpopular in China as it is anywhere else. If the original question was what the source of all the government's money is, the answer will no longer be the sale of land use rights. Even when land use rights do begin to expire in significant numbers, as noted earlier, Chinese law is unclear as to whether these rights must be renewed upon expiration of their initial term and whether the holder must pay an additional fee to the government if the holder does have automatic renewal rights. So even if China does budget the remaining land judiciously, it will not necessarily be able to raise additional funds by renewing or reconveying land use rights a couple of decades from now.

Other Sources of Funds

The Chinese government official who spoke so openly about China's reliance on the proceeds of the sale of land it had previously nationalized offered two additional reasons why China's real estate market has grown so quickly. Bond financing has stimulated Chinese real estate development, although this official indicated that the amount of bond financing is relatively small. In addition, "our own income" has been beneficial, by which he was referring to the frequent use of Build–Operate–Transfer (BOT) financing.[227]

In a typical BOT deal, a private entity is authorized to build a public project, such as a toll road or a bridge. The private entity is permitted to operate the project for a specified period of time, perhaps twenty years, so that it can recoup its costs and earn a profit through the imposition of user fees, such as tolls. At the end of the stated time period, the project reverts to government control. In a similar way, private entities that agree to construct quasi-public facilities may be awarded desirable land use rights nearby. In effect, they are being paid in kind for their provision of a public facility. One real estate expert stated that these types of projects initially became popular in Hong Kong and have spread from there to the mainland. In Shanghai, the Xintiandi historic preservation project apparently ran at a loss for the first several years after it opened, as its developer anticipated, but that developer also received valuable land use rights to neighboring downtown land.

Sources of Funds: A Summary

It thus appears that most of the loan financing and other financial support available to real estate developers and government entities in China—and, in fact, most of the support for China's overall development during the past two decades—has been borrowed or seized from past, present, and future generations of Chinese. Past generations of property owners involuntarily supplied their land to the government, which now is selling it off at an enormous profit. The land is a necessary input for real estate developers, while the sale proceeds are essential to government units struggling to provide vital services to a huge and demanding population. Today's Chinese are placing some of their savings in low-rate accounts at banks that lend to developers. They are also paying taxes that are used directly to furnish new infrastructure and indirectly to support insolvent banks. These citizens may also be paying somewhat higher prices for goods if the government is, in fact, meeting currency shortfalls by simply printing more of it. Future generations of Chinese will pay the rest of the bill if they pay higher taxes years from now, if they otherwise provide the funds that the government will need to repay its obligations, and if they must renew their expiring land use rights at unexpectedly high prices. China's people, then, have been and will be the source of the funds needed to support China's recent rapid development.

---

227 For a more detailed discussion of BOT transactions, see *infra* notes 312–16 and accompanying text.

The Stability of the Chinese Banking Sector

Most banks operating in China are owned or controlled by the Chinese government. These banks' lending decisions are at least as likely to reflect official government policy as astute business judgment. This unusual set of motivations causes the Western observer to wonder whether China's banks are financially viable. Since the competition facing the typical Chinese bank is almost entirely domestic, and thus responsive to the same internal political stimuli, China's banks appear to have little to fear from their local competitors. The same non-business factors that cause one bank to make a poor business decision likely cause that bank's rivals to make similarly poor business decisions. As one group of knowledgeable commentators has noted:

> Banks remain the predominant mechanism by which savings are intermediated to investment .... [T]he banks in general have made only modest progress toward operating on a commercial basis. They have high cost structures and limited risk assessment skills, and suffer from seemingly endless corruption. As a result, the earning power of the banks remains modest—especially for those that have not been recapitalized through government funds and must still provision for non-performing loans.[228]

A bank also is a business, however. It collects money from its borrowers, who are paying interest on their loans, and must pay interest to its own depositors from these collections. If China's banks make too many loans that are financially unwise, then at some point they may become insolvent. The government may be able to sustain these banks temporarily with infusions of funds—these banks are, after all, tools of the state and can be kept afloat with general operating revenues from the government. But if huge, money-losing banks are on China's balance sheet, they could become an enormous drain on China's economy over time.

This business pressure is compounded by the government's continuing insistence on funding projects that it deems worthy.[229] The financial demands of depositors combined with the policy mandates of the government seem to be causing China's banks to lend briskly. This may help to explain why loan officers must meet lending quotas based on volume rather than on the ultimate success or failure of the projects being funded. Several different experts confirmed that the modus operandi of Chinese banks seems to be to lend first and worry later. When

---

228 BERGSTEN, GILL, LARDY & MITCHELL, supra note 12, at 25.

229 *See* Richard Wu, *The Changing Regime for Regulating Loans of State Owned Banks in China: Towards a System of Prudential Banking*, 26 UCLA PAC. BASIN L.J. 107, 112–13 (2009) (describing the close linkages between the Chinese government and the banking industry until changes in loan regulations were implemented in the early 1990s, and arguing that the problem has been reduced somewhat since then).

I asked one lawyer how the system manages to work, he replied, "As long as the economy keeps growing ...."

Estimates of the proportion of nonperforming loans vary. I frequently heard knowledgeable experts—several affiliated with Chinese banks—state that 30–40 percent of loans held by Chinese banks are nonperforming. One bank attorney told me that the official estimate is in the 20–23 percent range. A Western attorney advised me that one of his clients, who purchases nonperforming loans from Chinese financial institutions, believes a more accurate number would fall in the 40–50 percent range. A Chinese expert summarized the issue more tersely: all banks in China are insolvent. Nearly every expert stated that the four leading Chinese banks, which control a huge segment of the lending market, are insolvent. Another Chinese banker denied the existence of the problem altogether.

In an effort to address the problem of nonperforming loans, the Chinese government established four asset-management companies in 1999.[230] The four largest banks in China began the process of transferring the weakest loans in their portfolios to these asset-management companies, thereby improving the financial stability of the transferor banks. It is widely assumed that these transfers were consummated as a precursor to public offerings of the stock of the four banks. These transfers did not solve the problem, of course; they simply shifted the nonperforming loans to the four new government-controlled entities. To the extent the government later needed to inject cash into its ailing financial sector, only the form of the problem changed. Instead of supporting four banks with large numbers of nonperforming loans, the government bolstered the four asset-management companies.

Several experts informed me that the asset-management companies attempted to sell some of these nonperforming loans to foreign banks at steep discounts.[231] The overseas buyers of these loans were gambling that they would be able to recover a higher percentage of the face value of these debts. The Chinese government, meanwhile, was able to cap and liquidate its losses on these loans, giving up

---

230 *See* Bing Wang & Richard Peiser, *Non-Performing Loan Resolution in the Context of China's Transitional Economy*, in URBANIZATION IN CHINA: CRITICAL ISSUES IN AN ERA OF RAPID GROWTH, *supra* note 5, at 271, 273, 275–76, 282–83 (tracing the history of China's asset-management companies and comparing them to the Resolution Trust Corporation in the United States); *China's Asset Management Companies Face Reform Pressure*, PEOPLE'S DAILY ONLINE, Aug. 10, 2005, http://english.peopledaily.com.cn/200508/10/eng20050810_201498.html (providing background on the four asset-management companies and discussing problems with their management and control).

231 *See, e.g., Business Brief—China Cinda Asset Management: Recovery of $6.7 Billion Is Made from the Disposal of Bad Loans*, WALL ST. J., Dec. 29, 2005, at B4 (describing the sale of nonperforming loans with a face value of 290 billion yuan, formerly held by China Construction Bank and China Development Bank, for a price of 54.18 billion yuan); *ICBC Transfers Loans to Huarong*, WALL ST. J., June 1, 2005, at A12 (describing the transfer of $30 billion of nonperforming loans from a leading Chinese bank to an asset-management company, as a prelude to ICBC's public offering of its stock).

the slim possibility of recovering more of the loan proceeds down the road and receiving instead a small but certain payoff now. By providing capital to the banks that held these loans and then disposing of the loans at such a steep discount, the government indirectly subsidized the banks' earlier poor lending decisions, many of which were made under government pressure to fund projects the government deemed meritorious.

One way or another, the government—though not necessarily the same arm of the government—is footing part of the bill for unwise decisions made by Chinese lenders in the past. The net expense may differ little from the price the government might have paid had it funded some of these projects directly or even built them itself. Note that one governmental entity may be profiting at the expense of another. For example, a municipal government may have benefited from the construction of a factory that, while unsuccessful overall, employs numerous local residents and reduces the local government's burden of supporting them. If the lender that holds a nonperforming loan to that company opts to sell this loan to an asset-management company rather than seeking to enforce it, the state-supported lender and the state-supported asset-management company share the ultimate loss, while the municipal government entity continues to enjoy the benefit.

When a bank suffers a loss in China, that state-owned entity is indirectly passing these costs along to the entire population. The ultimate sources of these funds are the same as those noted earlier, and include income tax revenues, transfer tax revenues, sales of land use rights, bond financing, and user fees and tolls. It is therefore critically important to China that it maintain current rates of growth in the real estate market, which serves as the wellspring for many of these revenue streams. Bank regulators have also taken other steps to strengthen China's banks, such as by raising capital adequacy targets.[232]

Several real estate experts, while acknowledging the problems facing China's banking sector, argued that the banks' problems do not arise from real estate loans. Real estate developers nearly always pay off their loans. Most of their projects, particularly residential developments, are sold upon completion, so the developers retire their debts quickly and move on to the next project. The buyers, meanwhile, are generally owner-occupants or investors, and they are able either to make their mortgage payments or to flip the properties quickly and at a profit. These experts claim that as long as real estate prices continue to increase, the rate of nonperforming real estate loans is likely to remain small.

All of these experts seemed dismissive of the idea that real estate prices might ever drop precipitously, a phenomenon unknown in the modern iteration of the Chinese real estate market. If such an event were to occur, China's lenders might suffer even more than they already have, because of their earlier failures

---

[232] Luo Jun, *China Said To Raise Biggest Banks' Capital Adequacy Targets*, BLOOMBERG BUSINESSWEEK, Apr. 26, 2011, http://www.businessweek.com/news/2011-04-26/china-said-to-raise-biggest-banks-capital-adequacy-targets.html (announcing new targets of 11.7 percent or 11.8 percent, depending on the bank).

to make credit decisions based on a mortgagor's actual capacity to repay. Such an occurrence, however painful in the short term, might eventually lead to the maturation of the residential lending industry, with loan decisions based on an applicant's actual salary, job history, and credit record.

The true sources of the banks' bad loans, according to these experts, are state-owned enterprises, foreign joint ventures, and wholly foreign-owned enterprises; one expert argued that nonperforming automobile loans account for a growing part of this problem as well. The Chinese government has significant reasons for ensuring that many of these loans continue to be repaid, even if it means using general tax revenues for the repayments. Some of the companies that might otherwise collapse are high-profile Chinese brand names, and it could shatter confidence in the emerging Chinese market, both at home and abroad, if the government were to allow a well-known company to fail. China has at least as much interest in ensuring the survival of some if its banner companies as the United States had in bailing out General Motors or Chrysler.

More critically, some of China's state-owned companies provide thousands of their workers with housing, education, health care, a reliable retirement income, and all the other benefits that used to be known as the "iron rice bowl." If too many of these companies were to close their doors, "chaos in the countryside," as one expert phrased it, might threaten the viability of China's government and the supremacy of the Chinese Communist Party. China's government probably is more concerned about avoiding problems that could lead to its own downfall than it is about any of the other issues it faces today.

Some of the nonperforming loans in sectors other than real estate are relatively recent in origin and were certainly made after the international community began to focus on the fragility of the Chinese financial sector. To some extent, this likely reflects the continued importance of personal connections in obtaining loans, particularly those loans that might not be forthcoming based solely on the underlying quality of a project. Even putting aside the persistence of the *guanxi* problem, however, it is clear that the government wants the banks it controls to keep some antiquated factories afloat even if the resulting loans worsen the health of the banks themselves.

By rescuing companies that cannot pay their debts, China is indirectly supporting more than just its banking industry. It truly is keeping its entire social welfare system afloat. China's leaders seem to recognize this fact clearly, and their real concern is what might happen if China's economy slows down to the point that the government is simply unable to keep these enterprises alive any longer. One real estate developer's answer to my question of whether China's banks are stable—"They must be!"—succinctly captures the combination of hope and faith that so many Chinese appear to feel.

Chapter 8
Preselling and Reselling of Residential Units

The Huge Demand for Urban Residential Units

The average Chinese citizen, worried about supporting himself and his family in the future and no longer protected by a reliable social safety net, is estimated to save 30–40 percent of his or her annual income. There are few investment vehicles in which average investors can place these savings. Bank accounts pay low interest rates, the volatile Chinese stock markets in Shanghai and Shenzhen are viewed with considerable trepidation, and strict currency controls limit the ability to invest outside China. That leaves real estate, and during the market peak in the late 1990s and early 2000s, residential real estate units were the hottest of commodities.[233]

The fact that work units no longer provide housing to their employees has forced many Chinese to buy their own residences. By 2010, 84.3 percent of Chinese owned their dwellings; by comparison, the rate in the United States was 66.2 percent in 2000.[234] Moreover, middle-class Chinese with some money to invest have been buying apartments as investments, often flipping them within a few months of purchase so they can pay off their acquisition loans, recognize their gains, and, perhaps, buy more apartments. As one expert informed me, "In Shanghai, if you own only one apartment, you do not belong to the middle class. If you own two or more, you can step into the middle class." A second expert agreed, stating, "People with two or more homes are rich."

At the peak of the market, I was told, units were appreciating at an annual rate of as much as 50 or even 100 percent. One colleague told me that he had purchased his home in Shanghai's Pudong New Area at a price of 13,000 renminbi (RMB) per square meter and that within three years it had appreciated to a value of 30,000 RMB per square meter. Many purchasers sell their real estate investments and reinvest the proceeds in other units. Refinancings in which the owner recoups its initial cash investment or more, so common in the United States prior to the recent real estate crash, are nearly unheard of in China.

As a result of the fact that so many apartments are purchased solely for investment purposes, a high percentage of residential units in urban markets such as Shanghai—including many that are held as second or third homes by their owners—have never been occupied. These units serve instead as symbolic vaults

---

233 For a more detailed discussion of the investment options available to Chinese citizens, see *supra* notes 206–14 and accompanying text.

234 Man, Zheng & Ren, *supra* note 56, at 6–7. Even among the lowest income decile, the home ownership rate in China in 2010 was 79.3 percent. *Id.* at 7.

for wealth accumulation. Urban residential units in China are typically built without many of the interior features that an American buyer (or building inspector) would consider standard, such as doors and plumbing fixtures, with this finishing work left to the purchaser of the unit. If a Chinese unit is being held vacant as an investment, this finishing work may remain incomplete for an extended period. The investors who hold these unfinished units plainly do not expect to generate any rental income and are not counting on receiving regular cash flow from the units. Rather, their investment return will come entirely in the form of appreciation in the value of the property.

Given how quickly China's middle class has grown during the past two decades, and given how difficult it is to find, clear, and rebuild on desirable urban land, the residential real estate market has not been able to keep up with the demand for units in which to invest. These factors have contributed to the sharp spike in prices for urban residential units. China's new capitalist class has thus received a first-hand lesson in the laws of supply and demand.

Overseas investors have augmented this domestic demand. As foreign investors began to discover the Chinese residential market, prices for new units rose even further. These purchasers from Hong Kong, Taiwan, North America, and Europe had numerous reasons for wishing to invest. Some, like the domestic investors, simply did not want to miss this promising investment opportunity while it was still available. Others predicted—with only partial accuracy—that the Chinese renminbi would have to appreciate against Western currencies, meaning that they would make money on the currency exchange even if the unit's value stayed the same or dropped somewhat.

The Chinese government partially de-pegged the renminbi from the US dollar on July 21, 2005, at a time when one dollar purchased 8.27 RMB. During the next three years, the dollar gradually depreciated to a range of 6.81–6.85 RMB, where it held steady after July 2008.[235] For the two years that followed, China pegged the value of the renminbi to that of the dollar, but under pressure from the Obama administration, China once again allowed the renminbi to appreciate in June 2010.[236] The renminbi has drifted up slightly since then against the dollar, with a US dollar buying only 6.33192 RMB on November 9, 2011.[237] The fact that China has not yet dramatically revalued the renminbi may have the effect of keeping these overseas real estate investors in the market and attracting new ones, in the belief that a greater revaluation, though deferred, is inevitable. The United

---

[235] Qing Wang & Steven Zhang, *An Exit Strategy for the Renminbi*, MORGAN STANLEY—GLOBAL ECONOMIC FORUM (June 10, 2009), http://www.morganstanley.com/views/gef/archive/2009/20090610-Wed.html.

[236] Keith Bradsher, *China Signals a Gradual Rise in Value of its Currency*, N.Y. TIMES, June 20, 2010, at A1.

[237] EXCHANGE RATE DATA (AMERICAN DOLLAR, CHINESE YUAN) (Nov. 9, 2011), http://www.x-rates.com/d/CNY/USD/data120.html (last visited Dec. 4, 2011).

States government regularly asks China to revalue its currency, and China regularly declined until its modest June 2010 actions.[238]

In addition to all of the urban residential units that are built primarily as investment commodities, many other apartments are occupied by their owners. China's huge and swelling urban population is living somewhere, and many city residents are eager to improve their living standard by moving to newer and more modern dwellings. For many Chinese, as for many Westerners, their home is both their place of residence and their most significant investment. China's new Property Rights Law confirms and describes the rights of the owners of these units, in language that will sound familiar to the owner of a Western condominium.[239] And as one newspaper account has amusingly observed, urban Chinese men find it easier to attract mates if they own an apartment.[240]

Developers have found themselves in the enviable position of not being able to meet this huge demand for urban residential units. Despite government limits on the ability of non-residents to relocate to Shanghai, high demand for residential units—many of which will remain unoccupied—has rapidly driven up their price. In the earlier days of the modern residential real estate market in China, there were few restrictions on so-called presales, in which the developer would sell the unit to the buyer before completing it. Developers were able to presell residential units at or above the original asking price as soon as they placed them on the market, long before they built these units. During the peak of the market in China, until about 2008, it was not unusual for prospective buyers to line up around the block to sign contracts to purchase units off the plans whenever a new project was announced.[241]

---

238 *See, e.g.*, Edward Wong & Mark Landler, *China Rejects U.S. Complaints on its Currency*, N.Y. Times, Feb. 5, 2010, *available at* http://www.nytimes.com/2010/02/05/world/asia/05diplo.html (noting, before China's actions in June 2010, that economists then believed the renminbi to be undervalued by 25–40 percent as against the dollar, and that the gap was the widest it had been since July 2005).

239 *See* Wuquan Fa [Property Rights Law], arts. 70–83 (enumerating the rights of owners of individual residential units within larger buildings).

240 Andrew Jacobs, *For Many Bachelors in China, No Property Means No Dates*, N.Y. Times, Apr. 15, 2011, at A1 ("Although there are few concrete ways to measure the scope of involuntary bachelorhood, more than 70 percent of single women in a recent survey said they would tie the knot only with a prospective husband who owned a home.").

241 *See, e.g.*, Michael Schuman, *Bubble Trouble: Why Real Estate Is China's Biggest Headache*, Time, Nov. 16, 2009, *available at* http://www.time.com/time/world/article/0,8599,1939768,00.html (describing prospective purchasers of residential units bringing chairs and folding beds so they could camp outside a real estate sales office for two days); *see also Underhanded Property Sellers Targeted*, China Daily, Mar. 23, 2011, http://www0.chinadaily.com.cn/china/2011-03/23/content_12211828.htm (describing misleading sales techniques and new efforts to combat them, and quoting Premier Wen Jiabao as stating, "'Morality should flow in the blood of property developers'").

These buyers did not wish to miss a short-lived opportunity to purchase a unit in a new residential development.[242]

Government Attempts to Limit Presales

A bubble mentality such as this created numerous opportunities for corner-cutting or even outright fraud by developers, and the government took steps to try to restrain this speculative frenzy.[243] Different real estate experts provided somewhat different descriptions of these government-imposed limitations and the effect they have had, possibly reflecting their own personal experiences, variations in the application of these new rules, and evolution of these restrictions over time and in different locations. One expert, for example, stated that units may no longer be presold without government consent, and that this consent is not available until the building is two-thirds completed or until the building has been topped off. Another expert told me that the building had to be at least 60 percent complete, and a third one told me 70 percent. The first of these experts noted that before this limitation was instituted, buyers would frequently execute purchase contracts and then assign their contractual right to buy the apartment at a profit while the unit was being built. The assignee of these contract rights would, in turn, flip the contract to yet another buyer. Meanwhile, the developer minimized its risk and locked in its own profit before breaking ground. Thus, the Chinese market had already matured to the point that it had learned to commodify not only real estate, but also the more ethereal contractual right to acquire real estate in the future.

Limitations on presales are designed to reduce the number of times an executory contract can, practically speaking, be assigned before the unit is even finished. One expert noted, though, that the demand for residential units is so great that developers nonetheless continue to presell units before the point in the construction process when presales are officially permitted. Prospective buyers are apparently so anxious to acquire units that they knowingly and willingly

---

242 The real estate craze that has gripped China for much of the past two decades bears some resemblance to the frenzy surrounding initial public offerings in the United States during some parts of that same 20-year period. *See, e.g.*, Peter Edmonston, *Google's I.P.O., Five Years Later*, N.Y. TIMES DEALBOOK (Aug. 19, 2009, 12:15pm), http://dealbook. blogs.nytimes.com/2009/08/19/googles-ipo-5-years-later/?scp=1-b&sq=google+ipo&st=nyt (noting that Google's valuation immediately after its initial public offering was $27 billion, but that it was worth more than $140 billion five years later).

243 *See, e.g.*, Chengshi Fangdichan Guanli Fa [Law on the Administration of Urban Real Estate], art. 45 (requiring, since 1995, that four conditions be met before developers may presell residential units: (i) payment of the fee for the land use right and receipt of the ownership certificate; (ii) receipt of a permit for construction; (iii) completion of 25 percent of construction; and (iv) registration with the local government and receipt of a certificate permitting presales; the seller also must submit the sales contract for public registration and must apply any sales proceeds it receives toward construction).

sign contracts that violate government restrictions on presales. In theory, if only occasionally in recent Chinese practice, unit values might go down during the construction period. If this were to happen, the ultimate contract assignee, who will have paid a premium to acquire the contractual right to purchase the unit at a price that seemed low at the time, will now suffer a loss. His cost for the unit—the price at which he acquired rights under the flipped contract—will now exceed the market value of the unit. Such a buyer will be tempted to deny the existence of the contract, arguing that the developer contracted to convey something that, under these new restrictions, it did not yet have the legal power to transfer.

Shanghai has established an official website that lists all developers that have received government permission to sell units in partially completed buildings. The website displays the number of units available along with the asking price for each. Even with recent attempts at transparency such as these in place, developers continue to try to drive up the price of individual units. One professional stated that some developers will engage in sham sales of new units to business associates, trying to create the illusion that a building is more popular than it actually is. Interested outside buyers then are forced to acquire units from these intermediaries, who retain a portion of the profits. The intermediaries, in essence, are buying the units in bulk at wholesale prices and reselling them individually at retail, sharing the markup with the developer while adding to the hype that surrounds the building. Developers apparently believe that this approach stimulates demand for the project and increases the total profit on the units.

It is important to note that the execution of a contract by the developer and the unit buyer holds a somewhat different significance in China than Westerners are accustomed to. In the United States, a contract of sale typically memorializes the agreement between the parties, sets forth the representations of the parties and the conditions precedent to each party's obligation to close, and provides remedies for breach. All of this may be true as well in China, but one American expert referred to Chinese contracts as merely the first phase in a negotiation process that continues after the parties have signed the document. American negotiations largely come to an end with the execution of the contract, but the contract is seen as only the middle of the negotiation process in China. Buyers of Chinese units who wish to terminate a contract, for example, regularly claim that conditions have changed sufficiently to release them from their contractual obligations. This may also be the case in the United States, of course, but the existence of a fully-executed contract probably has a greater impact on settlement negotiations or court action than it would in China, given the differing legal and social expectations in the two nations.

The Presale Process and the Timing Problems It Creates

Once the unit can legally be marketed, the developer is free to enter into presale contracts with buyers. Upon execution of the contract, the developer generally requires the buyer to pay a significant portion of the purchase price—sometimes as high as 50 percent—immediately or soon afterwards. The contract also establishes a payment schedule for the balance of the buyer's obligation, with the buyer making the final payment before occupancy. One consultant described buyers as receiving their key when they make the final payment. This payment schedule leaves the buyer in an undesirable position if the developer fails to complete the building, having paid for all or a large portion of the unit only to learn that the developer cannot complete it.

The Law on the Administration of Urban Real Estate, which dates back to 1995, appears to provide the buyer with some protection. As a condition to preselling a dwelling unit, the developer must, among other things, obtain permission to presell the home. In addition, the developer must submit the presale contract for registration in the public record. Moreover, "[t]he proceeds obtained from the presale of commercial houses must be used for the relevant construction purposes."[244] Public registration protects the buyer against multiple sales or further mortgages by the developer, and the statute also provides the buyer with some comfort that the sale proceeds will be used for construction purposes. In fact, developer malfeasance of this sort appears to be rare. The Chinese real estate market is only about two decades old and has been quite successful for nearly all of that time period. During this era, most residential development projects have been completed, and construction lenders tend to finish projects on behalf of the rare defaulting developers.

The Borrower's Need for a Loan

Many Chinese borrowers, like their counterparts elsewhere, do not have the financial capacity to acquire their residence outright and need to borrow a substantial portion of the acquisition price. Even those buyers who are in a position to buy their units outright, including some investors, may prefer the leveraging opportunities that borrowing funds provides. In the absence of a formal lending industry, borrowers would either have to accumulate the entire purchase price before buying a home or borrow part of the price in the informal market, perhaps from relatives and friends. Rather than doing this—or doing only this—many Chinese borrowers expect to borrow significant sums from institutional lenders at the time they buy their home and plan to pay off this debt from their future earnings over a period of years.

A modern residential mortgage market has existed in China since at least 1998. The People's Bank of China regulates loan-to-value ratios and interest rates, and mandates verification of borrowers' incomes. All mortgage loans carry adjustable rates. This residential mortgage market has been extraordinarily successful. As a

---

244 *Id.*; *see also id.* art. 46 (stating that "matters concerning the transfer of unfinished presale commercial houses that the buyers have purchased shall be prescribed by the State Council"). For a general discussion of the issue of presales, see Gregory M. Stein, *Private and Public Construction in Modern China*, 12 SAN DIEGO INT'L L.J. 5, 21–37 (2010).

result of this success and the generally dynamic real estate market, the People's Bank has tinkered with these variables in an attempt to limit growth to a more measured pace.[245]

Western lenders worry about extending a large loan to an untested borrower who possesses few assets beyond the real estate she will purchase with the borrowed funds. This is why these lenders demand a security interest in the property that will be purchased with the borrowed funds. The property the buyer will purchase with the borrowed funds often is the only asset the borrower owns that is valuable enough to repay the debt. This is the reason most borrowers need to borrow the acquisition funds in the first place, and it is also why the lender will quite reasonably demand a first priority security interest in this real estate. Chinese lenders are certainly no less concerned about repayment. However, the Chinese model, in which the buyer of a new residential unit pays all or most of the purchase price before the unit is completed, raises obvious legal and practical timing questions for both the buyer and the buyer's acquisition lender.

The typical Chinese residential buyer, who intends to borrow most of the funds she needs to acquire the unit, will have to procure these funds and deliver them to the developer before the buyer owns an asset of sufficient legal stability or economic value to pledge to her lender. Lenders will either refuse to lend on these terms or will have to extend a loan that is inadequately secured. If construction is not complete, the principal amount of any acquisition loan will almost certainly exceed the value of the partially constructed home at the time of the loan. The practice of lending to residential buyers before construction is complete would place Chinese acquisition lenders in a position of far greater risk than their Western counterparts. If a developer fails to complete a building in which many of its buyers have already used borrowed funds to pay the developer a significant part of the purchase price, the borrowers are likely to default on their loans and their acquisition lenders will be forced to foreclose on security that is worth less than the debt, assuming Chinese law even allows them to foreclose at all.

In many ways, a mortgage crisis of this type would be far more serious—and also more foreseeable—than the mortgage crisis currently facing American lenders. American lenders, by and large, extended loans that arguably were adequately secured at the time they were made, but property values subsequently depreciated faster than the loan balances could be reduced. By contrast, Chinese lenders in the situation just described would be extending loans that are undersecured from the outset. Chinese lenders are aware of this problem, of course. They presumably recognize that a buyer's "equitable" interest in a partly constructed unit may not be sufficiently well established, or sufficiently valuable, to be able to serve as adequate security for the repayment of an acquisition loan.[246]

---

245 *See generally* Deng & Fei, *supra* note 205, at 125–26, 128 (describing the growth of the modern Chinese residential mortgage market).

246 Although I refer to this type of title as "equitable," as it would be in common law practice, it is unlikely that Chinese law recognizes equitable title. The buyer simply

The Interests of Local Governments

Chinese bankers are nonetheless under great pressure to lend, as I was reminded repeatedly. Part of this pressure reflects the fact that local governments must house many newcomers even as they improve the quality of the existing housing stock for long-time residents. To meet these twin goals, the government is anxious to build new residential units as quickly as possible.[247] In recent years, the government has preferred to leave much of this construction task to the private sector. As a result, local governments pressure banks to lend to private developers and also to the ultimate buyers of individual residential units.

These local governmental units also want to see their home-grown real estate developers succeed, in part because it is good for the local economy and in part because many of these developers are well connected at the local government level. New construction leads to jobs for local residents and increased collection of fees and taxes and may in turn encourage still more economic development. Local governments may also have a more immediate financial stake in the real estate market. These government entities frequently serve as equity holders in the limited liability companies that are developing property within the jurisdiction and thus benefit directly when local projects are financially successful.[248]

Even when they do not have an ownership interest in the project itself, local governments profit enormously from the sale of the underlying land use rights. In fact, one of the most important effects of the creation of the land use right has been the access that local governments now have to the income stream that the sale of these rights provides.[249] One expert I interviewed estimated that approximately 20 percent of total national fiscal revenue derives from the sale of land use rights, with the number in Shanghai and Beijing approaching 50 percent. This reality often places local governments at odds with the central government, which has good reasons for wanting to keep the real estate boom from becoming too

---

does not own the unit yet. *See supra* notes 190–91 and accompanying text (discussing the mortgageability of lots on which construction is ongoing); JESSE DUKEMINIER ET AL., PROPERTY 552 (7th ed. 2010) (describing the common law concept of equitable conversion, and noting, "The buyer is viewed in equity as the owner from the date of the contract ....").

247 Under the Law on the Administration of Urban Real Estate, "The State shall ... support the development of construction of residential houses so as to gradually improve the housing conditions of residents." Chengshi Fangdichan Guanli Fa [Law on the Administration of Urban Real Estate], art. 4; *see also id.* art. 29 ("The State shall adopt preferential measures in aspects such as taxation to encourage and support real estate development enterprises to develop and construct residential houses.").

248 *See supra* notes 108–15 and accompanying text (discussing government participation in real estate ventures).

249 *See* Chengri Ding, *Policy and Praxis of Land Acquisition in China*, *in* URBANIZATION IN CHINA: CRITICAL ISSUES IN AN ERA OF RAPID GROWTH, *supra* note 5, at 77, 84–85.

explosive.[250] Moreover, some benefits may accrue to individuals who work for the government as well. Government officials may openly invest in and profit from local real estate development projects, or they may receive direct or indirect benefits under the table.

The Interests of the Lenders

Banks also have their own incentives to lend to residential borrowers aggressively. Chinese banks need to cover the interest payments they owe to their depositors. Even though banks pay low rates on savings accounts, the Chinese population is large and growing, its wealth has increased greatly during the past two decades, and its savings rate is extremely high. Individual savings that have not been invested in real estate may well be sitting in accounts at Chinese banks, and the banks must pay interest on these deposits.

As previously discussed, the incentive system that Chinese banks use can encourage lending even when it is not financially advisable. Bank officers must meet lending quotas, on which their annual bonuses depend. Banks reward employees' decisions to make loans, even if those loans are financially unwise. These banks are under pressure to lend money as fast as they can, and there are few consequences to lending officers if a particular loan later proves to be a poor one. Moreover, banks, like developers, have seen many good years recently and may view high default rates more as a theoretical possibility than as an actual prospect to be greatly feared. Chinese banks have a high rate of nonperforming loans; I heard estimates of these troubled loans that ranged from 20–50 percent. But Chinese experts repeatedly emphasized that many of these loans were extended to obsolete state-owned manufacturing enterprises and that few of China's troubled loans are secured by real estate. In fact, some struggling state-owned enterprises have been bailed out by real estate developers that have been willing to pay huge amounts to acquire them, simply to obtain the right to use the underlying land.

Earlier Resolutions of these Timing Problems

Urban residential buyers are in a position in which they want to acquire real estate and generally must borrow money to do so, and Chinese lenders face strong internal and external incentives to make these loans. So the Chinese market for residential real estate loans has no shortage of willing borrowers and lenders. These two facts do not resolve the legal and timing questions noted above,

---

250 Local governments may go to great lengths to hide the revenues they receive from the sale of land use rights, since a percentage of the sale proceeds must be turned over to Beijing. *See* Weiping Wu, *Urban Infrastructure and Financing in China*, *in* URBANIZATION IN CHINA: CRITICAL ISSUES IN AN ERA OF RAPID GROWTH, *supra* note 5, at 251, 265 (noting local governments' preference for "behind-the-door negotiation" over "transparent forms of bidding and auction at market rates").

however: developers require buyers to pay all or most of the purchase price to them before they have completed construction of the unit, while lenders sensibly want to receive mortgages on completed units when they extend large real estate loans to consumers who have few other assets. These demands by the developer for early payment also create difficult cash-flow problems for the would-be buyer, who may have to borrow funds and even begin to repay this loan on a unit she cannot yet occupy, even as she continues to pay the mortgage or rent on her current dwelling. The Chinese Property Rights Law, which dates back only to 2007, is vague as to how consumer mortgage loan transactions secured by unfinished units can proceed, and various experts in China provided me with different—and not entirely persuasive—answers to this important question.

One expert insisted that the unit buyer receives an ownership certificate covering her land use right even before the unit is completed, to be followed by a second certificate for the unit itself after the developer completes construction. The borrower mortgages the first of these certificates to her lender while construction is progressing, thereby securing the acquisition loan even before the unit is ready for occupancy. This statement is legally plausible, as explored below, but it fails to account for the fact that the portion of the value of the completed unit that is allocable to the underlying land use right will represent only a small portion of the value of the entire completed unit for which the buyer must obtain acquisition funds. Thus, the borrower must still borrow an amount that greatly exceeds the value of the asset she has available to mortgage—the first of these two land use right certificates—and any lender that is willing to extend such a mortgage loan will be undersecured almost from the outset.

Under China's Property Rights Law, a buyer may apply for "pre-notice registration," which serves as notice of the buyer's interest in the property prior to the official transfer of the land use right.[251] This registration presumably prevents the seller from later deciding to convey the property to a higher bidder, by putting the prospective second buyer on notice of the first buyer's interest. However, the initial buyer's registration lapses if the transfer of the land use right is not registered "within three (3) months from the date on which such registration can be registered."[252] The law does not appear to distinguish between a land use right for the underlying land and a land use right for the unit itself, nor does it clarify whether pre-notice registration creates a property interest that can legally be mortgaged. The law also states, "The establishment ... of property rights due to such actions as legal construction ... of houses shall become valid and effective upon the occurrence of such actions."[253] This last provision seems merely to indicate that the holder of a land use right is also the owner of a unit that is later built on that land from the time the unit is built.

---

251 Wuquan Fa [Property Rights Law], art. 20 (China).
252 *Id.*
253 *Id.* art. 30.

The Property Rights Law does make clear in Article 180 that both the land use right to the building lot and the houses and other structures built on that lot are mortgageable.[254] Article 182 then goes on to state that a mortgage of either the lot or the house on the lot automatically functions as a mortgage of both.[255] This Article, however, appears to assume that the structure already exists at the time of the mortgage, which means that Article 182 does not necessarily prohibit the type of bifurcated mortgage—arising before or during the construction process— that is described above. By contrast, Article 200 states, "When land use right of construction lot is mortgaged, newly built houses on the land are not mortgaged property."[256] The clear import of this last Article is that lots on which houses are to be built are to be treated differently from lots on which houses already exist. This implication is buttressed by the last sentence of the Article, which states that the value of a house that is built on a lot that is already mortgaged does not accrue to the mortgagee upon foreclosure.[257]

One must also question whether the lender to the unit buyer will be willing to accept a mortgage of the certificate for the underlying land use right, given that the to-be-completed unit still is legally owned by the developer that is building it and also remains subject to that developer's own construction financing. This means that, in addition to the fact that the value of the certificate is less than the amount of the unit buyer's total debt, the unit still is owned by someone other than the buyer and may be subject to a substantial senior lien arising from the developer's construction activities. Finally, the expert who explained this financing structure acknowledged that it may not be legal, even as he affirmed that it is common practice. Note, however, that there does not appear to be anything in the Property Rights Law prohibiting this type of loan financing structure.

The Current Approach to Presales

A knowledgeable real estate expert explained to me what he believes to be the current state of Chinese practice with respect to residential presales. He also noted that mandatory changes to this process are under consideration, reflecting public and government sentiment that the current presale process leaves unit buyers exposed to unwarranted risk. Real estate developers may not begin to presell units in a new building until the building is 25 percent complete. This 25 percent figure refers only to construction costs and excludes the price of the land use right itself. Thus, the developer must have invested nearly half of the total cost of building the

---

254   *Id.* art. 180.
255   *Id.* art. 182.
256   *Id.* art. 200.
257   *Id.*; *see also* Chengshi Fangdichan Guanli Fa [Law on the Administration of Urban Real Estate], art. 52 (China) (containing a similar provision).

unit before it can be marketed: the roughly 30 percent of the typical budget that is required to obtain the land use right, plus one-fourth of the remaining 70 percent.

Once the developer reaches this 25 percent threshold, it can apply for permission to begin preselling units, which takes fifteen days to receive. The developer will begin to advertise shortly afterwards. This is the point at which prospective buyers line up around the block, the developer holds a lottery, and the winners may select their apartments in sequence, based on their review of building plans and, perhaps, their inspection of a model apartment. Each buyer also must pay a nominal amount of the purchase price at this point, which is nonrefundable but will be credited against the price. One month later, the buyer must put up the rest of the first 20 percent of the price. Two months after that, the buyer must pay the entire balance of the purchase price.

This last payment deadline is the point at which the buyer's cash-flow problems become apparent, since she is borrowing the funds to pay the balance of the purchase price long before she can occupy the unit or mortgage it to the acquisition lender. Moreover, the buyer will also have to begin to repay this acquisition loan three or four months before the apartment is completed and ready for occupancy. So there is a period of three or four months late in the construction process when the buyer bears the costs of carrying two residences: the mortgage on the new one and the mortgage or rent on the one she is soon to vacate.

The borrower cannot mortgage the unit to the acquisition lender at the time of this last payment deadline, because she does not yet own the apartment and thus does not have the legal capacity to mortgage the unit. But she can record a notice of the future mortgage, which will automatically become a mortgage when the buyer acquires the land use right for the completed unit. Of course, this notice is junior to the developer's construction loan. That priority problem is somewhat less problematic that it might at first seem, because the developer's construction lender often also serves as the acquisition lender to the various unit owners.

Nonetheless, this lender is now overextended. It has lent construction funds to the developer and also acquisition funds to the buyer. This buyer has paid the entire purchase price for her unit to the developer, but the developer has not yet repaid the construction lender. To protect itself against developer insolvency, the lender also obtains a personal guarantee of completion from the developer, or perhaps from one of the developer's creditworthy principals. Another expert advised me that, in the few cases in which developers had actually defaulted in a setting such as this, the government had invited a replacement developer to complete the project, and that developer had contributed additional funds and then negotiated with the unit buyers to share this additional cost. Under the circumstances, the unit buyers were relieved to obtain the apartment for which they had already paid, even at an increased cost, and in many cases the unit had appreciated during the construction process.

Note also that in troubled projects of this type, the developer may have fallen behind in its payments to contractors. Contractors have preferential lien rights, which seems fair, given the inherent vulnerability of their position.[258] However, this preference favors the unpaid contractor over the residential purchaser who has prepaid for an incomplete unit.

In the end, the developer's desire to require buyers to pay for the unit in full before it is complete amounts to a form of buyer financing of the seller's construction project. The developer, in effect, is borrowing money from its eventual buyers by requiring them to prepay for their units before they can benefit from them. This reduces the amount that the seller must borrow from its construction lender, thereby reducing the seller's interest costs. The buyers, who must carry two units concurrently, are taking greater risks and are paying more than the stated acquisition price for their units, by subsidizing the developer's soft costs. And the buyers' lenders also are taking greater risks. One agent indicated to me that when he bought his own home, the bank was willing to lend him funds to pay for the unit before it was completed, but he was never able to make clear to me what security the lender received while the apartment was under construction. During this fourteen-month period, however, the agent was making scheduled payments on an incomplete apartment at the same time that he was continuing to pay rent on his existing dwelling. He acknowledged the risk and expense he incurred but stated that he had no alternative if he wished to become a homeowner.

There is nothing irrational about a financing structure such as this, but the buyer needs to recognize that the price set forth in the contract of sale actually understates the total cost that the buyer will pay. As long as institutional lenders—or informal lenders such as members of the buyer's extended family—are willing to provide loans to the units' ultimate buyers before the units are complete, and are willing to bear whatever legal risks this structure continues to present under current Chinese law, this payment structure works as well as any other, and it appears to have succeeded in recent years in China. The presale arrangement may be more cumbersome than it needs to be, but if it has become prevalent and buyers of new homes have come to expect it, they can factor the risks and costs it presents into their purchasing and borrowing decisions. At least one expert suggested to me that this current structure, while not actually supported by Chinese law, is viewed as desirable by the government because it is effective in maintaining social stability among the millions of people who want to buy new homes. Meanwhile, the law and practice in this area of Chinese real estate law appear to be continually developing as the market matures. In fact, there is some suggestion that presold homes are actually somewhat less expensive today than homes that are completed before sale, which implies that the parties may have learned to deduct imputed interest costs from the price for which the unit would otherwise sell.[259]

---

258   *See supra* Chapters 4, 7 (discussing the fact that contractors are often forced to accept slow payment from developers as a means of obtaining the work and thus are indirectly financing some developers' projects).

259   Deng & Fei, *supra* note 205, at 131.

Resales of Urban Residential Units

The fact that new urban residential units can later be resold profitably demonstrates that there is also a significant resale market in addition to the market for new units. In fact, the market for new units is driven in large part by the success of the resale market, with many buyers of new units expecting to cash out as quickly as possible. The reason the resale market is so vibrant—to the extent these two markets can even be distinguished—is the same as the reason why new units sell so quickly: the possibility of significant and speedy gains from transferring residential units. Moreover, the fact that the unit to be resold already exists and the buyer can inspect a completed apartment rather than waiting for development to proceed eliminates the construction and lending risks described above that the buyers of new units face.

The lender to this buyer similarly obtains a mortgage interest in an existing unit. Thus, mortgaging existing units upon resale presents none of the complexities described above. I was told by several Chinese lawyers that the transfer and loan process for existing residential units is convenient, quick, and safe, even for the typical lay investor who is unfamiliar with the relevant law.

Buyers of resales tend to be urban dwellers who cannot afford the presale process and its requirement that the buyer carry two dwellings at once, or who simply cannot afford costlier new apartments in the neighborhoods in which they wish to live. Rather than buying a new unit in a less desirable location, these buyers choose to purchase a second-hand unit that is more centrally situated. Some of these buyers are urban residents who have just received government compensation for the loss of their former dwelling. In addition, some resold units may be rented out, perhaps to rural migrants who need a place to live in the city or to recent college graduates who cannot yet offer their own home.

Recent Government Attempts to Slow the Residential Real Estate Market

In an effort to cool the overall residential real estate market, including sales of both new and existing units and pre-completion flips of new units, the government has raised interest rates, imposed new taxes, strengthened other lending requirements, and stepped up tax enforcement. China's benchmark interest rate rose steadily in 2006 and 2007, peaking at 7.47 percent. It then dropped dramatically over a five-month period to 5.31 percent in January 2009, presumably out of concerns about the global economic crisis, before creeping back up to 6.56 percent in July 2011.[260] Interest rates are higher for second homes, to discourage the acquisition of multiple investment units. This policy is intended to make more dwelling units

---

260 *China Interest Rate*, TRADING ECONOMICS (July 2011), http://www.tradingeconomics.com/china/interest-rate (last visited Nov. 7, 2011).

available more cheaply for first-time buyers who plan to occupy the apartments they purchase.

The government has increased existing transfer taxes and gains taxes and has imposed new ones. Buyers must pay a transfer tax equal to 1.5 percent of the purchase price. In addition, if the seller is transferring the unit within five years of initially acquiring it—a time limit that was recently increased from two years—the seller pays an additional transfer tax of 5 percent. I was told that this tax was originally a gains tax, levied only on the seller's profit, but was amended to become a transfer tax, calculated as a percentage of the entire sale price. To discourage investment in luxury units, the government assesses the latter tax on units larger than 144 square meters even after the seller has owned the unit for five years, and these larger units pay the former tax at a rate of 3 percent rather than the standard 1.5 percent. At about the same time that these new taxes became effective, banks increased their minimum downpayments on residential units from 20 percent to 30 percent, with some banks requiring even larger initial payments.

These policies, most of which were implemented before the recent global crisis, have apparently been somewhat successful, slowing down appreciation of residential units as the government had hoped to do. Moreover, investors who had purchased units with the goal of selling them at a profit within a few months likely ended up holding these units for longer than they intended. Recent global conditions have led to a brief reversal of some of these policies, with the government apparently concerned about slowing the real estate market down too much.

Chapter 9
Commercial Construction and Commercial Leasing

Lending Submissions, Credit Decisions, and the Commercial Construction Process

The commercial real estate development market in China operates in a manner that is not completely surprising to the American lawyer who is familiar with US construction methods. A Chinese real estate developer assesses the local market in an effort to determine whether a particular real estate project will be profitable. The developer approaches lenders and seeks to borrow the largest amount of money it can, thereby maximizing its leverage and overall return. If the developer plans to hold the completed building as rental property, it begins to look for tenants; if it plans to sell individual units to owners, it starts trying to sell them before the units are built. The developer also will enter into a contract with a construction company to build the structure.

In short, the overall goals and methods of Chinese real estate developers are similar to those of Western developers.[261] And current Chinese law makes it clear that real estate developers may profit from their projects. For example, Article 135 of the Property Rights Law states, "The owner of the right to the use of land for construction use shall, according to law, be entitled to possess, utilize and obtain profits from the State-owned land, and have the right, by utilizing such land, to build buildings and their accessory facilities."[262] There are important distinctions, however, between Chinese and Western developers, reflecting dramatic differences in law, history, culture, and custom. This chapter will compare and contrast the approaches taken by Western and Chinese real estate developers.

Commercial Lending Revisited

Early in the project, a Chinese real estate developer that seeks funding for construction must obtain a project loan, which is analogous to an American

---

[261] "China's construction industry is a mainstay of the Chinese economy and is projected to become the largest construction market in the world by 2010." ASHLEY HOWLETT, PRC CONSTRUCTION LAW—A GUIDE FOR FOREIGN COMPANIES 3 (2006).

[262] Wuquan Fa [Property Rights Law], art. 135.

construction loan.[263] The experts that I met with emphasized the fact that a borrower seeking a project loan from a lender is required to produce four documents. These documents all focus on legal requirements rather than on the financial viability of the project that is being developed. Thus, they do not assist the lender in determining whether the loan is likely to be repaid. Rather, these submissions are designed to ensure that the project complies with applicable laws.

First, the prospective borrower must provide the project lender with the land use right certificate, which serves as documentary evidence that the borrower owns the land use right covering the land on which the project will be built and can mortgage it. The contract for assignment of the land use right is required to set forth certain statutory terms, including the size of the parcel, the nature of the land, and the uses that are permitted on the land.[264] The purchaser's use rights appear to vest upon registration of the land use right, at which point the purchaser receives the land use right certificate.[265] Any change thereafter in the use of the land requires government approval.[266] Ownership of the land use right automatically incorporates the right to mortgage the land use right, as long as the term of the mortgage does not exceed the remaining term of the land use right.[267] The developer's possession of this certificate proves to the project lender that the borrower has paid the government for the land use right. In common law terms, this certificate is analogous to the developer's deed or ground lease, but with some elements of a restrictive covenant included.[268]

Second, the loan applicant must provide its prospective lender with a zone certificate, which states how many buildings are permitted on the lot and sets forth the permitted height and bulk of those buildings. This document, like the land use right certificate, serves some of the same purposes as the common law deed and restrictive covenant, but here the focus is on the number and size of the proposed structures rather than on their uses.

Third, the would-be developer must provide its project lender with a land zone certificate. This certificate confirms that the proposed use is permissible. Finally, the developer must present the building or construction permit. Possession of this permit indicates not only that the building is permitted within the zone, in terms of both its size and its use, but also that the local government has granted the

---

263 This chapter focuses primarily on the construction process. For a more general discussion of the relationship between borrowers and lenders in China, see *supra* Chapter 7.

264 Wuquan Fa [Property Rights Law], art. 138.

265 *Id.* art. 139.

266 *Id.* art. 140.

267 *Id.* arts. 143–44.

268 The ground lease analogy is an imperfect one, as previously noted. *See supra* notes 81–86 and accompanying text. The restrictive covenant analogy is also an unsatisfactory one: although Chinese land use right certificates include restrictions on use, thereby creating a weak resemblance to a restrictive covenant, the owner of the underlying land and holder of the enforcement right is the government. In some senses, then, the use limitations contained within a land use right certificate more closely resemble zoning restrictions.

developer permission to build. This document serves many of the same purposes as the building permit that American jurisdictions typically require.

In the early days of the modern Chinese real estate market, before lenders required these four submissions, lending standards were widely viewed as lax. Developers pushed hard to borrow and develop so they could maximize their profit; lenders lacked the experience, desire, and incentive to know which loan applications should be approved; and projects proceeded whether or not they were financially viable. As a result, the developer would profit if the project was successful, while the bank suffered most of the risks of failure. Moreover, these banks were state-controlled rather than private, which meant that their focus was more on the political desirability of any given project and less on the ability of a development to generate profits for its developer and lender.

This informality in Chinese lending standards created the impression that officers of state-controlled lenders would help their well-connected developer friends obtain loans, with the banks quietly absorbing any losses that resulted if the project did not turn out as well as hoped. While this perception may have been richly deserved in many cases, there is also no doubt that Chinese lenders were inexperienced in these early days of the modern Chinese real estate market. This perception has changed considerably, though not completely, as the Chinese real estate market has matured. More formalized and standardized lending requirements also have served to put a needed damper on a market that had been overheated.

The four documents that lenders require today all pertain to legal requirements and demonstrate to the project lender that the developer may proceed to construct the building. Prospective borrowers often provide little else to the lender. Notably, most project lenders do not appear to require the more detailed financial information that a Western construction lender would demand in making its credit analysis of the borrower's application for funds. Chinese lenders are verifying that the project is legal and may proceed, but are not predicting whether it is desirable or will succeed.

To be sure, the very nature of the four required submissions provides the project lender with considerable comfort that the borrower is creditworthy. A borrower that owns a land use right, for example, demonstrates that it already has marshalled the resources needed to acquire and pay for a desirable and valuable asset. Thus, the borrower will already have made a considerable capital contribution to its own project before it seeks to borrow funds for construction. If the land was previously occupied, the borrower also will have had to bear the extra expense of relocating the prior occupants. The borrower that owns the land use right has already made a financial commitment to the project that may represent 30 percent of the total project budget, and sometimes even more than that.[269]

---

269 The experts I interviewed were not in agreement as to whether a land use right can be mortgaged as security for the repayment of a loan to be used to acquire that very right. *See supra* notes 190–91 and accompanying text.

Although they will not serve as security for repayment of the loan, the other three documents do offer the project lender additional comfort that the developer will be able to complete the job successfully. Before Chinese lenders began requiring the four submissions described in the text, they demanded only evidence that the borrower possessed the land use right for the property. I was told that the number of nonperforming real estate loans—always relatively small—dropped further after lenders began requiring the three additional submissions.

Nonetheless, this submission package required by Chinese lenders is markedly sketchier than the set of documents a Western construction lender would demand. A Western lender would certainly insist on reviewing the domestic equivalent of these four documents, to assure itself that the borrower owns the land and may legally build the proposed structure on it. If the borrower could not demonstrate that it had received one or more of the corresponding documents already, the lender would make the obtaining of the outstanding documents a condition precedent to the lender's obligation to advance any of the construction loan proceeds. Western borrowers, of course, often submit a construction loan application before they even acquire the land on which the structure is to be built.

But Western construction lenders would demand considerably more than just the legal assurances that these types of documents offer. A Western lender would insist on reviewing the borrower's market research showing that there is a need for the proposed structure in the relevant market; the borrower's income analysis showing the cash flow that the building will generate over time;[270] a study of the feasibility of the design; and a wide range of other financial and technical submissions. Before it makes its underwriting decision, this lender will want to confirm that the borrower has "run the numbers," and will want to verify these numbers for itself, as a means of forecasting whether the project can succeed.

There are several possible explanations why Chinese project lenders are so much less demanding than their Western counterparts. To begin with, some of the experts I interviewed were careful to distinguish between minimum lending requirements and actual lending requirements. Banks may not be required to see anything more than the four documents enumerated above, but some demand more anyway. The four documents thus constitute a threshold that banks are free to—and do—exceed. Perhaps developers who lack experience or who have not worked with a particular bank must submit a wider range of materials than developers with whom the lender has enjoyed a successful relationship in the past. In addition, Chinese project lenders know that loan applicants have already committed a significant amount of capital just to be able to acquire the land use right and obtain the three other documents. An American borrower that receives a nonrecourse loan with a 95 percent loan-to-value ratio has far less at risk than the typical Chinese borrower does, and the Chinese lender may justifiably feel more comfortable.

---

270 Mike E. Miles et al., Real Estate Development: Principles and Process 177 (4th ed. 2007).

Chinese lenders also know that many real estate developments in China are built with the idea that they will be conveyed to the ultimate occupants upon completion, if not sooner. This is particularly true of urban residential projects. Most new residential projects in China's rapidly expanding cities are conveyed under a legal structure that is comparable to the Western condominium, rather than rented out.[271] The developer begins marketing individual units as soon as it is legally permissible, often signing contracts with purchasers early in the construction process. These downstream purchasers pay a significant portion of the purchase price at the time they execute their contracts, often make additional payments during construction, and fulfill their entire financial obligations at or before completion of the building.

If a project such as this is successful, as most have been so far, the developer will have transferred most or all of the units by the time construction is complete. The developer will be in a position to cash out and repay the project loan as soon as the building is finished, and the developer–lender relationship will last for a year or two, at most. This means that neither the developer nor the project lender has much concern with the continuing viability of the project. The risk of post-construction depreciation falls almost entirely on the buyers and their respective acquisition lenders. If the value of the units were to drop during the construction process, of course, the original developer and its project lender might suffer losses. For example, the percentage of buyers who breach their acquisition contracts will rise as the value of the units drops. But residential units have appreciated consistently during the past two decades, and problems such as this have arisen only infrequently.

Chinese and American Construction Lending Contrasted

By contrast, many loans for construction of urban multi-family residential projects in the United States are made to developers that intend to hold the property for rental income after it is completed. In some cases, the construction lender plans to stay on as the borrower's permanent lender. More commonly, the construction loan will be "taken out" by a permanent loan from a long-term lender such as an insurance company or pension fund.

In American projects in which the construction loan will be taken out by an unaffiliated entity once construction is complete, one may ask why the construction lender cares what happens to the project after its own loan has been repaid. The answer is that the construction lender knows that its ultimate source of repayment is the permanent lender's funding of the permanent loan. Even though the permanent lender typically commits to this loan before construction begins, its commitment ordinarily includes a lengthy list of conditions precedent to its funding obligation. Many of these closing conditions focus on the continued financial viability of

---

271 Wuquan Fa [Property Rights Law]), arts. 70–83 (discussing the attributes of this type of residential legal structure).

the borrower and the successful completion of the project in accordance with the original plans and specifications.

In cases such as these, the two lenders and the developer often enter into a tripartite agreement at the outset, addressing many of the permanent lender's concerns. For example, the permanent lender commonly conditions its obligation to fund the permanent loan on the developer's having met certain legal and financial tests. The construction lender, in turn, will worry that the permanent lender might choose not to fund the permanent loan (and thereby pay off the construction loan) if the developer cannot meet these conditions by the time construction is complete. Therefore, the construction lender has a strong incentive to address these same requirements in the tripartite agreement or in its construction loan agreement with the developer, and it ordinarily holds the developer to the same standards as the permanent lender does. This is true even though the permanent lender may be focusing on issues that will not arise until long after the construction loan has been repaid. This greater concern by both of the lenders about the continuing viability of the project probably goes a long way toward explaining the American construction lender's more searching due diligence review of the developer's pre-construction projections about the property.

Loans Secured by Commercial Rental Property

With respect to commercial properties, the picture in China is more mixed. As with residential property, many commercial projects are sold upon completion, often in individual units, and thus are analogous to commercial condominiums in the West. But commercial properties in China are somewhat more likely to be held by the developer for rental income. Project lenders that are advancing money to developers that plan to hold a completed commercial project for rental income ought to be extremely concerned with the developer's long-term prospects.

It is worth noting that in cases in which the developer intends to continue to hold the property after construction, it is more common in China than in the United States for the project lender also to serve as the permanent, or cash-flow, lender. In other words, if the project is going to be held for rental income, not only must the initial lender worry more about the project's success over time, that lender also is more likely than in the United States to be the cash-flow lender that will suffer directly if the project fails. This fact does not alter the overall issue, of course, for rather than satisfying the lengthy closing conditions of an independent cash-flow lender that will be taking out the project loan and thereby repaying the project lender's funds, one would expect that the borrower instead must satisfy the nearly identical concerns of the unitary project/cash-flow lender from the outset. Rather than worrying that the cash-flow lender will not provide the funds the project lender expects to receive as repayment, this project lender instead should be equally worried that the developer itself will never be able to repay the loan.

Nonetheless, when I asked more than one Chinese expert about the extent to which project lenders look more toward the long term when analyzing loan applications from developers that are building rental properties, the general reaction to my question was bafflement. One lawyer advised me that developers have concluded that Chinese banks are flexible on this issue—far more flexible than Western lenders would be—and generally do not impose stringent conditions on their funding obligations. This phenomenon may be explained in part by the fact that some of the larger real estate developers and most major lenders are state-owned or state-controlled. Thus, their business decisions may focus on political and social considerations and not just on a project's bottom line.[272]

In at least some recent cases, Chinese commercial developments that will be held for rental income are owned by entities in which one of the stakeholders is foreign and is expected to put up a significant percentage of the cash that will be needed to develop the property. Loan-to-value ratios in these projects are likely to be fairly low, which may give lenders to these entities increased confidence that the loans are safe. The lenders have less money at risk, while the borrowers, including their overseas investors, have more to lose.[273]

Another possible explanation for Chinese lenders' willingness to lend after only a cursory review of a fairly short list of submissions is the fact that China's history as a nation with a modern real estate market is quite short. The process of construction and permanent lending that is so familiar to Western lawyers evolved before the development of China's modern real estate market. China's current market dates back only to the late 1980s, and Chinese lenders have seen mostly good times since then. China certainly has a large number of nonperforming loans, but those loans tend to arise in industries other than real estate. It is quite possible that the relative absence of market troughs during the careers of today's Chinese real estate professionals has led them to believe that conditions can never get any worse than they have been during the last twenty years. In short, China's lenders may believe, perhaps naively, that they have lived through the worst market conditions they will ever have to endure, and they simply may not see any point in demanding more information from prospective borrowers.

Finally, and perhaps most importantly, one should always keep in mind that the lending industry in China is largely controlled by the Chinese government. Western lenders, by and large, are privately owned entities.[274] Their shareholders

---

272 *Cf.* Bing Wang & Richard Peiser, *supra* note 230, at 272 (recognizing that loans to state-owned enterprises account for most of the nonperforming loans in China).

273 For a general discussion of the moral hazard problem that high loan-to-value ratios can create, see Gregory M. Stein, *The Scope of the Borrower's Liability in a Nonrecourse Real Estate Loan*, 55 Wash. & Lee L. Rev. 1207, 1239–44 (1998).

274 The Obama administration went out of its way to reassure the public that measures designed to bail out America's troubled banking industry did not constitute government nationalization of these banks. *See, e.g.*, Paul Krugman, *Banking on the Brink*, N.Y. Times, Feb. 23, 2009, at A27 (arguing for a more direct nationalization of the banks, while lamenting that "[t]he Obama administration, says Robert Gibbs, the White House spokesman, believes 'that a privately held banking system is the correct way to go'").

are investors who will become dissatisfied if too many of the lender's loans perform poorly. Chinese banks, by contrast, lack profit-oriented private shareholders who can serve as corporate watchdogs. Rather, these banks are controlled by a government that is influenced by many factors in addition to the profit motive, ranging from political necessity to outright corruption.[275] If a project will produce an outcome that is politically desirable—perhaps by increasing tax revenues, moving a large number of workers from state-owned industries to the private sector, or bringing glory to a local government official who wants to leave his mark on a city—it may get a green light even if it is not financially meritorious in the Western sense.

None of this discussion is meant to suggest that Chinese lenders simply extend credit heedlessly. Each bank is bound by its own internal credit policies, which are set by its board of directors. In addition, Chinese banks are subject to government oversight. While these regulators do not approve each loan, they do inspect banks regularly and issue warnings if a bank has too many nonperforming loans on its books. Nonetheless, Chinese banks may be more willing than their Western counterparts to forgo profits on individual loans in order to meet other, non-business needs.

In addition, several different experts advised me that, while Chinese lenders typically do not demand the types of feasibility studies and market analysis that Western lenders would require, some developers nonetheless undertake this type of due diligence anyway. These studies are for internal use only and give the owner's equity holders a clearer sense of the viability of the project before they risk their own funds. This two-track system reflects the fact that the quasi-capitalist owner has interests that differ dramatically from those of the socialist-government-affiliated lender. Thus, the submissions to the lender are presumably designed to persuade the lender that the project is politically defensible, while the internal reviews are designed to convince the investors that the project will be profitable.

Specific Provisions of Project Loans

Project loans tend to have shorter terms in China than they do in the West. Chinese real estate developers typically request project loans with a term of twelve months, a duration that will strike the Western real estate expert as frighteningly short. In part, these short terms may reflect the fact that construction in China proceeds at a frenetic pace, with job sites often operating around the clock and with local

---

275 *See, e.g.*, Peter S. Goodman, *Lessons the Teacher Forgot*, N.Y. TIMES, May 17, 2009, at WK1 ("In China, ventures may be spectacularly unprofitable, yet enrich everyone lucky enough to get a piece .... Soon enough, [a] trophy skyscraper [can descend] into financial disaster, but the developers, bankers and party officials have already extracted their riches, and for long afterward they will still enjoy them.").

concerns about neighborhood disruption taking a back seat to the desire to complete the project as quickly as the laws of physics will allow. And as previously noted, these quick construction schedules also reflect the fact that loans of this duration are considered short-term loans, which means that they lead to less in the way of application formality and a lower level of loan oversight. If the building is not complete when this short term expires, it is fairly easy for the borrower to receive an extension from its project lender, and the loan will still be treated as short term from an administrative perspective.

If a lender agrees to provide a project loan to a developer, that loan will typically be for a principal amount of roughly 60 percent of the project budget. As in Western construction loans, the Chinese project lender does not ordinarily advance this amount to the borrower in a single lump sum. The provision of a single payment at the outset would make the loan nearly impossible for the lender to monitor. It also could easily lead to the unexplained disappearance of the funds before the project is completed, although some experts noted that this does occasionally occur anyway. Conversely, the provision of a single payment at the end of the project would create insuperable cash-flow problems for the developer. Rather, the project loan is usually disbursed in stages as construction progresses. Recall as well that the Property Rights Law authorizes "mortgages of maximum amount," but does not define this term.[276] In some cases, the borrower may be able to negotiate for a modest lump-sum payment at the beginning of the loan term. In addition, one developer indicated that borrowers with sufficient experience or sufficiently close connections with bank officials may be able to negotiate more favorable terms than these.

The Construction Process

The construction process itself also follows a pattern similar to that employed in the West. The developer enters into a contractual agreement with a general contractor. This general contractor, in turn, may subcontract portions of the work to companies with more specialized skills. However, the payment process in China differs significantly. More than one expert complained that Chinese real estate developers are notoriously slow to pay their contractors. As previously noted, a contractor may not receive any payments at all until it has completed one-third of the work, and the contractor may receive little or no interest on these payments as they are accruing.[277]

---

276 Wuquan Fa [Property Rights Law], arts. 203–07; *see also* Danbao Fa [Guaranty Law], art. 59 (China) (defining "mortgage of maximum amount" as a mortgage in which "the mortgaged property shall be used to secure the creditor's claims which occur successively during a given period of time and to the extent of the total amount of the claims").

277 *See supra* Chapter 4 for a discussion of how general contractors may come to hold an equity interest in the development entity; *supra* Chapter 7 for a discussion of this

The result of this practice is that the contractor acts as an informal construction lender, advancing money for materials and labor for which it is reimbursed only weeks or months later. Although I pressed several professionals on the question of whether these payments were actually overdue, or whether the contractor had simply agreed to accept a delayed payment, I was not able to obtain a reliable answer to this question. Either way, though, the contractor is incurring obligations to its suppliers and workers which it must either meet before receiving payment from the developer (presumably by borrowing funds itself) or defer paying (thereby shifting this burden to its employees, subcontractors, and materials suppliers). Whichever pattern is present, someone involved in the construction process is indirectly financing the developer's project, perhaps at its own expense.

Contractors may well build these hidden financing costs into the prices they demand for construction work. A contractor that knows it will face this problem and agrees in advance to accept deferred payments anyway, or that negotiates its construction contracts under the assumption that it will be paid slowly, may attempt to include imputed interest in its bids. To the extent that the developer accepts a contractor's bid that has been increased to reflect these interest payments, the developer is paying the cost for its own slow payments. Numerous experts confirmed, however, that in China's cut-throat construction market, contractors do not have the market leverage to price this financing cost into their jobs.[278]

At the same time, even in a very competitive market, contractors must recover these costs one way or another if they are to survive. It is easy to believe that China's large construction workforce, much of it made up of workers from the provinces, is not in a position to protect itself against contractor employers that fail to pay wages in a timely fashion. These workers may not initially recognize how slowly they will be paid, or they may recognize this fact and nonetheless accept wages that are effectively lower than they appear. To the extent that they are surprised by slow receipt of wages from their employers, and thereby effectively underpaid, these workers may have little recourse, particularly since many of them have migrated to cities in which they cannot work legally. These workers may be the parties that ultimately bear most of the financial burden of slow payments from developers.

Commercial Leasing in General

The rental market in modern China is considerably less active and advanced than an observer might guess, given how energetic the overall real estate market has

---

problem from the lender's perspective.

278 *Cf.* Tang & Liu, *supra* note 177, at 222 n.30 (suggesting that many Chinese contractors are state-owned and thus have considerable leverage when working with developers).

become in the past quarter-century.[279] Despite the hyperactivity in China's real estate sector, much of the real estate that has been developed since the late 1980s consists of units that are owner-occupied or, in some cases, owned-but-unoccupied. As previously noted, residential units have become an investment commodity, and many owners hold their units vacant, purely for their investment value.

Similarly, just about any resident of China who seeks newer and more modern accommodations for her own use would rather own than rent her home, in the belief that property values are appreciating so rapidly that to do otherwise would be financially foolish. Whenever possible, a prospective owner scrapes together a downpayment and buys a unit as soon as she can. Developers quick to notice this trend have built units that they attempt to sell as rapidly as possible. The preference that both investors and occupants have shown for buying residential units does not appear to trouble residential developers, who are able to cash out of their projects more quickly than they would if they held them for rental income. These developers can skimp on construction quality, knowing that the repair or replacement costs that will inevitably surface down the road will be borne by someone other than themselves, and they can lock in their profits immediately rather than relying on the vicissitudes of an immature and fickle residential rental market.

The picture in the commercial market is somewhat more muddled, as noted earlier. Although a surprising number of commercial units are owned, the commercial rental market is far more active than the residential rental market. For example, some of the high-end shopping malls built recently in major cities are rental properties, similar to some American malls. In a typical case, the mall will be constructed by a state-owned enterprise—sometimes with a foreign partner—and the retail occupants will be tenants rather than owners. In these cases, the ownership enterprise bears a greater investment risk than it would have if it had sold the commercial units. If tenants fail to pay their rent, the landlord may find that its financial obligations, including debt service, exceed its ability to pay them. Thus, to the extent the economy takes a turn for the worse in the future, a developer that owns and rents out its property is bearing much of the risk of this economic downturn, while a developer that has already sold the units has cashed out of the project and ended its risk. The ownership enterprise retains any appreciation, of course. If the property increases in value, the developer enjoys these gains, both by raising the rent it charges when leases come due for renewal and by benefiting from the enhanced property value when it sells the project later on.

Because the Chinese government often owns a partial interest in these rental projects, many experts view this ownership structure as the Chinese government's method of receiving some of the investment gains from the expanding real estate sector. In essence, the government acts very much like a private real estate

---

279 *See generally* Gregory M. Stein, *Commercial Leasing in China: An Overview*, 8 CORNELL REAL EST. REV. 26 (2010) (describing the construction lending process and commercial leasing).

investor. It functions as a large and not-too-silent partner that shares in the equity appreciation of an enormous nationwide real estate development project.[280] Of course, the government also could, and sometimes does, benefit from its investments by selling off units right away, pocketing or reinvesting its gain.

It appears that smaller local developers are more inclined to sell off their completed projects than are larger or more established developers. These smaller entities face greater difficulties in obtaining project loans. They generally need all the cash they can get their hands on and often will find it impossible to move on to their next project until they cash out of their previous one. Larger developers, by contrast, have the staying power, bank balance, and connections with lenders and government officials to be able to hold their completed projects while continuing to invest in new projects. The market is also driven to a considerable degree by the identity of the ultimate occupant. Large overseas chains, particularly those that operate big-box stores, have shown a recent preference for owning their Chinese locations. Wal-Mart and Ikea, for instance, are concerned about the short durations of leases and rapid increases in rentals.[281]

Commercial Leasing in Mixed-Use Projects

Some large retail malls are built as components of even larger mixed-use projects. In Shanghai, for example, a typical upscale shopping mall might occupy the lower five stories of one building in a much larger, multi-building complex that also includes twenty or thirty office floors plus a hotel and cinema. One expert suggested to me that the rental retail component in a complex of this type might be losing money, but the other portions are likely to be profitable enough to offset these retail losses. If a single entity owns more than just the retail part of the building, it is likely to be making money on its total real estate investment. The owner may view the retail area as something of a trophy property that is highly visible to upscale Chinese shoppers and foreign visitors, with this portion of the property subsidized by the office and hotel portions. A mall such as this may even serve as a loss leader for the project as a whole. Although it loses money on its own, it increases the project's attractiveness to office tenants and hotel guests who spend elsewhere within the complex, much as retail shops and restaurants located in resorts may lose money but are essential to the overall success of the resort.

Even if the retail portion of a mixed-use project seems to have low foot-traffic, as many do, it may be losing less money than the casual observer would guess.

---

280 Chinese law seems to authorize this type of public–private joint venture. Wuquan Fa [Property Rights Law], art. 67.
281 Bonnie Cao & Michael Wei, *Wal-Mart, Ikea Lead Retailers' Push in China Land-Buying as Rentals Surge*, BLOOMBERG NEWS, July 4, 2011, http://www.bloomberg.com/news/2011-07-04/wal-mart-ikea-lead-retailers-push-in-china-land-buying-as-rentals-surge.html.

High-profile international retailers have been willing to overpay for prime locations to some extent, even if they know from the outset that these sites will lose money. They simply want to be able to add trendy Shanghai to their list of locations. These high-end stores, with few shoppers and little merchandise, may serve more as billboards for these chains than as traditional, profitable retail locations.

Cash-Flow Lenders and Commercial Leasing

If a developer plans to sell a new project immediately upon completion, the project lender knows this from the outset and expects to receive repayment promptly. By contrast, cash-flow lenders have to maintain an ongoing relationship with the developer, in its capacity as landlord, perhaps for a prolonged period. Cash-flow lenders should be quite concerned with the developer's creditworthiness, history, and experience. Banks—and, for that matter, developers—apparently are more likely to perform thorough feasibility studies in these cases. Given that future rental income will be used to pay off the developer's loans, these lenders take a more careful look at the rental market, the identity of potential future tenants, and the ability of these tenants to pay rent to their landlord throughout the terms of their leases. One knowledgeable expert advised me that developers of successful commercial buildings held for rental income typically recoup their cash investment within ten years and that the default rate on cash-flow loans of this type is extremely low.

Another expert advised me that the typical term for a cash-flow loan on a commercial rental building is three to five years, somewhat shorter than a comparable loan term in the United States. These short terms imply that many cash-flow loans must be refinanced. Perhaps these shorter terms reflect concern among Chinese cash-flow lenders about the likelihood of receiving repayment from borrowers who are holding commercial property for rental income. These lenders may view the Chinese commercial rental market as volatile and may seek to reduce their long-term risk accordingly, notwithstanding the dramatic and consistent appreciation in property values in China during the past two decades. Or perhaps Chinese cash-flow lenders are wary of longer loan terms simply because they have so little experience with this type of lending.

Commercial Lease Provisions

Lease terms in Chinese commercial projects are typically much shorter than in comparable Western projects. Office leases to mid-sized business tenants in China tend to have terms of two or three years, and rarely more than five years. Thus, commercial tenants in China are regularly searching for space and relocating into new quarters. If real estate values increase rapidly, as they have in many Chinese cities in recent years, tenants take the risk of rent increases when they need to renew their leases. By contrast, leases in Western markets are usually for considerably longer terms and frequently include renewal options.

Western landlords thus face the risk that the rent will seem low by the end of the term. They may mitigate this risk by including periodic rent escalations, along with provisions that require the tenant to share in any increases in the landlord's costs for taxes, insurance, and maintenance of common areas. Chinese leases, by virtue of their shorter duration, would seem to present far less of a need to include these types of provisions. Larger multinational corporations do tend to seek longer lease terms—perhaps ten or twenty years—a fact that may reflect the greater real estate experience these non-Chinese entities have accumulated in markets outside China.

Tenants believe that landlords have far more power than tenants and have better connections with government officials and the police. For these reasons, tenants generally do everything they can do to pay their rent on time. They know that serious breaches of their leases will lead to eviction, a remedy they wish to avoid. If a tenant does default, the lease typically allows the landlord to commence a legal action in court or to arbitrate. Landlords may receive contract damages or liquidated damages and may also seek to have the tenant evicted. The landlord's method of eviction depends on the terms included in the lease. Landlords may be able to exercise self-help to remove the tenant and also can seek a court order compelling the tenant to vacate the premises. One expert described a fairly harsh self-help process in which the landlord can use its security guards to evict a tenant in default. This process appears even more drastic than the self-help remedy that used to be common in the United States but which has fallen into widespread disfavor in recent years.[282]

---

282 *See, e.g.*, Berg v. Wiley, 264 N.W.2d 145 (Minn. 1978) (departing from the common law rule by holding that landlords may not exercise self-help to remove a tenant that is still in possession).

Chapter 10
Infrastructure: Building and Paying for Roads, Bridges, Subways, and Airports

The Murky Distinction Between Public and Private in China

Real estate development in modern China is not just a private enterprise. This reality may arise, at least in part, from China's recent attempts to harmonize the private right to use property with the public ownership of land that its nominally socialist system still requires. For example, Article 3 of China's Property Rights Law states, "During the primary stage of socialism, the State shall adhere to the basic economic system, with public ownership playing a dominant role and diverse forms of ownership developing side by side."[283] This Article also requires the state to "develop" the public portion of the economy, but only to "encourage, support, and guide the development of" the private sector.[284]

The government has been the leading participant in a national undertaking to upgrade basic public infrastructure for at least the past two decades.[285] China's local governments invest in infrastructure to meet public demand, to improve productivity, to provide financial benefits to these governments themselves, and to comply with national law. Thus, a significant portion of the construction in China today is public construction, initiated, planned, and largely executed by various levels of government for a primarily public purpose. Public projects such as these tend to proceed quite rapidly. For example, Shanghai's Pudong Airport was conceived and built in just over two years. By comparison, Denver's recently completed international airport took nearly six years from initial outlays to official opening. In addition, there is typically little or no public input, as "[p]ublic participation in general has never been an established feature of the development process in China."[286]

---

283 Wuquan Fa [Property Rights Law], art. 3.
284 *Id.*
285 *See, e.g.*, Jae Ho Chung, *Recipes for Development in Post-Mao Chinese Cities: Themes and Variations*, in CITIES IN CHINA: RECIPES FOR ECONOMIC DEVELOPMENT IN THE REFORM ERA, *supra* note 101, at 1, 2 (noting that, in the earlier days of China's real estate modernization process, local governments played an even more important role because of a "shortage of bourgeois entrepreneurs and private business groups") (footnote omitted).
286 Gerrit Knaap & Xingshuo Zhao, *Smart Growth and Urbanization in China: Can an American Tonic Treat the Growing Pains of Asia?*, in SMART URBAN GROWTH FOR CHINA, *supra* note 136, at 11, 23.

China's infrastructure, which was never adequate to begin with, is crumbling from decades of neglect prior to the 1990s. It is being stressed by a growing and more demanding citizenry. Local governments in China know that they must provide a diverse range of services to a huge population that is insisting on higher levels of comfort. This population includes the tens of millions of rural migrants who have been relocating to cities each year in search of construction and factory jobs. These governments have also come to recognize that improved infrastructure leads to increased productivity.[287] For these reasons, governments at all levels, and local governments in particular, have been eager to update and expand their existing housing stock, upgrade substandard roads and bridges, and build new subways and airports.

Investment in infrastructure helps China's people, but it may also pay financial dividends to the local governments that provide it. "Urban infrastructure is considered to be a good form of public investment because it can increase revenue from land leases."[288] Not only do local governments raise abundant revenue by selling land use rights, they also have relative freedom as to how they spend these proceeds. "Revenues generated from public land leasing were regarded as extra-budgetary revenue, and their disposal was completely in the hands of local governments. Land revenues are the biggest share of extra-budget revenues, which play an extraordinary role in financing local governments."[289] The central government also is becoming increasingly cognizant of the environmental dangers it must address without delay and has encouraged public green projects as diverse as generating cleaner power and providing more public space.[290]

China's City Planning Law seems to compel cities to engage in infrastructure planning. This law, which "shall be observed when the plan for a city is being formulated or implemented, or when construction is being carried out within a planned urban area,"[291] demands that "[t]he construction of items of urban infrastructure as defined in the plan for a city shall be incorporated into the plan for national economic and social development ... and shall be carried out step by step in a planned way."[292] When urban areas are being redeveloped, "special attention

---

287 "[I]mproved public infrastructure probably increases the productivity of all private factors .... For this reason, improvements in the public physical infrastructure in Chinese cities will be necessary for urban labor productivity to approach levels in the developed world." Jeffrey S. Zax, *Efficiency in China's Urban Labor Markets*, in URBANIZATION IN CHINA: CRITICAL ISSUES IN AN ERA OF RAPID GROWTH, *supra* note 5, at 209, 227.

288 Wu, *supra* note 250, at 258.

289 Ding, *supra* note 136, at 123 (footnote omitted).

290 Robert Ash, *Managing China's Arable Land Resources in an Era of Sustainability*, in URBANIZATION IN CHINA: CRITICAL ISSUES IN AN ERA OF RAPID GROWTH, supra note 5, at 117, 139 (noting how the government's "increasing emphasis on sustainability and harmony" may be undercut by rural migration and the stresses it can place on infrastructure, the environment, and social order).

291 Chengshi Guihua Fa [City Planning Law], art. 2.

292 *Id.* art. 6.

shall be given to the construction of the infrastructure and public facilities so as to enhance the multiple functions of the city."[293] The City Planning Law also requires the making of "a scientific forecast" from "actual conditions."[294]

The Influence of the Public Sector on "Private" Development

The above discussion draws an artificially sharp distinction between public and private development of Chinese real estate, and assumes that infrastructure can be described as purely public while other, more profit-oriented projects can be contrasted as entirely private. But although public entities have the desire, responsibility, and capacity to engage in infrastructure development, it is essential to remember that even so-called private development in China frequently has a significant public element. The government exerts significant control over all aspects of the Chinese real estate market. As a result, projects that would be considered primarily private in the West necessarily import some of the characteristics of public projects when they are undertaken in China. One expert reminded me that while, to Americans, "private" means that the government is not involved, "in China, the government is everywhere."

This government dominance of the entire real estate market manifests itself in a variety of ways. The government controls the sale of land use rights and uses this power to influence what is built and where. For example, Article 10 of the Law on the Administration of Urban Real Estate states, "Granting of the land-use right must conform to the overall planning for land utilization, urban planning and the annual plan for land to be used for construction."[295] Similarly, Article 4 of the Land Administration Law states, "The State applies a system of control over the purposes of the use of land."[296] Government bodies thus both supervise transfers of the right to use land and designate the uses to which that land can be put.

The government influences the land market by other means, as well. All of the major domestic lenders are controlled by the government. Real estate development entities frequently have government stakeholders. And every developer's need for

---

293   *Id.* art. 27.

294   *Id.* art. 13.

295   Chengshi Fangdichan Guanli Fa [Law on the Administration of Urban Real Estate], art. 10.

296   Tudi Guanli Fa [Land Administration Law], art. 4. A variety of other Chinese statutes also require the government to control how land is used. *See, e.g., id.* art. 1 (describing the purposes of the law, including "protecting and developing land resources" and "making rational use of land"); *id.* art. 3 (stating that to "use land rationally ... is China's basic policy" and calling on the government to plan uses of land accordingly); *id.* art. 17 (requiring "People's governments at all levels [to] draw up overall plans for land utilization" to foster "national economic and social development"); *id.* art. 44 (requiring that certain formalities be met before agricultural land may be converted to other uses); Chengshi Fangdichan Guanli Fa [Law on the Administration of Urban Real Estate], art. 25 ("The development of real estate must be strictly subjected to the urban planning.").

guanxi ensures that even developers without government stakeholders maintain close links to government officials. For these reasons, all development in China is, to a significant degree, public development. Moreover, this uncertain boundary between public and private can lead to ambiguity as to who bears responsibility for various public improvements.[297]

Even in a development that is wholly or largely owned by a private entity, the government may insist that the private developer supply infrastructure that is ancillary to the private development. The government routinely demands that developers build roads and sidewalks and install necessary utilities, just as most American jurisdictions would do. If a developer plans to construct a residential complex, it may also be compelled to include the green space and parking for which its development will increase demand. In this way, the public is not compelled to bear the costs of externalities that the developer has created.

In thriving regions such as Shanghai's Pudong New Area, a new project may be sufficiently profitable as a whole that a developer will jump at the chance to acquire land use rights despite significant and expensive government-imposed requirements. In cases such as these, the government may require the developer to construct off-site improvements with a more tenuous nexus to the new development. These obligations resemble the exactions or impact fees that some American jurisdictions impose but may display a considerably higher level of government intrusion.[298] Developments in urban areas also may require expensive and controversial relocations of current occupants and demolition of existing structures. Such relocation and demolition may be undertaken by the developer, the government acting at the developer's expense, or the two acting in concert. These relocations are becoming more and more contentious, and thus more expensive. For example, a heavily publicized settlement of an expropriation claim occurred in Chongqing in 2007, after a lone couple held out for additional compensation while continuing to occupy their house in the middle of an otherwise fully excavated construction site.[299]

The private development of land that is currently used for agricultural purposes is particularly problematic and will trigger even more intrusive government review and involvement, as discussed earlier. China's Property Rights Law severely

---

297 *See* Randall Crane, *Public Finance Challenges for Chinese Urban Development*, *in* URBANIZATION IN CHINA: CRITICAL ISSUES IN AN ERA OF RAPID GROWTH, *supra* note 5, at 237, 239 (observing that "service responsibilities, capacities, and costs change as cities grow, especially where the line between the public and private sectors is increasingly fluid").

298 *See, e.g.*, Wu, *supra* note 250, at 259–60 (discussing China's "infrastructure connection fee"). For a general overview of the law of exactions and impact fees, see ROBERT C. ELLICKSON & VICKI L. BEEN, LAND USE CONTROLS: CASES AND MATERIALS 634–35 (3d ed. 2005) (discussing exactions and describing the limits on exactions as "a central issue in land development law"). The authors continue by supplying greater detail on this topic. *Id.* at 635–79.

299 *See "Nail House" in Chongqing Demolished*, CHINA DAILY, Apr. 3, 2007, http://www.chinadaily.com.cn/china/2007-04/03/content_842221.htm (news account with photos).

limits the ability to convert agricultural land to other uses, stating, "The State adopts special protection with regard to the agriculture land, strictly limiting the transfer of agriculture land to construction land so as to control the total quantity of the construction land."[300] The expropriation of "basic farmland" requires State Council approval,[301] which indicates just how concerned the government is about the social dislocation that the loss of farmland might cause. "Since farming is their primary income source, quality of life for farmers depends on the amount and quality of land they own. Land acquisition (for urbanization, for instance) means that villagers lose farmland, which in turn reduces their economic well being."[302] Nonetheless, extensive further urbanization is inevitable in China, and other government land use policies encourage it.[303]

Common Interests of Developers and Local Governments

All of these public attributes of private development can create difficulties and costs for Chinese developers, conflicts of interest for local government officials, and problems for Chinese society more generally. Given how much money local governments earn from the sale of land use rights and how these governments have come to rely on developers for constructing essential infrastructure, there is great pressure to allow intensive development. As one author notes, "Driven by financing interest [*sic*], local government forms a coalition with developers despite the fact that government is expected to supervise the real estate business

---

300 Wuquan Fa [Property Rights Law], art. 43; *see also* Tudi Guanli Fa [Land Administration Law], art. 4 (requiring that the State "rigidly restrict conversion of land for agriculture to land for construction" and "give special protection to cultivated land"); *id.* art. 18 (prohibiting "people's governments of provinces, autonomous regions and municipalities directly under the Central Government [from reducing] the total area of the cultivated land within their own administrative regions").

301 Tudi Guanli Fa [Land Administration Law], art. 45; *see also* Erik Lichtenberg & Chengri Ding, *Assessing Farmland Protection Policy in China*, *in* URBANIZATION IN CHINA: CRITICAL ISSUES IN AN ERA OF RAPID GROWTH, *supra* note 5, at 101, 101 (discussing the Chinese government's concern about the loss of farmland and describing the failure of government measures introduced to stem these losses); *id.* at 107 (observing that "losses of cultivated area to urban uses have been concentrated in the most productive farming areas of the country"); Lin & Ho, *supra* note 132, at 106 (observing, "The most striking feature separating recent land use change from the long-term trend since 1949 has been the net loss of large quantities of cultivated land.").

302 Meng & Li, *supra* note 176, at 126.

303 Ash, *supra* note 290, at 139 ("In the face of massive surplus farm labor, low agricultural labor productivity, and widespread rural poverty, accelerated urbanization has been a touchstone of China's development strategy. There is no doubt that the process of urbanization will continue.").

and overcome market failure. Consequently, problems caused by the immature market are worsened by the coalition of power and money at the local level."[304]

This same author notes that, despite central government interest in addressing these problems, local government officials often work to undercut these national policies. For example, Shanghai's government lost an enormous amount of revenue when the central government implemented national policies in 2005 that were designed to slow the real estate market, and Shanghai quietly took steps to reverse these policies the following year.[305] Moreover, developers and local governments often prefer to expand at the urban fringe, regardless of whether this constitutes good urban or agricultural planning. Such expansion displaces farmers and creates sprawl, but it is usually cheaper to pay compensation to ousted rural residents than to their urban counterparts.[306]

This tension is by no means limited to governments in cities, with the same phenomenon evident in villages. "[L]and development undertaken by village committees can be understood as a set of strategies for strengthening local budgets ...."[307] Real estate development creates huge revenues for villages, and China's many rapidly urbanizing villages need this income stream, both to build infrastructure and to provide entitlements to residents.[308]

Construction of Infrastructure

The discussion in this chapter so far has described the quasi-public nature of some superficially private developments. These projects, though, have a non-government interest holder that is using its real estate expertise and its personal capital to build something it wishes to construct. The private developer presumably is motivated by the goal of turning a profit for itself. These developments are as private as current Chinese law and practice allow. The public developments on which the rest of this chapter will focus, by contrast, have purposes that are purely or largely public. They are built at the government's behest, by the government or at the government's direction, for the benefit of the public, and with little or no profit motive. Some of these projects are purely public. However, as the discussion that follows will demonstrate, many others of these supposedly public development projects have a quasi-private nature. They may be outsourced to private entities or

---

304 Tingwei Zhang, *Urban Development Patterns in China: New, Renewed, and Ignored Urban Spaces*, in URBANIZATION IN CHINA: CRITICAL ISSUES IN AN ERA OF RAPID GROWTH, *supra* note 5, at 3, 24.
305 *Id.* at 24–25.
306 *See* Knaap & Zhao, *supra* note 286, at 23.
307 Michael Leaf, *Chengzhongcun: China's Urbanizing Villages from Multiple Perspectives*, in URBANIZATION IN CHINA: CRITICAL ISSUES IN AN ERA OF RAPID GROWTH, *supra* note 5, at 169, 172.
308 *Id.*

otherwise have significant private components, further muddying the distinction between public and private in today's China.

This confusion may be at least partly intentional, as China struggles to harmonize free-market development with Communist principles. As already noted, Article 3 of the Property Rights Law states:

> During the primary stage of socialism, the State shall adhere to the basic economic system, with public ownership playing a dominant role and diverse forms of ownership developing side by side. The State shall consolidate and develop unswervingly the public sector of the economy and at the same time encourage, support and guide the development of the non-public sectors of the economy.[309]

Public–private partnerships of the type described in the text may thus reflect China's stated goal of merging socialist principles with the incentives that the desire to earn personal profit can create.[310]

The Influence of the Private Sector on "Public" Development

The discussion above demonstrated that private projects in China frequently exhibit substantial government intrusion. The analysis that follows, which examines projects that are supposedly public, will show that many of these ostensibly public infrastructure undertakings reveal significant private influence and participation. Nonetheless, several of China's huge infrastructure projects of the past twenty-five years have been undertaken largely by the government itself, and this chapter examines some of these more traditional public projects as well.

Even as powerful and monolithic a government as China's has needed to enlist the budding private sector. As the discussion below will demonstrate, the government funds some infrastructure projects by selling off land use rights to private developers. These private entities must buy the land they need from the government, which then uses the sales proceeds for the purpose of building infrastructure. Alternatively, the government may borrow funds for infrastructure projects from domestic banks and then use the proceeds of these sales of land use rights to repay those loans.

In addition, the government has afforded sizable tax breaks to domestic and foreign private companies that have chosen to locate in Special Economic Zones (SEZs). The government thereby suffers a short-term reduction in tax collections as a way of inducing private businesses to relocate in targeted areas. These businesses, it is hoped, will stimulate further development and, ultimately, increased tax revenues. When it wished to encourage the development of Shanghai's Pudong

---

309 Wuquan Fa [Property Rights Law], art. 3.
310 *See generally* XIANFA pmbl. (2004) ("The basic task of the nation is to concentrate its efforts on socialist modernization by following the road of Chinese-style socialism.").

New Area, for example, the government reduced the income tax that businesses that located in Pudong would have to pay to just 15 percent, as compared to 33 percent elsewhere in Shanghai.

And as noted earlier, the government sometimes uses its strength to provide more forceful inducements than these. When the government decreed that the Lujiazui district in Pudong was going to become Shanghai's financial center, it increased the likelihood that this project would succeed by granting business licenses to foreign banks that wished to open new offices in Shanghai only if they located in Lujiazui. Similarly, proprietors of international schools were advised that they would receive licenses to operate only in the Jinqiao area of Pudong, further increasing the likelihood that foreign businesses would choose to place their offices in this new area.[311]

Build–Operate–Transfer Projects

Rather than building infrastructure itself, the government may outsource this traditionally public function to private entities. China has authorized private entities to build some projects of this nature, such as toll roads; operate these projects for twenty or thirty years to recoup their costs and earn a reasonable profit; and then transfer control of the project back to the government at the end of this recoupment period.[312] This Build–Operate–Transfer (BOT) structure, seen most often in developing nations, is also used occasionally in the West. For example, Toronto recently financed construction of a new airport terminal by structuring it as a BOT. The use of BOT financing in China also helps to attract overseas investment.[313]

BOTs shift the initial construction costs to the private developer, along with some of the risk that project revenues will not cover the cost of construction debt service. They also defer the government's ability to collect the full revenues that the project generates and require the government to relinquish some control over the project for the duration of the BOT period. The private developer bears whatever share of the upside and downside construction and operational risk is set forth in the parties' written agreement, while the government can remove the cost of constructing the project from its books.

---

311 *See supra* notes 101, 126 and accompanying text.

312 Article 67 of the Property Rights Law implies that the government may enter into transactions of this type. Wuquan Fa [Property Rights Law], art. 67.

313 *See* Yeh, *supra* note 161, at 51–52 (noting the increasing prevalence of Build–Operate–Transfer projects in China and the ability of this mechanism to attract foreign infrastructure investment). For discussion of an American example of BOT financing, see J.K. Wall, *For Whom the Road Tolls: Public–Private Funding Model Is Gaining Speed*, INDIANAPOLIS STAR, Nov. 15, 2006, Business Section, at 1 (discussing proposed 75-mile toll road in Indiana to be financed privately and leased to a private operator for 75 years).

Public–private partnerships are relatively new to China and do not always proceed seamlessly. There may be legal and practical limits on the extent to which government bodies and private entities can work together. Shanghai has established a modern subway system from scratch in little more than fifteen years. Nonetheless, the placement of subway stations and the rail linkages to aboveground developments appear haphazard:

> Current regulations prevent the transit agency from involvement in property development above the ground. Therefore, there is no incentive for the transit agency to consider land use beyond its right-of-way. More often than not, the rail transit station and its neighboring land uses are simply adjacent to each other. There is lack of synergy and integration among them.[314]

The many layers of Chinese bureaucracy, such as those exhibited by Shanghai, contribute to this problem. Mixed-use, public–private projects do not currently "fit into any existing categories for development evaluation and building permit approval"[315] and, in fact, are not currently permitted under Shanghai's regulations.[316] Public–private partnerships may be able to contribute positively to harmonious uses of land and successful development of infrastructure, but China seems not to be taking maximum advantage of this development and financing technique.

I was also told of cases in which the government induced a private developer to build a public project that was not likely to generate sufficient revenues for the developer to recover its costs. The government typically persuaded the developer to undertake this project by promising the developer, either publicly or privately, that it would provide the developer with some other source of revenue that would more than offset development losses on the designated project. For example, the developer might construct a subway station that the government needed, despite the fact that the developer would not profit from the project, in exchange for receiving valuable land use rights adjacent to the station. In some ways, these are just unusual public–private partnerships, in which the money-losing infrastructure project is coupled with a loosely related venture that serves as an inducement to the private developer. But the examples that were described to me were not negotiated openly, and it is unclear whether they actually were permissible under applicable laws.

By building its own projects in specific areas and creating muscular incentives for the private sector to do the same, the government seeks to channel infrastructure

---

314 Ming Zhang, *Value Capture Through Integrated Land Use–Transit Development: Experience from Hong Kong, Taipei, and Shanghai, in* URBANIZATION IN CHINA: CRITICAL ISSUES IN AN ERA OF RAPID GROWTH, *supra* note 5, at 29, 40. The author, comparing Shanghai's efforts in these areas to those in Hong Kong and Taipei, calls the Shanghai example "primitive." *Id.* at 39.

315 *Id.* at 42.

316 *Id.* at 43.

development exactly where it wants it. Several experts told me that the government even subsidized the cost of residential land use rights in Pudong before the area became attractive to residents, essentially paying people to move into a new section of the city that the government desperately wanted to succeed. This combination of strong public action and guided private choice is common in China's modern era of redevelopment.

Funding Sources for Infrastructure Projects

Even when the government is building infrastructure on its own, it must find a funding source for these public developments. "[The] system does not now adequately stimulate own-resources (such as the property tax), while relying heavily on central revenues for local spending purposes."[317] Given the absence of a broad-based *ad valorem* property tax, local tax revenues are both low and unpredictable. As a result, "under the current taxation system, the revenue share for local governments is not commensurate with their responsibilities, such as providing major capital improvements and other local public goods for urban expansion."[318]

Government entities need a more reliable funding source, and they depend on banks to supply much of the capital for infrastructure projects. Although Chinese government entities that wish to build infrastructure are beginning to have access to capital markets, the government—particularly at the local level—more commonly borrows directly from domestic banks. Chinese banks lend to various levels of government with a high degree of comfort that the government will repay these loans. Some of this lender confidence may be misplaced.[319] However, the banks are government-controlled entities themselves, and they are relying, at bottom, on the full faith and credit of the Chinese government.

---

317   Crane, *supra* note 297, at 246.

318   Chengri Ding & Yan Song, *Property Tax for Sustainable Urban Development*, in SMART URBAN GROWTH FOR CHINA, *supra* note 136, at 57, 61.

319   *See, e.g.*, Simon Rabinovitch, *Moody's Warns on China's Local Debt*, FT.COM, July 5, 2011, http://www.ft.com/intl/cms/s/0/db8d296e-a702-11e0-a808-00144feabdc0.html#axzz1RL90R4jj (suggesting that China's latest audit of local governments understated their debt load, due in part to a recent surge in lending to local governments for infrastructure projects); Andreea Papuc, *Chinese Banks See Risks in 23% of $1.1 Trillion Loans*, BLOOMBERG NEWS, July 23, 2010, http://www.bloomberg.com/news/2010-07-23/china-banks-said-to-see-risks-in-23-of-1-1-trillion-public-project-loans.html (noting that "Chinese banks may struggle to recoup about 23 percent of the 7.7 trillion yuan ($1.1 trillion) they've lent to finance local government infrastructure projects"). *But see* Henry Sanderson, *China Regulators, Officials Aim to Ease Local Finance Vehicle Loan Concern*, BLOOMBERG NEWS, July 27, 2010, http://www.bloomberg.com/news/2010-07-27/china-regulators-officials-aim-to-ease-local-finance-vehicle-loan-concern.html (suggesting that the collateral and guarantees provided in connection with these loans provide adequate backing).

The government later repays these loans from two funding sources: sales of land use rights and revenues from user fees generated by the infrastructure project itself, such as subway fares and highway tolls.[320] When a local government entity conveys land use rights, Article 55 of the Land Administration Law states that the central government receives 30 percent of the funds the sale generates, while the local government retains the remaining 70 percent.[321] One Chinese lawyer told me, however, that the central government allows the local government to keep, for its own local purposes, 70 percent of the central government's 30 percent share. This means that the local government receives 91 percent of the total purchase price in the end. Article 55 goes on to provide that both portions of the payment must be used exclusively "for developing cultivated land."[322] By contrast, Article 19 of the Law on the Administration of Urban Real Estate requires that "[a]ll the fees for granting the land-use right shall be turned over to the State Treasury and incorporated into the budget so as to be used for the construction of urban infrastructure and for land development."[323]

The people with whom I spoke gave no indication that the last clause of Article 55 of the Land Administration Law, requiring that sale proceeds be used for the development of cultivated land, is actually being enforced. But even if this provision does apply and is being followed, the use of these funds for the purposes specifically enumerated in the law would free up other funds that might otherwise have been dedicated to these goals to be used for other important governmental purposes, including infrastructure development. A local government's desire to fund infrastructure projects is often the primary motive for that government's sale of land use rights in the first place. Investment in infrastructure, in turn, makes additional urban land available for development and increases its value.[324] The government has also become concerned that more of the funds from the sale of land use rights be used for educational purposes. The State Council recently ordered that one-tenth of the profits from land sales be spent on education.[325]

The favorable apportionment of the proceeds of the sale of land use rights creates additional incentives for local governments to maintain high property values and

---

320 *See generally* Wu, *supra* note 250, at 257–62 (discussing the financing sources that are available for infrastructure projects).

321 Tudi Guanli Fa [Land Administration Law], art. 55 (2004).

322 *Id.*

323 Chengshi Fangdichan Guanli Fa [Law on the Administration of Urban Real Estate], art. 19.

324 *See* Yeh, *supra* note 161, at 45 ("Land-related revenue is used to improve urban infrastructure, which in turn can improve accessibility and open up new land for development. This process increases land value, which then increases government revenue, providing further capital for building more infrastructure.").

325 Wang Huazhong, *Education to Get Land Transfer Windfall*, CHINA DAILY, July 4, 2011, http://www.chinadaily.com.cn/china/2011-07-04/content_12825850.htm (noting that, even with this increased funding, Chinese educational spending lags behind that of the United States, northern Europe, and Japan).

sell off land use rights quickly.[326] The hotter the local real estate market, the more valuable the rights to the land; the quicker the local government sells off these valuable assets, the more rapidly it generates funds for capital construction. These infrastructure projects then fuel further price acceleration for local real estate. In fact, one academic advised me that the modern Chinese land use right evolved as the government initially sought ways to raise funds to invest in infrastructure. The government needed money for public projects and concluded that it could transfer the right to develop land that it controlled and then invest the proceeds generated by these transfers in public works.

Recent Major Infrastructure Projects

Huge, high-profile infrastructure projects have become the norm in China, as each generation of Communist Party leaders tries to leave its mark on the nation, just as emperors did during dynasties past. These projects typically involve significant investment by the private sector, catalyzed by government incentives. The government jump-started China's recent economic boom by creating a small number of SEZs and using tax breaks and other economic incentives to encourage private investment. One of the most striking of these is the city of Shenzhen, located just across the border from Hong Kong, which was designated as the first SEZ in 1979. Shenzhen grew from a small rural village with 20,000 residents to a modern city of approximately eight million people in just three decades.[327] Initially, the government designated four cities and one province as SEZs, adding many more as the experiment proved successful.

In the late 1980s, Pudong was a relatively inaccessible portion of Shanghai Municipality, located east of the Huangpu River and occupied mainly by farms, warehouses, and scattered residences.[328] On April 18, 1990, the government proclaimed the Shanghai Pudong New Area project, to be built in this sparsely populated district. The National People's Congress announced that the Pudong area would be developed at a rapid pace, "to make Pudong one of the international centers for economy, finance and trade, to open up further the cities along the

---

326 "The revenue-sharing agreement between the local and central governments is blamed for problems such as chaotic and uncoordinated development .... Local government officials, interested in raising revenue, sell land use rights beyond the level of municipal need .... These overzealous practices yield profound, negative, long-term consequences." Ding & Knaap, *supra* note 55, at 23.

327 Note that some of this population growth is due to a significant expansion of the geographical area of the city. For a discussion of the nearby SEZ city of Dongguan, with a recent history much like that of Shenzhen, see LESLIE T. CHANG, FACTORY GIRLS 17–43 (2008) (describing Dongguan from the perspective of some of the migrant women who work in that city's factories).

328 *See* TIM CLISSOLD, MR. CHINA: A MEMOIR 243 (2004) (recalling "seeing the occasional water buffalo squelching around in the mud" in Pudong in the early 1990s).

Yangtze River ... so as to accelerate to a new stage the development of the Yangtze River Delta and the regions along the river."[329]

By 2003, Pudong had been redeveloped into a modern and largely urbanized area with 2.7 million permanent residents. In that short time span, the government built and catalyzed the construction of a city the size of Chicago directly across the river from the existing city of Shanghai. Government construction of infrastructure came first, with private development following fairly quickly. The government also made strong efforts to encourage foreigners with needed talents to relocate to Pudong, particularly overseas Chinese living in Hong Kong, Taiwan, and the West. Domestic Chinese with similar talents were heavily recruited to Pudong as well. One Western lawyer summarized the government's top-down approach to projects of this type as "Let There Be Pudong!"

Pudong continues to flourish. Pudong International Airport opened in 1999; shortly thereafter, the government ordered all international carriers to fly only to Pudong, rather than to the older and more centrally located Hongqiao Airport.[330] The Asia-Pacific Economic Cooperation annual meeting was held in Pudong in 2001. China's first magnetic levitation train began operation early in 2004, with trains from Pudong Airport reaching speeds of 270 miles per hour. The former site of the 2010 World Expo straddles the Huangpu River, with about three-quarters of the land area of the Expo located in Pudong and the remainder of the site located in the older Puxi section of Shanghai.

Redevelopment projects of this type are not free of social cost, of course. The clearing of the land for the Shanghai Expo required the relocation of 18,000 households and 270 businesses and caused an increase in housing prices throughout the city.[331] More generally, the success of projects such as the Pudong redevelopment likely encouraged similar ventures, in which incumbent residents lost their land and received only modest compensation in exchange, while real estate developers and corrupt government officials garnered dramatic financial benefits.[332] This does not necessarily imply that projects such as these should not be pursued, or that they are destined to fail. After remarking on the huge amount of public money spent in Pudong with little regard to whether it is an economically viable project, for example, one commentator asks, "[S]hould one bet against Pudong? Maybe not."[333]

One of the exhibits in Shanghai's Planning Museum does an outstanding job of summarizing the approach cities such as Shanghai have taken toward the modernization process. Although the language of the exhibit legend would seem out

---

329   PUDONG NIAN JIAN 2004 [PUDONG YEARBOOK 2004] 8 (2004).

330   As part of the tourism upswing resulting from the 2010 Shanghai World Expo, some international service was restored to the newly renovated Hongqiao.

331   HSING, *supra* note 148, at 111.

332   YASHENG HUANG, *supra* note 137, at 227.

333   TED C. FISHMAN, CHINA, INC.: HOW THE RISE OF THE NEXT SUPERPOWER CHALLENGES AMERICA AND THE WORLD 31 (2005).

of place as the description of any Western democracy's efforts to upgrade its facilities, in China it serves as a fitting summary of the government's effort to rally public support for a major nationwide public endeavor. The exhibit describes Shanghai's overall credo as follows:

> [W]e will make [a] great effort to develop various social undertakings, strengthen the construction of socialist spiritual civilization, constantly make innovations of spiritual civilization, satisfy the people's increasing demand for spiritual culture, and raise the overall quality of the citizens and the civilization development of the city, so as to provide incentive [sic] for Shanghai's modernization drive.

PART III
Law and Development in China

Chapter 11
China's Other "Other Path": Confounding the Predictions of Development Economics

China's Recent Pattern of Legal Development

One of the principal themes of this book has been how Chinese real estate professionals operate against a legally uncertain background. Part II offered numerous examples of lawyers who needed to represent their clients in settings in which there was no law or no unambiguous law. They devised new legal structures with the hope that the law would later be construed in a way that ratified the approach they had already taken on their clients' behalf. Sometimes other lawyers would imitate an earlier deal, figuring that a technique that had already been tried once without challenge was less likely to be questioned in the future. Over time, a tentative method would develop into a more common course of doing business. Perhaps no problems would ever arise. Or perhaps if problems ever did arise, a court deciding a case in which a lawyer followed this increasingly common practice would simply endorse it, thereby giving judicial approval to those professionals who might wish to mimic it in the future.

Beginning to Fill the Legal Gaps

As time went by, the National People's Congress approved more and more legislation in substantive areas that had not previously been fully addressed. Many of these laws were developed in somewhat piecemeal fashion. The General Principles of the Civil Law (GPCL), effective in 1986, filled some of the huge legal holes that had been unplugged since at least 1949, though not as extensively as some had hoped. As one commentator later noted, "It was therefore decided to extract from the draft civil code some relevant general principles and to enact them as the GPCL, which is to serve as a basic framework for the operation of the existing civil law enactments and for further development."[334] The General Principles of the Civil Law did recognize "the owner's rights to lawfully possess, utilize, profit

---

    334 CHEN, *supra* note 23, at 243 (footnote omitted); *see also* MO ZHANG, CHINESE CONTRACT LAW: THEORY AND PRACTICE 9 (2006) (describing the original intention of drafting a more comprehensive code, which was followed by the realization that there was too much legal uncertainty to do so at such an early date).

from and dispose of his property."[335] But at the time the General Principles of the Civil Law became effective, "Chinese legal thinking about property rights ... had not yet matured; there also existed ideological obstacles regarding whether the affirmation of property rights ... would challenge the socialist principle of public ownership of the means of production."[336]

Other laws were enacted rapidly, to address problems that were threatening to become crises. The Land Administration Law, which was adopted in 1986 and amended in 1988, 1998, and 2004, provides a good example. Commenting on this law, one pair of authors observes,

> The purpose[] of these changes in the law was to prevent a collapse into anarchy in the land markets by ensuring that changes of use and occupation would have to be approved and registered and that the state would retain the right to recover land required for public works or the needs of state-owned enterprises.[337]

In the years that followed, laws were adopted in numerous other substantive areas relevant to the real estate market.[338] The State Council enacted the "Provisional Regulations on Assigning and Transferring the Urban State-Owned Land-Use Right" in 1990, which had the important effect of setting maximum durations for the grant of land use rights. The Law on the Administration of Urban Real Estate became effective in 1995, and the Guaranty Law was implemented in the same year. China also adopted a more detailed Contract Law, a Construction Law, a Tender Law, and other statutes relating to commercial business relationships. Most significantly, the Property Rights Law became effective in 2007, unifying and clarifying several disparate strands of property law and filling in still more holes in China's legal mosaic. The 2007 Property Rights Law, however, is China's first legislation since before 1949 to address property rights comprehensively.

Many of these laws, in the course of augmenting China's legal structure, merely ratified the practices that lawyers had already developed, used, and repeated in prior years, or implemented them with only minor modifications. In other cases, newer laws actually challenged existing practices, or at least failed to buttress them. In some of these cases, the newer rules, when actually tested, have given way to the previously established practices that contradict them.

---

335 Ming Fa Tong Ze [General Principles of the Civil Law], art. 71; *see generally* CHEN, *supra* note 23, at 248–53 (summarizing the provisions of the General Principles of the Civil Law that relate to property).

336 CHEN, *supra* note 23, at 249.

337 Li Ling & David Isaac, *Development of Urban Land Policies in China*, *in* THE IMPACT OF CHINA'S ECONOMIC REFORMS UPON LAND, PROPERTY AND CONSTRUCTION, *supra* note 7, at 16, 21.

338 *See generally* 3 CHINA BUSINESS LAW GUIDE 87,151–52 (2005) (listing and summarizing various Chinese laws that pertain to property rights); HOWLETT, *supra* note 261, at 291–574 (reproducing the full text of several of these laws, in English and Chinese).

China's legal development has thus been an ongoing back-and-forth among several different interest groups. Business people in China wish to undertake potentially lucrative transactions for which the legal system previously offered no roadmap, and they regularly rely on the unrecognized business and legal structures that Kellee Tsai has labeled "adaptive informal institutions."[339] Lawyers, who have been gradually developing proficiency by trial and error, need to represent their clients effectively within an uncertain legal climate, and they help their clients develop these new business and legal models. Local officials want to encourage development while possibly profiting personally along the way.[340] Legislators wish to continue to improve China's economic landscape without challenging—and perhaps even by endorsing—business and legal practices that have already been adopted with apparent success.[341] Judges, who may lack detailed knowledge of the subject matter of the disputes they face, have frequently been willing to ratify informal business practices that appear to be working successfully on the ground. "This was not about a textbook approach in which farsighted government officials first establish all the right institutions ... and then let global markets magically grow the country. Instead, this was about something far more ad hoc, far messier, and far more difficult to interpret at the time."[342]

China, then, has seen remarkable economic development since the 1980s, including in the field of real estate. This is true despite the fact that much of this development took place at times where there was little or no relevant law, or when a new law was so untested that none of the participants in a particular transaction could be certain what that law meant or how remaining questions would be answered. Throughout this period, the legal system was developing rapidly, often

---

339 KELLEE S. TSAI, CAPITALISM WITHOUT DEMOCRACY: THE PRIVATE SECTOR IN CONTEMPORARY CHINA 9, 19 (2007). Tsai argues further that "grassroots interactions are an equally central, and easily overlooked, component of the causal processes underlying formal institutional change and durability." *Id.* at 202. This is true even when the relevant actors are not overtly seeking to change existing institutions. *Id.* at 208.

340 *Id.* at 9 ("In the course of their everyday interactions, China's local officials and business owners devised novel ways for local enterprises to operate, which in turn attracted elite-level attention in sanctioning, post hoc, changes in the country's economic and political institutions."); Andrew G. Walder & Jean C. Oi, *Property Rights in the Chinese Economy: Contours of the Process of Change*, in PROPERTY RIGHTS AND ECONOMIC REFORM IN CHINA 1, 21 (Jean C. Oi & Andrew G. Walder eds., 1999) ("Bureaucratic behavior is not static and immutable, and analysis of economic change therefore requires an understanding both of officials as economic actors and of the varying incentives, constraints, and resource that shape their opportunities and choices.") (footnote omitted).

341 TSAI, *supra* note 339, at 40; *see also* LUBMAN, *supra* note 13, at 175 ("The Chinese experience demonstrates the difficulties of introducing new legal institutions that are at best unfamiliar and at worst inconsistent with the political and social context into which they have been thrust.").

342 STEINFELD, *supra* note 68, at 23–24 (footnote omitted).

responding to business practices that had already been adopted without formal legal recognition.

The Sequencing of Legal Development and Economic Growth

These observations about China's recent economic growth appear to contradict the predictions of law and development theory. Although this theory is complex, and will be described in greater detail below, the basic idea is simple: legal and institutional development must precede economic growth. Business people will not be willing to invest in a legal environment in which no one is certain exactly what a contract is or how it will be construed; who owns title to various assets and what that ownership implies; how security interests will be enforced; and what will happen if one of the parties becomes bankrupt. In particular, a legal system must offer strong and predictable property rights if it wishes to foster significant economic development. Investors need a reasonably high level of certainty and comfort before they will commit their assets. A nation at China's early stage of legal and institutional development will supposedly be unable to attract significant investment until it adopts business laws that offer predictability and establishes a judiciary that will enforce those laws consistently. The traditional theory and the observations about China that appear to conflict with it are the subject of Part III of this book.

This chapter will proceed as follows. In the next section, I will offer an overview of law and development theory, focusing most prominently on the widely held belief that institutions such as strong and predictable property rights are an essential prerequisite to economic development. The section following that one will then refer back to earlier chapters to recall the many ways in which China's incontrovertible growth during the past two to three decades seems to contradict this theory.

The next chapter will continue the discussion of development economics in China by offering numerous possible explanations of how the facts that seem to contradict the theory could potentially be harmonized with it. I seek neither to discredit the theory nor to argue that modern China cannot possibly exist. Rather, I will suggest different ways in which the theory might be modified or the supposed facts might be reinterpreted. Given the enormous breadth of topics such as "law and development" and "rule of law," I will attempt to focus almost exclusively on those aspects of these wider topics that are most germane to real estate law and to recent Chinese progress.

All of this brings to mind the old joke about the three economists who find themselves lost while hiking. One of them pulls out a map, scrutinizes it, and then says to the others, "Do you see that mountain over there? Well, according to this map, we're on it!" The goal of these two chapters in Part III is to examine the ways in which the map might need to be modified or the users might be misinterpreting it.

Law and Development Theory

Those who seek to foster economic growth in less-developed countries have followed an approach that has continued to evolve since World War II. In the earlier decades of this era, there was a strong belief that wealthier states needed to help their less affluent counterparts modernize themselves. This period, which David Trubek and Alvaro Santos have called the "First Moment," "focused on the role of the state in managing the economy and transforming traditional societies."[343] Modern laws were needed to jump-start the economy and to bring about social change. In many instances, those new laws emphasized the importance of human and civil rights. In addition, wealthier nations would need to provide enormous infusions of cash to their less well-to-do neighbors. The Marshall Plan is a classic example of this First Moment approach to economic development.[344]

During the 1970s and 1980s, this approach faded as neoliberal economics grew in influence. This Second Moment was characterized by a strong belief that reliance on private markets would lead to economic growth. Developing nations merely needed to integrate themselves into the burgeoning international economy. During this Second Moment, the focus of international agencies, including the World Bank, shifted from public law to private law. There was a particular emphasis on the importance of predictable contract and property rights, and "Rule of Law" became the watchword. Nations that adopted strong, reliable, and consistently enforced laws—particularly in the areas of contracts and property—would be better positioned for economic development and growth. Civil and human rights were de-emphasized during this era.[345]

The Third Moment began during the 1990s and continues today. It is characterized by a belief that the purely economic focus of the Second Moment is simply too narrow. Markets have limits and need to be carefully regulated by the government, and strong institutions matter. Under this view, development is seen as incorporating more than just economic growth, also factoring in human freedom, participation, and flourishing. There is a much greater focus on alleviating economic inequality and ensuring that any economic growth benefits all members of a society by reducing poverty. Legal reform is seen as more than just an instrumental tool designed to bring about economic development. Law reform is also desirable in and of itself, in that it helps humans to reach their

---

343 David M. Trubek & Alvaro Santos, *Introduction: The Third Moment in Law and Development Theory and the Emergence of a New Critical Practice*, in THE NEW LAW AND ECONOMIC DEVELOPMENT: A CRITICAL APPRAISAL 1, 2 (David M. Trubek & Alvaro Santos eds., 2006).

344 *See* Frank K. Upham, *From Demsetz to Deng: Speculations on the Implications of Chinese Growth for Law and Development Theory*, 41 N.Y.U. J. INT'L L. & POL. 551, 560–62 (2009) (noting that this approach, which succeeded so estimably in the case of the Marshall Plan, failed when employed in other nations in later years).

345 Trubek & Santos, *supra* note 343, at 2–3.

fullest potential in both the economic and non-economic realms.[346] As Gregory Alexander has noted in the American context,

> property is the material foundation for creating and maintaining the proper social order, the private basis for the public good. This tradition, whose roots can be traced back to Aristotle, has continuously understood the individual human as an inherently social being, inevitably dependent on others not only to thrive but even just to survive.[347]

China's modern development began during the Second Moment and continues today. To many observers, China's recent strong growth contradicts the Second Moment development model that insists that strong and predictable institutions, such as contract and property rights, must exist before a nation's economy can blossom. In order to assess the degree to which China contradicts this model, it is important to review exactly what the model predicts.

Douglass North and the New Institutional Economics

The leading proponent of the belief in strong property rights is Douglass North. In his influential 1990 work, *Institutions, Institutional Change, and Economic Performance*, which led to the emergence of the "New Institutional Economics" movement, North defines institutions as "the rules of the game in a society or, more formally, ... the humanly devised constraints that shape human interaction."[348] These institutions can be formal, such as written laws, or informal, such as customs, traditions, and taboos. "Institutions, together with the standard constraints of economic theory, determine the opportunities in a society. Organizations are created to take advantage of those opportunities, and, as the organizations evolve, they alter the institutions."[349] Society, then, can benefit from strong institutions, which include both formal law and less formal methods of interaction. And

---

346 *Id.* at 6–18.

347 GREGORY S. ALEXANDER, COMMODITY AND PROPRIETY: COMPETING VISIONS OF PROPERTY IN AMERICAN LEGAL THOUGHT 1776–1970, at 1–2; *see also id.* at 2 ("All of these understandings of property share, however, a commitment to the basic idea that the core purpose of property is not to satisfy individual preferences or to increase wealth but to fulfill some prior normative vision of how society and the polity that governs it should be structured.").

348 DOUGLASS C. NORTH, INSTITUTIONS, INSTITUTIONAL CHANGE AND ECONOMIC PERFORMANCE 3 (1990).

349 *Id.* at 7. North refers to this as "a feedback process." *Id.*; *see also* LUBMAN, *supra* note 13, at 1 ("Studying the links between legal institutions and economic reform in post-Mao China can help us to better understand relations between state and society generally.").

informal institutions will often have a greater influence on economic development than will more formal rules, as some have argued is the case in China.[350]

In North's view, humans wish to cooperate so they can all benefit economically. In smaller, more traditional societies, this cooperation is governed by informal institutions. People abide by conventions and norms, which are a part of the society's heritage. Even in the most basic of societies, order "is the result of a dense social network where people have an intimate understanding of each other and the threat of violence is a continuous force for preserving order .... Deviant behavior cannot be tolerated in such a situation."[351] Of course, different societies develop their own specific norms and conventions.

As societies grow and become more complex, there is an increasing need for individuals to transact with strangers. The particular local norms on which each of the parties is accustomed to relying may not be fully shared by the transacting parties. "Therefore a second general pattern of exchange has evolved, that is impersonal exchange, in which the parties are constrained by kinship ties, bonding, exchanging hostages, or merchant codes of conduct."[352] Among other features, development of these societal norms minimizes transactions costs, thereby paving the way for future transactions.

Finally, with further growth, trade becomes mostly impersonal, and contracts must be enforced by neutral third-party arbiters. In fact, proper enforcement of contracts is essential to bringing rule-of-law improvement to any country.[353] This more complex type of arrangement "has been the critical underpinning of successful modern economies involved in the complex contracting necessary for modern economic growth .... A coercive third party is essential .... Indeed, effective third-party enforcement is best realized by creating a set of rules that then make a variety of informal constraints effective."[354] As Harold Demsetz noted earlier,

---

350 Donald Clarke, Peter Murrell & Susan Whiting, *The Role of Law in China's Economic Development*, in CHINA'S GREAT ECONOMIC TRANSFORMATION 375, 403 (Loren Brandt & Thomas G. Rawski eds., 2008); *see also* WERNER MENSKI, COMPARATIVE LAW IN A GLOBAL CONTEXT: THE LEGAL SYSTEMS OF ASIA AND AFRICA 592 (2d ed. 2006) (noting that "any attempts by the state in China to determine people's conduct through imposing codes from above ... will always only remain one of several influences on the consciences of individual Chinese people.").

351 NORTH, *supra* note 348, at 39.

352 *Id.* at 34–35.

353 KENNETH W. DAM, THE LAW–GROWTH NEXUS: THE RULE OF LAW AND ECONOMIC DEVELOPMENT 93 (2006); *see also* ALICE H. AMSDEN, THE RISE OF "THE REST": CHALLENGES TO THE WEST FROM LATE-INDUSTRIALIZING ECONOMIES 286–87 (2001) ("In the early stages of development, institutions in the form of markets are rudimentary, and the formation of secure property rights is part of the evolution toward deeper and more perfect market structures.").

354 NORTH, *supra* note 348, at 35; *see also* MANCUR OLSON, JR., THE LOGIC OF COLLECTIVE ACTION: PUBLIC GOODS AND THE THEORY OF GROUPS 16–19 (1965) (describing how primitive societies form kinship groups, while modern societies form larger associational

discussing property law, "Property rights ... derive their significance from the fact that they help a man form those expectations which he can reasonably hold in his dealings with others. These expectations find expression in the laws, customs, and mores of a society."[355]

At this point in a society's growth and development, many of the original informal constraints have been subsumed by more formal rules which, in turn, are interpreted in accordance with social customs and norms. No subgroup within such a complex society is powerful enough to maintain control, and political compromise is necessary. Rules will continue to evolve, but future changes will likely be incremental and evolutionary, as there is institutional resistance to formal changes in the rules and inertial resistance to modifications of norms. North describes institutional norms in these contexts as having "great survival tenacity."[356] At this point in an advanced society's development, North observes,

> Political rules broadly define the hierarchical structure of the polity, its basic decision structure, and the explicit characteristics of agenda control. Economic rules define property rights, that is the bundle of rights over the use and the income to be derived from property and the ability to alienate an asset or a resource. Contracts contain the provisions specific to a particular agreement in exchange.[357]

Hernando de Soto and the Informal Economy

Peruvian economist Hernando de Soto, writing at about the same time as North, espouses similar views. His groundbreaking work, *The Other Path: The Invisible Revolution in the Third World*, emphasizes the importance of the informal economy in nations such as Peru, with their inadequate systems of legal property rights.[358] Describing rights that sound similar to adverse possession rights in Anglo-American law, de Soto observes how informal occupants might move onto property they do not own, gradually receiving increased recognition of their legal

---

groups); Bruce A. Ackerman, *Foreword: Talking and Trading*, 85 COLUM. L. REV. 899, 899 (1985) ("the law may allow us to achieve a form of mutual understanding that permits us to proceed with the business of life without undertaking the impossible task of befriending the world").

355 Harold Demsetz, *Toward a Theory of Property Rights*, 57 AM. ECON. REV. 347, 347 (1967).

356 NORTH, *supra* note 348, at 91; *see generally id.* at 68, 89–91.

357 *Id.* at 47.

358 HERNANDO DE SOTO, THE OTHER PATH: THE INVISIBLE REVOLUTION IN THE THIRD WORLD 12 (1989) ("We can say that informal activities burgeon when the legal system imposes rules which exceed the socially accepted legal framework—does not honor the expectations, choices, and preferences of those whom it does not admit within its framework—and when the state does not have sufficient coercive authority.").

status over a prolonged period of time—perhaps twenty years—during which their expectancy rights are inexorably increasing. These occupants construct buildings that are unlikely to be removed, and the value of their property and their more generalized feeling of security continuously increase, thereby encouraging still further development. Eventually, their rights may become legally recognized, perhaps through negotiation.[359] A significant part of the problem, in de Soto's view, arises from insufficiently developed title registration systems, which leave the poor with uncertain property rights and an inability to obtain secured credit for investment purposes.[360]

Informal norms, then, can be extremely strong, particularly when they must substitute for an official legal structure that is not up to the task of meeting public demand. "The process of development we have been discussing shows that people are capable of violating a system which does not accept them, not so that they can live in anarchy but so that they can build a different system which respects a minimum of essential rights."[361] Unintentionally foretelling events that would begin to occur in China soon afterwards, de Soto notes how informal occupants from rural areas of Peru have gradually enhanced their own property rights in the urban neighborhoods to which they have relocated. De Soto even goes so far as to label this process "a long march toward private property," likely reflecting Peru's Maoist political crisis of that era as much as China's own Long March.[362]

Nations such as Peru, then, have never successfully navigated the transition from primary reliance on informal norms to primary reliance on established laws applied by neutral arbiters. The economy has grown well past the point where most transactions are among people of a common background who can rely on more traditional enforcement norms, but the legal structure has failed to keep pace. As a result of the legal system's failure to adapt to the nation's growth, informal participants in the economy of a nation such as Peru not only technically violate the law, they also incur such non-productive costs as avoiding punishment, remaining small enough to avoid detection, and bribing officials.[363] Thus, the lack of a well-established legal structure serves as a waste of resources in an already poor nation and a drag on an economy that is not as productive as it otherwise might be.

De Soto proposes a solution. "It is essentially these three elements—property rights, contracts, and an extracontractual legal system—that a good law should

---

359   *Id.* at 23–27.

360   Hernando de Soto, The Mystery of Capital: Why Capitalism Triumphs in the West and Fails Everywhere Else 6 (2000); *see also* Dam, *supra* note 353, at 135–36 ("The farmer cannot mortgage his property where no legal infrastructure protects it or describes its metes and bounds. And if he cannot mortgage his property, he cannot borrow to improve his property, or to buy more land, or to start a new business.").

361   De Soto, *supra* note 358, at 55.

362   *Id.* at 57.

363   *Id.* at 152–58.

provide. The absence of such a law creates an extremely burdensome set of costs which informals must bear in exchange for not paying the costs of formality."[364] More secure rights, and particularly more secure property rights, will give informal participants in the economy a greater incentive to invest more, which will, in turn, benefit economic performance as a whole.

In Western nations, this process has already occurred, though not always rapidly or consciously. Citing earlier work by North and others, de Soto observes that Western contract law developed through informal custom, with authorities ultimately giving their blessing to trade practices that had become prevalent without prior legal recognition. "[I]nstead of trying to shape reality to its wishes, the state converted into legal norms practices which had proved their feasibility."[365] By doing so, the authorities reduced uncertainty and encouraged still more investment. This process not only grants formal recognition to the property rights held by the poor, it also frees up these newly minted property owners to grant security interests in this asset that is now recognized as property.[366]

In fact, poor Peruvians may be leading the nation in an economically productive direction by informally adopting changes that prove productive and that the state later endorses because of their proven success. Without that official state recognition, though, the poor will continue to operate in an economy that places them at a significant disadvantage. "All the evidence suggests that the

---

364   *Id.* at 158; *cf.* Clarke, *supra* note 57, at 96 (arguing that property rights are considerably more important than contract rights because "the fear of confiscation of one's property by government makes a very large number of growth-enhancing investments impossible"). *But see* Daniel W. Bromley, *Formalising Property Relations in the Developing World: The Wrong Prescription for the Wrong Malady*, 26 LAND USE POL'Y 20 (2008) (arguing that failed legal and political systems are far more harmful to individual land occupants than is the absence of formal legal tenure).

365   DE SOTO, *supra* note 358, at 179. *But see* Alfred L. Brophy, *Hernando de Soto and the Histories of Property Law*, *in* HERNANDO DE SOTO AND PROPERTY IN A MARKET ECONOMY 51, 52 (D. Benjamin Barros ed., 2010) ("de Soto advances a particular reading of U.S. history regarding property that gives more attention to informal property systems in the evolution of property rights in the United States than is warranted.").

366   *See* DE SOTO, *supra* note 360, at 46 ("What creates capital in the West, in other words, is an implicit process buried in the intricacies of its formal property systems.); *id.* at 157 ("Property is not the assets themselves but a consensus between people as to how those assets should be held, used, and exchanged."). *But see* Ezra Rosser, *Anticipating de Soto: Allotment of Indian Reservations and the Dangers of Land-Titling*, *in* HERNANDO DE SOTO AND PROPERTY IN A MARKET ECONOMY, *supra* note 365, at 61, 61 ("The allotment experience of Indian tribes suggests that unqualified faith in the transformative power of land-titling is misguided and highlights the particular dangers disadvantaged groups face when their land rights are formalized as individual ownership rights."); Rashmi Dyal-Chand, *Leaving the Body of Property Law? Meltdowns, Land Rushes, and Failed Economic Development*, *in id.* at 83, 90–92 (questioning whether recent low-income recipients of land rights in nations such as Senegal and Cambodia will enjoy anything more than ephemeral development gains).

legal system may be the main explanation for the difference in development that exists between the industrialized countries and those, like our own, which are not industrialized."[367]

Randall Peerenboom and the Rule of Law in China

Leading China scholar Randall Peerenboom has carefully examined modern China's growth in light of these more global theories of law and development. At the outset of his work, *China's Long March toward Rule of Law*, Peerenboom states his goal of explaining China's recent explosive economic growth during a time when the legal system was still developing rapidly. He argues that we cannot simply assess China's current development in light of economic models that arose in other contexts. We must instead determine what has worked, and will continue to work, for China.[368] This China-specific analysis might then help us to refine our overall model of law and development as we continue to apply it in other contexts. As Peerenboom would note in another work several years later, "China's success calls into question the wisdom of spending billions of dollars on promoting rule of law and good governance modeled on the legal systems and political institutions found in Euro-America."[369]

Peerenboom correctly notes that any analysis of this type must begin by defining exactly what "rule of law" means.[370] A thin theory of rule of law "stresses the formal or instrumental aspects of rule of law—those features that any legal system allegedly must possess to function effectively as a system of laws, regardless of whether the legal system is part of a democratic or nondemocratic society, capitalist or socialist, liberal or theocratic."[371] A thin theory of rule of law is typically believed to include such features as procedural rules for making laws, transparency, general applicability, clarity, prospectiveness, consistency, stability,

---

367 DE SOTO, *supra* note 358, at 185.

368 PEERENBOOM, *supra* note 2, at xiii; *see also* Frank Upham, *Mythmaking in the Rule-of-Law Orthodoxy*, *in* PROMOTING THE RULE OF LAW ABROAD: IN SEARCH OF KNOWLEDGE 75, 75 (Thomas Carothers ed., 2006) ("The foundation of my argument is that law is deeply contextual and that it cannot be detached from its social and political environment."); Mo Zhang, *The Socialist Legal System with Chinese Characteristics: China's Discourse for the Rule of Law and a Bitter Experience*, 24 TEMP. INT'L & COMP. L.J. 1, 5 (2010) ("The rule of law as developed in China does not seem to follow any traditional Western patterns but rather it is encumbered by Chinese legal traditions that might make many Westerners uncomfortable.") (footnotes omitted). Zhang attributes this difference, in part, to China's strong desire for social and political stability. *Id.* at 42.

369 RANDALL PEERENBOOM, CHINA MODERNIZES: THREAT TO THE WEST OR MODEL FOR THE REST?, at 3 (2007).

370 PEERENBOOM, *supra* note 2, at 2–21.

371 *Id.* at 3.

fairness in application and enforcement, and a reasonable level of acceptability to the public.[372]

By contrast, thick theories of rule of law "begin with the basic elements of a thin concept of rule of law but then incorporate elements of political morality such as particular economic arrangements (free-market capitalism, central planning, etc.), forms of government (democratic, single party socialism, etc.), or conceptions of human rights (liberal, communitarian, 'Asian values,' etc.)."[373] Thick theories of rule of law, then, are more value-laden: they necessarily contain all of the bare-bones elements of a thin theory but also privilege certain normative beliefs as to where these clearly stated and fairly enforced laws should be guiding a society.

A thick theory of rule of law needs to make decisions about the relative importance of contested values, such as the role of government and the inviolability of individual rights. But simply making these normative choices is not necessarily preferable. For example, as Pitman Potter has noted, if we begin with the assumption that the state is the owner of all land, then the right to use land remains subject to the state's discretion. Such a system might comport with even a thick rule of law, but individual property rights will always yield to state ownership.[374] Similarly, as Thomas Carothers notes, "Some Asian politicians focus on the regular, efficient application of law but do not stress the necessity of government subordination to it. In their view, the law exists not to limit the state but to serve its power."[375]

Institutions matter to Peerenboom, just as we saw that they do to Douglass North. Peerenboom argues in a later work that while political ideology may have slowed China's growth, the bigger problem for China is that it lacks the established institutions—such as an independent judiciary—needed to apply and enforce its rapidly expanding body of laws. Thus, even essential reforms may need to be implemented at a measured pace.[376]

Peerenboom also focuses on the manner in which various reforms must be sequenced, noting that other successful Asian states "moved slowly on economic, political, and legal reforms. They paid attention to the conditions required for success. They experimented .... [R]eformers were crossing the river by feeling the stones, hoping not to end up on their backsides with wet pants."[377] With these

---

372 *Id.* at 65.

373 *Id.* at 3.

374 Pitman B. Potter, *Public Regulation of Private Relations: Changing Conditions of Property Regulation in China*, in THE DEVELOPMENT OF THE CHINESE LEGAL SYSTEM: CHANGES AND CHALLENGES, *supra* note 178, at 51, 56.

375 Thomas Carothers, *The Rule-of-Law Revival*, in PROMOTING THE RULE OF LAW ABROAD: IN SEARCH OF KNOWLEDGE, *supra* note 368, at 3, 5.

376 PEERENBOOM, *supra* note 369, at 218, 230–32.

377 Randall Peerenboom, *Rule of Law, Democracy and the Sequencing Debate: Lessons from China and Vietnam*, in LEGAL REFORMS IN CHINA AND VIETNAM: A COMPARISON OF ASIAN COMMUNIST REGIMES 29, 44 (John Gillespie & Albert H.Y. Chen eds., 2010).

definitions and parameters established, Peerenboom then proceeds to examine the extent to which China's recent moves toward some form of rule of law comport with or contradict modern theories of law and development, an analysis to which this chapter and the next one will return.

The Third Moment

This introductory discussion of evolving theories of law and development cannot conclude without returning to Trubek and Santos's Third Moment, which emphasizes human flourishing in addition to economic expansion. One of the earlier proponents of this view, Amartya Sen, argues that development is not merely economic, but also personal:

> Expansion of freedom is viewed, in this approach, both as the primary end and as the principal means of development. Development consists of the removal of various types of unfreedoms that leave people with little choice and little opportunity of exercising their reasoned agency. The removal of substantial unfreedoms, it is argued here, is *constitutive* of development.[378]

By expanding the focus to encompass personal freedoms in addition to supposedly more objective economic factors, Sen's approach is more specific to individual contexts and cultures. "The exercise of freedom is mediated by values, but the values in turn are influenced by public discussions and social interactions, which are themselves influenced by participatory freedoms."[379]

The absence of a social safety net leads to poverty, which is not merely a status of low income, but also a deprivation of the ability to reach one's potential. To Sen, therefore, poverty refers to an entire life and not simply to a low wage status.[380] And the traditional approach of development theory has been too narrow, in that it focuses only on income, without also factoring in inequalities in employment, health care, education, and social status.[381]

Questions of freedom regarding property rights cannot be severed from questions of how that property is distributed. As Charles Lindblom notes, "[I]t is not at all obvious that free exchange makes (or leaves) the less propertied members of that society free."[382] Those with less property will have trouble acquiring more. "Nor if we are all born into a world in which property rights are already assigned, as indeed they are, does it follow that exchange supports our freedom unless we

---

378 Amartya Sen, Development as Freedom xii (1999) (emphasis in original).
379 *Id.* at 9.
380 *Id.* at 87.
381 *Id.* at 108.
382 Charles E. Lindblom, Politics and Markets: The World's Political–Economic Systems 46 (1977).

own a great deal."[383] And as David Kennedy writes, "[C]alls for the 'formalization' of property entitlements ... only obscure the distributive choices involved in constructing a private law regime—choices which ought rather to be carefully analyzed for their impact on economic growth and development."[384]

Sen does not conclude that we need to abandon the unfettered market economy. Rather, he argues for supplementing the free market with institutions that counteract the ability of "the powerful to capitalize on their asymmetrical advantage."[385] In a society that provides a greater measure of equality of more than just income, all participants will enjoy fuller and richer lives.[386] And those citizens who have now become full participants in society by virtue of this enhanced equality will, in turn, have to fulfill the civic responsibilities that this full participation implies.[387]

Joseph Stiglitz goes a step further, contending that markets are not only inequitable, but also inefficient—in other words, government intervention is needed to help markets function properly. In *Making Globalization Work*, he focuses specifically on international trade and the economic globalization of recent decades, arguing that politics has prevented globalization from attaining its potential. The market does not operate freely; rather, nations with advanced economies set up trade rules that lock in their own pre-existing advantages.[388] The modern global market may have helped some nations, but it has not helped most people, including in those nations that have benefited overall.[389] And Stiglitz reserves particular praise for China, which has managed to head off many of the problems globalization typically exacerbates by imposing tight government controls on the economy.[390]

Stiglitz argues that trade liberalization in recent years has not brought about the growth it promised, while creating social upheaval in developing nations such as Mexico. In part, this is because trade pacts such as the North American Free Trade Agreement are neither free nor fair and lead to an unequal division of the gains from trade. In part, it is because developing nations that are supposed to benefit

---

383 *Id.*

384 David Kennedy, *Some Caution about Property Rights as a Recipe for Economic Development*, 1 ACCT., ECON., & L. 1, 42 (2011), *available at* http://www.bepress.com/cgi/viewcontent.cgi?article=1006&context=ael; *see also* AMSDEN, *supra*, note 353, at 19 ("There is a broad consensus among political economists that income distribution has a major bearing on economic development ....").

385 SEN, *supra* note 378, at 142.

386 *Id.* at 144.

387 *Id.* at 284.

388 JOSEPH E. STIGLITZ, MAKING GLOBALIZATION WORK 4 (2006); *see also* PEERENBOOM, *supra* note 369, at 16 ("[S]ome critics in developing states have portrayed the attempts of the US and other developed states to promote democracy as motivated by economic self-interest rather than concern for people in developing countries.").

389 STIGLITZ, *supra* note 388, at 8–9. Stiglitz worries that "globalization might be creating rich countries with poor people." *Id.* at 9.

390 *Id.* at 10–11.

do not have the social safety net in place required to assist those whose lives and livelihoods are disrupted by the dramatic changes freer trade inevitably brings. And in part, it is because some of these developing nations do not have the educational and technological infrastructure to benefit from rapid economic growth.[391]

Finally, Jeffrey Sachs examines why some nations seem to have stagnated economically while others have prospered. In *The End of Poverty: Economic Possibilities for Our Time*, he focuses on the causes of this uneven growth, arguing that technology explains much of the gap between the world's rich and poor nations.[392] All of the world's nations were poor two centuries ago, all have become much wealthier, some have grown at a much more rapid pace than others, but those that have lagged can still catch up.[393] Focusing specifically on China's rapid economic growth in recent decades, especially in comparison to that of Russia, Sachs makes the claim that "China is likely to be the first of the great poverty-stricken countries of the twentieth century to end poverty in the twenty-first century."[394]

Sachs is particularly critical of de Soto's argument that the solution to the problems faced by lower-income countries is the establishment of a more reliable system of titles and deeds.[395] Numerous countries such as China and Vietnam have achieved rapid economic growth in recent decades without clarifying titles to the degree that de Soto claims to be necessary, and several East Asian economies have attained high income levels by following other routes.[396] Sachs concludes that de Soto's analysis is too simplistic, in that it fails to factor in such other relevant factors as "initial incomes, education levels, fertility rates, climate, trade policy, disease, proximity to markets, and the quality of economic institutions ...."[397] Only by expanding the analysis to include these additional ingredients can an observer determine which factors lead to which problems in different nations and how each of these problems can then be solved. Sachs views this global war on poverty as the current generation's major challenge.

To What Extent Is China Following Law and Development Theory?

Throughout Part II, I noted the wide variety of ways in which Chinese real estate professionals have managed to prosper since the mid-1980s. Much of this success

---

391 *Id.* at 61–66. Stiglitz notes that China actually had a huge advantage over Mexico in this last regard, by virtue of its much larger investment in research. *Id.* at 65–66.
392 JEFFREY SACHS, THE END OF POVERTY: ECONOMIC POSSIBILITIES FOR OUR TIME 31 (2005).
393 *Id.* at 29–31.
394 *Id.* at 168.
395 *Id.* at 321 (citing DE SOTO, THE MYSTERY OF CAPITAL, *supra* note 360).
396 *Id.*
397 *Id.* at 322.

occurred during a time when China had a shortage of relevant business laws and little experience consistently and fairly enforcing the laws it did have. This apparent success obviously calls into question many of the predictions of law and development theory that I have just described. The discussion that follows in this section will summarize some of the observations presented in Part II that appear to call development theory into question, at least as it is applies to China. In the next chapter, I will seek to address these seeming inconsistencies.

Land Use Rights

Chapter 3, which examined the contours of the land use right, offers a pair of illustrations of ways in which the recent growth of China's real estate industry seems to contradict law and development theory. First, although the 1988 constitutional amendments implicitly recognized land use rights, and laws adopted in the years that followed answered some of the open questions about the status of property rights, the uncertainties that implicit constitutional recognition created were not significantly reduced until the Property Rights Law became effective in 2007. Thus, much of China's breakneck legal development occurred at a time of significant doubt as to what it meant to own the right to use land in China.

Before 1988, the precursor to the land use right was protected only under contract law. Contract rights are less stable than property rights, and the holder of this contract right presumably could collect damages from the government if the government breached but did not enjoy the more robust protections of property law. The 1988 constitutional amendments provide another example of Chinese legal development catching up with actual transactions. Note, though, that the mere constitutional recognition that the right to use land is transferable is a slender reed on which to construct the entire modern Chinese real estate industry.

Thus, before 1988, real estate professionals had virtually no legal assurance that the government would recognize their right to use land. Between the 1988 constitutional amendments and the 2007 effective date of the Property Rights Law, these same professionals were functioning in a legal environment whose contours were only gradually becoming clear. Law and development theory predicts that real estate development would be unlikely to proceed at the rapid pace actually seen in China during most of this two-decade period.

Similarly, Chapter 3 also discusses the question of whether land use rights are automatically renewable upon expiration and, if so, how the price for the renewal will be established. Land use rights were not legally acknowledged until 1988 and they generally last for forty, fifty, or seventy years, depending on the use to which the land is being put. This means that China's young real estate market has not seen these renewal questions arise as often as they will when the first round of land use rights begins to expire. In fact, the issue will probably surface before the first wave of expirations begins, as owners of aging buildings seek to refinance their property for renovation or other purposes. Lenders will likely be reluctant to lend if their security is a building that is located on land subject to a use right that is soon to expire. At this point, the government can expect to hear from the holders of land use rights that have not expired yet but are nearing the end of their term.

There have been some cases in which rights with terms shorter than the legal maximums have come up for renewal and the government has willingly extended the terms, although it was under no legal obligation to do so. The more pressing issue will arise when local governments, which are so heavily dependent on the proceeds of sales from land use rights, begin to run out of desirable land to sell and must begin to look for other sources of revenue. Will these governments seek to fund their operations by imposing fees upon current users of land whose initial terms are up for renewal?

As already noted, Article 149 of the Property Rights Law appears to require the government to renew land use rights when the property is being put to residential use.[398] However, this provision does not state the term for which the right must be renewed, it does not state whether the government can collect another fee for renewing this land use right, and it does not state how any such fee is to be calculated. Moreover, this Article does not unambiguously apply to other types of uses.

Chapter 3 has already illustrated a variety of different ways in which a renewal fee might be calculated. The more important point here is that no one knows which, if any, of these options will prove true, and yet the real estate market does not seem to be terribly worried by this uncertainty. Law and development theory argues that strong and predictable property laws are essential for real estate development. But in China, developers have been building industrial, commercial, and residential structures at a remarkable rate without having any idea whether they will continue to own the right to use the land on which their buildings are located after perhaps only forty years.

Ownership Entities

Chapter 4, which examined the ownership entities that are commonly employed in the Chinese real estate market, provides another useful example of Chinese real estate development preceding, or occurring concurrently with, Chinese legal development. Numerous sources insisted to me that the true pioneers in this field—both in the real estate market and in the more generalized maturation of small manufacturing enterprises—were the residents of Wenzhou, as the end of that chapter notes. Years before Chinese law permitted business enterprises of these types to exist, the Wenzhounese were informally creating business organizations to pool their individual investments. One pair of commentators describes the Wenzhou model as one in which "the traditional household became the foundation for a dynamic manufacturing and trading system which spread out from hamlets

---

398 Wuquan Fa [Property Rights Law], art. 149; *see also supra* notes 91–98 and accompanying text (discussing the uncertainty as to what will happen when land use rights begin to expire in large numbers).

and townships to embrace the whole country."[399] Although these investors risked losing their investments if the government failed to recognize the validity of their rudimentary business entities, they were willing to take the chance.

To some degree, the people of Wenzhou may have been desperate for change and viewed the post-Mao era as a brief opening during which experimentation was more likely to be tolerated. In this sense, they were learning how to exercise their voice at a time when exiting the underlying system was not a realistic alternative.[400] They may have hoped for profits that would be large enough to offset the risks they were taking: if the potential gains were sufficiently great, then the total risk (the product of the amount invested and the weighted average of the predicted returns) might be warranted. They may also have had some basis for viewing local officials as generally supportive of this type of experimentation.[401]

To the extent that the people of Wenzhou ever contemplated whether government officials would later acquiesce to informal practices they had already decided to employ, it was probably more with the hope that they could obtain post hoc official recognition for what they were already doing and less for the thrill of crafting new legal structures. And by virtue of being the first to experiment and to succeed, the Wenzhounese may have foreseen that they would build natural competitive advantages for themselves in the future, based on their earlier and more extensive experience in these business fields.[402] Nonetheless, the Wenzhou investors appear to have been perfectly willing to risk considerable personal resources, not to mention the displeasure of local government officials, in an extraordinarily unsettled legal environment.

Ted Fishman has written about the risks the Wenzhounese were taking at this time:

---

399   Keith Forster & Yao Xianguo, *A Comparative Analysis of Economic Reform and Development in Hangzhou and Wenzhou Cities*, in CITIES IN CHINA: RECIPES FOR ECONOMIC DEVELOPMENT IN THE REFORM ERA, *supra* note 101, at 53, 57; *see also* Corinna-Barbara Francis, *Bargained Property Rights: The Case of China's High-Technology Sector*, in PROPERTY RIGHTS AND ECONOMIC REFORM IN CHINA, *supra* note 340, at 226, 227 (noting how community norms served as an adequate substitute for property rights laws in the early days of China's redevelopment).

400   *See* ALBERT O. HIRSCHMAN, EXIT, VOICE, AND LOYALTY: RESPONSES TO DECLINE IN FIRMS, ORGANIZATIONS, AND STATES 30 (1970) ("Voice is here defined as any attempt at all to change, rather than to escape from, an objectionable state of affairs ....").

401   *See* TSAI, *supra* note 339, at 197.

402   *See, e.g.*, David L. Wank, *Producing Property Rights: Strategies, Networks, and Efficiency in Urban China's Nonstate Firms*, in PROPERTY RIGHTS AND ECONOMIC REFORM IN CHINA, *supra* note 340, at 248, 271 (noting that "a process of transformation in which political reform proceeded more slowly than market reform gave Chinese entrepreneurs advantages in forging networks across local state-society borders to enhance business and stimulate the economy.").

> Starting a private business in China was illegal. As with all illegal businesses that thrive despite the law, it took a combination of will, political skill, business acumen, and a readiness to game the system in any imaginable way, employing secrecy, bribes, and a facility with the law that could recast otherwise illegal ventures into businesses that fit some legal construct acceptable to those policing the local economy .... The entirety of China's budding private sector mushroomed under the same sort of restrictions faced by American bootleggers and speakeasies during Prohibition.[403]

Wenzhounese investment, occurring in the very early days of the modern Chinese economy, seems to contradict the predictions of law and development theory.

As economic development spread to other parts of China during the 1980s and 1990s, investors in other parts of the nation followed the pattern established in Wenzhou. Although these other examples were more significant on a national level, and involved far greater levels of overall investment, the fact that they happened later may suggest that they occurred during a period when the legal environment, though still somewhat opaque, was becoming more settled. In other words, though far more was at stake overall, the relative investment risks these later investors undertook may already have been starting to diminish during this period.

Presales

Chapter 8 illustrated the uncertainties about timing and cash flow that surround the typical purchase of an urban residential unit. Developers require that their purchasers put up most or all of the acquisition funds before the unit is complete, meaning that the purchaser must carry the new, not-yet-complete unit while incurring living expenses somewhere else. To the extent the purchaser is borrowing funds for this purchase, it has only a shaky form of security in the new unit to offer to its mortgage lender. Uncertainties of this magnitude might well be disabling in Western markets. But it is no exaggeration to state that tens of millions of residential units have been developed and sold in China under precisely this level of legal uncertainty. This Chinese reality directly contradicts the predictions of law and development theory, which hold that strong and reliable property rights are a prerequisite to the smooth functioning of the real estate market.

Each of the examples offered in this section, drawn from current and prior Chinese real estate practice, illustrates ways in which the growth of the Chinese real estate industry appears to have occurred at a time when the legal structure was too wobbly to support it. Traditional law and development theory maintains that considerably more legal maturation should have occurred before this type of economic growth could have happened. The next chapter addresses this apparent anomaly.

---

403 FISHMAN, *supra* note 333, at 63.

Chapter 12
Harmonizing Law and Development Theory with China's Actual Progress

Is China Following the Law and Development Model?

The previous chapter introduced traditional law and development theory. Douglass North, as we saw, argues that strong contract law enforced by neutral arbiters is a "critical underpinning" for the development of a nation such as China, with its huge and impersonal economy that is part of an even larger global marketplace. A nation like China that is on the road to economic development also needs other strong rule-of-law protections, such as a reliable and consistently enforced law of property. Hernando de Soto echoes these views, observing how the failure of a society to move from reliance on informal norms to dependence on established and fairly enforced laws can place a drag on the overall economy. Randall Peerenboom and others focus more specifically on China's unique case and the degree to which China seems to be pursuing the development pattern that North, de Soto, and others have predicted.

Yet that chapter also proceeded to illustrate that China does not, in fact, appear to be following this traditional development pattern. Therefore, this chapter seeks to explain this incongruity. Drawing on the discussions in Part II of this book and their repeated emphasis on how China has developed its real estate market in practice and not just by statute, this chapter will seek to harmonize the traditional theory of law and development with what has actually happened in China's real estate market during the past two decades or more.

The Commentators Begin to Respond

Peerenboom worries about these seeming inconsistencies. He notes, "If the critics are right and rule of law is not necessary for sustained economic growth, at least in China, then one of the ruling regime's main incentives for promoting legal reforms will be undercut, calling into question the future of rule of law in China."[404] The Chinese leadership is keenly concerned with promoting economic growth, and if it concludes that it does not need the instrument of rule of law to attain that goal, it might abandon that tool in favor of others.

---

404 PEERENBOOM, *supra* note 2, at 450.

Peerenboom suggests several possible reasons why China does not seem to be following the pattern predicted by North and others.[405] China might actually be following the rule of law to a greater extent than has been acknowledged. Alternatively, investors might be acting irrationally when making their investment decisions, foolishly discounting risks more than they ought to. Another possibility is that rule of law might not be as essential as its supporters claim, either because the theory is misguided in general or because China is a unique case that does not fit patterns seen elsewhere. Finally, the theory might be correct, and China would have grown at an even more rapid pace had it protected property rights more strongly.

Donald Clarke similarly raises at least three possible explanations for this disharmony, which echo but do not precisely follow those suggested by Peerenboom.[406] First, the theory may be correct and the observations that do not seem to support it may be wrong or incomplete. In other words, property rights are essential and those rights are being adequately enforced in China. Thus, to the extent observers argue that China does not have an adequate system of property rights, or did not at the relevant times in the past, they are overlooking informal enforcement mechanisms that are sufficient.

Second, Clarke posits, the theory may be correct and the observations of Chinese growth may simply be wrong. This is not to suggest that China has not grown rapidly in recent years, but rather to argue that China might have grown even more rapidly had it not been held back somewhat by an inadequate system of property rights. Finally, China simply might be vivid proof that the theory is wrong.

Some Additional Possible Explanations

This chapter will offer several explanations of its own. Although it will integrate the work of Peerenboom, Clarke, and others, it will categorize the possible explanations in a somewhat different fashion and will suggest alternatives not directly raised by these other commentators. Drawing both on the work of scholars of law and development and on my own research into actual practices in the Chinese real estate market, the discussion that follows will propose several ways in which law and development theory still might be harmonized with recent Chinese experience.

This chapter will present and examine six alternative explanations. First, the traditional theory of law and development may simply be wrong. Second, the traditional theory may not be entirely wrong, but might need refinement. Third, China may actually be following the traditional theory of law and development, which means that observers have been misinterpreting the evidence that leads them to a contrary conclusion. Fourth, the traditional theory may be a Western construct

---

405   *Id.* at 462–63.
406   Clarke, *supra* note 57, at 91–92.

that cannot be transplanted into China. Fifth, it may make little sense to apply the traditional model to a nation that still retains so many features of its Communist past. Finally, and perhaps most importantly, we must remember that any model is just a model that does not apply perfectly in any given nation, especially one as unusual as China. This last explanation synthesizes elements of the first five and questions how well any paradigm can be expected to apply anywhere. These six possible explanations necessarily overlap. The correct account, if such a thing exists, may well be a hybrid of these various alternatives, which are themselves not as neatly distinguishable as the arguments that follow may initially seem to imply.

Law and Development Theory Is Wrong

The first possible explanation for the apparent inconsistencies between law and development theory and China's recent experience, as suggested above by both Peerenboom and Clarke, is that the theory is just wrong. China may demonstrate that economic growth is possible even in the absence of strong laws of property and contracts, just as the presence of fairly strong laws in some nations that have not enjoyed successful economic development might indicate that growth need not follow automatically from a more predictable legal system. Under this view, supporters of law and development theory are so wedded to their beliefs that they simply cannot see, or choose to ignore, all Chinese evidence to the contrary. In the words of Francis Fukuyama,

> it is perfectly possible to have "good enough" property rights and contract enforcement that permit economic development without the existence of a true rule of law in the sense of the law being the final sovereign. A good example is the People's Republic of China .... An abstract commitment to "rule of law" has not been necessary for the country to achieve double-digit rates of growth for more than three decades.[407]

One of the strongest advocates of this view, Frank Upham, observes that China's growth after 1978 occurred in a nation that lacked a fully effective legal system. He then bluntly notes, "For those interested in the relationship between law and economic development, however, it is almost as if those thirty years of growth have not taken place."[408] After observing that China has consistently resisted Western pressure to adopt the Washington Consensus—with its goals of freer markets and stronger property rights—Upham proceeds to point out that after the collapse of Western financial markets in 2008, "[o]ne can surmise that

---

[407] FRANCIS FUKUYAMA, THE ORIGINS OF POLITICAL ORDER: FROM PREHUMAN TIMES TO THE FRENCH REVOLUTION 248–49 (2011) (footnote omitted).
[408] Upham, *supra* note 344, at 553.

Chinese leaders must be pleased that they did not take *this* particular bit of Western advice."[409] Similarly, Upham views de Soto's examples as undercutting de Soto's own hypothesis. In arguing that Peru would benefit from more formalized rule-of-law structures, de Soto's principal illustration demonstrates how successful many Peruvian entrepreneurs have managed to become despite the absence of these structures.[410] China's example makes it "irrefutable" to Upham that a nation can enjoy considerable economic growth in the absence of strong laws and institutions.[411]

In the view of David Kennedy, supporters of law and development theory refuse to acknowledge how poorly it appears to apply to cases such as China.[412] This shortsightedness results from a failure to recognize that property rights are embedded within the social fabric of each individual society rather than being part of an underlying structure that predates and helps to form that society.[413] Thus, every society is involved in an ongoing struggle over the adjustment of property rights. Those who benefit from the current property allocation seek to leave it intact, while those who currently have less will advocate for change. The system of property law that results from this continuing tension mirrors the unique history of the particular culture, displaying, in Kennedy's words, "a dense network of entitlements reflecting specific social histories of allocative struggle."[414]

Kennedy does not necessarily reject traditional development theory, but he does express uncertainty as to the theory's comprehensiveness. He is not willing to go quite so far as to call the theory incorrect. Rather, his more modest goal, after reviewing the jarringly inconsistent case of modern China, is to remind observers "to hesitate before accepting conventional neo-liberal wisdom about the importance of 'clear' or 'strong property rights' [*sic*] for economic development."[415]

Clarke, Murrell, and Whiting make a point similar to Kennedy's, and perhaps even a stronger one. They initially argue that "the relationship between legal and economic development was bidirectional—a coevolutionary process," echoing Kennedy.[416] But later, they posit that, in fact, the relationship is exactly the opposite of that predicted by law and development theory. China's modern burst of growth began in the 1970s while the legal system did not begin to catch up until the 1990s. If anything, economic change spurred legal change, rather than

---

409 *Id.* at 575 (emphasis in original); *see also* LIEBERTHAL, *supra* note 109, at 6 (observing that the argument in favor of moving toward an American-style financial system, "once taken very seriously in Beijing, appeared fraudulent, and China's reluctance to accept it appeared retrospectively a mark of wisdom").
410 Upham, *supra* note 368, at 80–82.
411 Upham, *supra* note 344, at 576.
412 Kennedy, *supra* note 384, at 8–10.
413 *Id.* at 8–9.
414 *Id.* at 16.
415 *Id.* at 9.
416 Clarke, Murrell & Whiting, *supra* note 350, at 376.

the reverse.[417] Under this view, perhaps, the theory of law and development is not merely wrong, but exactly backwards.

Kevin Davis and Michael Trebilcock take a similar approach, although they acknowledge that informal norms in China may have taken the place of the more formalized legal systems seen in developed Western nations. To them, skeptics of law and development theory are correct to some degree but overstate their case. A legal system is just one method of social control, and informal norms and codes may serve as an adequate substitute, as they seem to have done in China.[418] Thus, while the theory of law and development may be wrong, it is also possible that the theory merely needs to be broadened to incorporate informal customs and rules. Clarke appears to agree somewhat, arguing that stable legal rights are a critical factor in economic development, but that property rights are more important than contract rights.[419] Note that the approach of Davis and Trebilcock—and perhaps that of Clarke as well—seems to disagree definitionally with that of North, who argues that informal methods of social control are merely one component of the overall institution of law. To North, then, the presence of these informal methods would support the law and development hypothesis, as they are just an alternative form of governing through the institution of law, defined in his more expansive manner.

These commentators all argue that traditional law and development theory may be completely wrong, and is, at minimum, partially inaccurate. The discussions in Part II of this book, drawing on actual Chinese experience, provide some evidence that these criticisms may be on the mark. During the 1980s and 1990s, real estate professionals were willing to make huge investments in property for which they held land use rights despite the fact that the legal status of these land use rights was unsettled. In other words, substantial economic development was occurring—in the core field of property law, no less—despite the absence of any formal government assurance that the developer of the property had the legal right to use the land. These professionals similarly made these investments without any clear idea as to what will happen to their property rights when the term of the land use right expires.

---

417 *Id.* at 399. The authors do, however, accept that some alternative to a formal property system—perhaps guarantees embedded in the political structure of China itself—might have provided investors with the necessary security prior to the 1990s. *Id.* at 400–03; *see also* Donald Clarke, Peter Murrell & Susan Whiting, *Law, Institutions, and Property Rights in China*, 129 WOODROW WILSON INT'L CENTER FOR SCHOLARS ASIA PROGRAM SPECIAL REP. 42, 42 (2005), *available at* http://www.wilsoncenter.org/topics/pubs/AsiaReport_129.pdf (finding that "economic actors use legal institutions such as courts to a perhaps surprising degree").

418 Kevin E. Davis & Michael J. Trebilcock, *The Relationship between Law and Development: Optimists Versus Skeptics*, 56 AM. J. COMP. L. 895, 932–33 (2008); *see also id.* at 934.

419 Clarke, *supra* note 57, at 93.

Perhaps the point when a newfangled land use right would expire seemed far off in the future at the time these developments began. But the right to use a parcel of land forty years in the future has a discrete value that can be calculated with a reasonably high degree of certainty. Maybe the early developers did not perform this calculation, or maybe they performed it and proceeded anyway. Either answer seems to contradict the traditional theory of law and development: they failed to assess the risk (despite the theory's prediction that they would), or they assessed the risk and were willing to accept it (despite the theory's prediction that they would not). These developers undertook significant investment in real estate in a legal climate that did not offer strong and enduring protection for property rights.

Law and Development Theory Is Not Entirely Wrong, but Needs to Be Refined

The second possible explanation for why China seems to contradict the theory of law and development is a softer version of the first one. Law and development theory may not be entirely wrong, but it might overstate the case and therefore need to be moderated. The traditional theory may be correct to some degree, and we may not have enough information to reach any firmer conclusion. Thomas Carothers laments, "The rapidly growing field of rule-of-law assistance is operating from a disturbingly thin base of knowledge at every level ...."[420] Moreover, there has been insufficient research assessing the impact of programs designed to foster the rule of law.[421] Several of the commentators discussed in the previous section, particularly Davis, Trebilcock, and Clarke, allude to this view, highlighting once again that the explanations offered in each section of this chapter may overlap with one another to some extent. The current section will examine whether the evidence supports the view that traditional law and development theory needs to be modified before it can be applied to China.

Randall Peerenboom argues that law and development theory is correct as far as it goes but that it leaves out other important causal factors. Most significant in China's case is the fact that strong macroeconomic policies and a high-quality business environment helped to foster rapid economic growth. Other factors also contributed to this economic progress, most notably the government's tight control over the valuation of the renminbi.[422] China certainly has adopted many of the

---

[420] Thomas Carothers, *The Problem of Knowledge*, in PROMOTING THE RULE OF LAW ABROAD: IN SEARCH OF KNOWLEDGE, *supra* note 368, at 15, 27. Carothers goes on to note the absence of "a well-grounded rationale, a clear understanding of the essential problem, a proven analytic method, and an understanding of results achieved." *Id.* at 28.

[421] Stephen Golub, *A House without a Foundation*, in PROMOTING THE RULE OF LAW ABROAD: IN SEARCH OF KNOWLEDGE, *supra* note 368, at 105, 131.

[422] Randall Peerenboom, *Conclusion: Law, Wealth and Power in China*, in LAW, WEALTH AND POWER IN CHINA: COMMERCIAL LAW REFORMS IN CONTEXT, *supra* note 69, at 272, 277.

legal reforms that law and development theory considers essential prerequisites to economic development, including the protection of land use rights and greater recognition of intellectual property, contract, labor, and bankruptcy rights. But these changes were not implemented initially with any clarity.[423] Law and development theory thus may partially explain China's recent economic expansion. But given that this growth in laws was slow and relatively late, other significant contributing factors must also have played a role.

Similarly, Kellee Tsai demonstrates that to the extent the legal system inadequately protects formal property rights, an informal system has evolved in China to plug these gaps. These informal norms, which she calls "adaptive informal institutions," serve as "routinized adaptations to the constraints and opportunities of various formal institutions."[424] Although Tsai at first seems to reject the predictions of law and development theory, noting that the speedy rise of the private sector predated legal reform by twenty years, she then emphasizes the ways in which these informal institutions substituted for the formal legal reforms that would follow. In fact, the development of these adaptive informal institutions often spurred the formal changes that came later.[425] Thus Tsai agrees with law and development theory only to the extent that she interprets "law" broadly enough to include informal institutions, as North does. If law and development theory focuses only on formal laws, by contrast, then China appears to contradict the theory.

These commentators provide illustrations of the ways in which law and development theory may be partially correct. Although they cannot endorse the theory wholeheartedly, in light of the contradictory evidence that China provides, they are willing to note ways in which the theory might be modified rather than abandoned. In the face of facts that do not support the theory, they are willing to tinker with the theory rather than discarding it.

There are two variants of the belief that law and development theory is partially correct but needs refinement to explain the Chinese case that merit examination here. The first variant argues that law and development theory may or may not be correct as applied to China but that it is premature to decide. China's modern economy is only about two decades old, and the jury is still deliberating. Peerenboom notes that "if one considers that rule of law took centuries to establish in Western states, the progress in China in less than thirty years is remarkable."[426] Kenneth Dam largely agrees that this view might be accurate:

---

423   *Id.* at 276.
424   TSAI, *supra* note 339, at x.
425   *Id.* at 45 ("I argue that the accumulation of informal interactions between local state and economic actors provided both the impetus and the legitimizing basis for these key reforms."). Tsai also notes, as de Soto had before her, that informal institutions enjoy fewer protections from government intervention and that subsequent formal endorsement by the government strengthens these institutions. *Id.* at 68.
426   PEERENBOOM, *supra* note 369, at 198.

All of these circumstances recall Zhou Enlai's famous answer to a question about the consequences of the French Revolution, "It is too early to tell." It is certainly too early to accept the notion that recent Chinese experience is a counterexample to the need for a focus on institutions in the developing world and, indeed, for a rule of law in China itself.[427]

Dam ends up by hedging, arguing that modestly reliable legal institutions can lead to some economic development but that more vigorous growth depends on establishment of stronger institutions.[428] Perhaps China is still stuck in its First Moment—in the midst of a large, internally funded Marshall Plan—and has not yet progressed beyond that point.[429]

The second variant holds that legal and economic development in any society is path-dependent. In an effort to explain why different societies have performed so differently over time, Douglass North emphasizes the importance of path-dependence and a nation's particular history. "We cannot understand today's choices (and define them in the modeling of economic performance) without tracing the incremental evolution of institutions."[430] This explains the failures of less-developed nations that attempted to modernize by adopting constitutions similar to the United States Constitution. "Although the rules are the same, the enforcement mechanisms, the way enforcement occurs, the norms of behavior, and the subjective models of the actors are not .... [This] will lead to widely divergent outcomes in societies with different institutional arrangements."[431] Thus, the law and development model must be refined to reflect the unique history of the culture in which it is being applied. Given the dramatic differences between Chinese and Western culture, history, and norms, it is not surprising that a model developed in the West would need to be modified greatly before it has significant explanatory value in China. I have touched on this topic already and will expand this discussion further below.

China Is Following Law and Development Theory

A third possible explanation as to why China appears to be contradicting law and development theory is that this appearance is inaccurate. In other words, to the extent that the evidence from China seems to fly in the face of the traditional theory, observers are misreading that seemingly contradictory evidence. Under this view, the theory remains robust, the evidence from China that supports the

---

427 DAM, *supra* note 353, at 277.
428 *Id.*
429 *See supra* notes 343–44 (discussing law and development theory and the First Moment).
430 NORTH, *supra* note 348, at 100.
431 *Id.* at 101.

theory is correct, and the counter-evidence that seems to contradict the theory can be explained away. In fact, much of the information that I gathered from Chinese real estate professionals seems to support this explanation, as I discuss below.

Support for this View among the Commentators

Yasheng Huang, for example, argues that China has followed the traditional law and development model. In his view, "The successes of the Chinese economy are a function of conventional sources—private-sector development, financial liberalization, and property rights security."[432] In fact, Huang makes the case even more strongly than that, arguing that to the extent Chinese growth has occasionally stumbled, it has been precisely because the government has intervened in a way that reduced these three sources of security. Huang also argues that China's development in recent decades has been intentional and formalized, not merely functionally efficient.[433] Thus, contrary to Bruce Dickson and Kellee Tsai,[434] he sees strong evidence of formal improvement in Chinese legal structures from the beginning, and not merely the growth of informal norms that gradually became institutionalized and formalized as their practical benefits became evident.

Randall Peerenboom, in his thorough description of the rule of law in China, appears to agree, at least to some extent. He suggests that there is considerable evidence that China has progressed toward a thin version of the rule of law, at a minimum.[435] Those that dispute this conclusion may perhaps have been hoping for greater political liberalization and democratization, which still may occur. But China has made considerable progress toward rule of law in the economic sphere, despite occasional problems and reversals, and most likely will continue to move in this direction in the coming years.[436] In response to those who argue that China contradicts the traditional law and development model, Peerenboom responds, "I

---

432 YASHENG HUANG, *supra* note 137, at 30. In his preface, Huang notes that "the true China miracle occurred in the 1980s and ... was a miracle created by the bottom-up entrepreneurship and considerable liberalization on many fronts. In the 1990s, there was in fact a substantial reversal of reforms." *Id.* at x.

433 *Id.* at 30 ("Chinese economic success is a result of a movement toward *manifestly and explicitly* efficient policies and institutions, not just a result of *functionally* efficient policies and institutions.") (emphases in original).

434 *See infra* notes 460–70 and accompanying text (discussing Dickson's work); *supra* notes 339–42, 424–25 and accompanying text (discussing Tsai's work).

435 PEERENBOOM, *supra* note 2, at 558 ("there is considerable evidence of a shift from a legal regime best characterized as rule by law toward a system that complies with the basic elements of a thin rule of law ....").

436 Peerenboom, *supra* note 377, at 32 ("A functional legal system has played an important part in growth in China .... The legal system also performs an enabling function by creating the basic infrastructure for transactions, including markets, security exchanges, mortgage systems, accounting practices and so on."); *see also* PEERENBOOM, *supra* note 2, at 559 ("Despite opposition and the occasional setback, China's legal system will continue

suggest that law has played a more important role in China's economic growth ... than is usually assumed; and, more importantly, law is likely to play an even greater role in the future in China."[437]

Edward Steinfeld also agrees, arguing that China is following a development path much like that of Taiwan in recent years. He views China as intentionally modernizing and internationalizing its economic structure. China is not merely opening itself up to the West. "Rather, it is absorbing our notions of governance and taking them as its own. Hence, the government's program [sic] of rule of law, political accountability, and increasing popular participation become something more than cynical rhetoric. They become an aspiration, an expression of values and intentions."[438]

Support for this View in my Field Research

Much of the research that I discussed in Part II can be construed in a way that supports the argument that China is following the traditional law and development model. In response to my questions about how China managed to modernize its real estate sector before enacting its first comprehensive property law, many of the professionals I interviewed took great pains to emphasize the various other laws that predated the 2007 Property Rights Law but managed to serve many of the same functions in piecemeal fashion. They repeatedly stressed the importance of the 1986 adoption of the General Principles of the Civil Law (GPCL), which gave investors greater faith in the enforceability of their contract rights.[439]

Despite the absence of any significant provisions addressing property law, the GPCL strengthened the confidence of investors—including foreign investors—that parties to contracts in China would respect those legal relationships and that Chinese courts would enforce them. As China continued to implement and enforce new business laws after the GPCL, overall levels of trust in the legal system continued to increase, and enactment of the Property Rights Law in 2007 was merely another step in a progression that had been under way for more than two decades.

These Chinese experts raise a valid point. The government's legal capacity to grant individuals the right to use land was incorporated into China's Constitution

---

to converge toward some form of rule of law. To the extent possible, the ruling regime will rely on incremental changes ....").

437 PEERENBOOM, *supra* note 2, at 19.
438 STEINFELD, *supra* note 68, at 230.
439 *Cf.* Mo Zhang, *From Public to Private: The Newly Enacted Chinese Property Law and the Protection of Property Rights in China*, 5 BERKELEY BUS. L.J. 317, 321 (2008):
> Indeed, the Property Law is a significant piece of legislation in China because it fills in the country's "legal blank" with regard to private property and property in general. Furthermore, it helps enhance the legal infrastructure of the country by establishing a framework that is badly needed for the regulation and protection of property rights.

in 1988. The maximum duration of land use rights was established by regulation two years later. Other commercial laws were adopted during the 1990s, each one further strengthening the legal structure needed to support sophisticated business transactions. Additional amendments to the Chinese Constitution in 2004 required that the government pay compensation for the expropriation of land. Finally, the Property Rights Law became effective in 2007. This succession of new laws reveals a clear pattern of increasing protection for private property rights, and it coincides with the rapid growth of China's real estate market.

While it is probably not possible to show a direct causal relationship between the expanding legal protection for property rights and the growth of the Chinese real estate market, it is clear that each of these laws was enacted in response to concerns that the absence of adequate legal protections might be slowing market growth. In fact, as Chapter 3 details, the Property Rights Law might have been enacted several years sooner but for concerns about the ability of the Chinese Communist Party to harmonize the provisions of that law with socialist doctrine. Thus while I have earlier portrayed the gradual legal recognition of the land use right as somewhat hesitant and unsteady, perhaps the existence of tolerable legal protection provided in other areas of business law combined with the knowledge that further property law enactments were under consideration offered the market adequate legal reassurance.[440]

Part II of this book provides considerable additional support for the argument that China truly is acting in the manner that traditional law and development theory predicts. Limited liability companies are the most common business form employed for the ownership of commercial real estate in China. As Chapter 4 illustrated, the Company Law that authorizes the creation of limited liability companies was adopted in 1993. China thus implemented a business law relatively early in its modernization phase allowing the creation of a legal structure that was necessary for successful real estate development. The discussion of urban planning in Chapter 5 noted that China's land use plans, top-down though they may be, have been mandated since the City Planning Law became effective in 1990. Again, China continued to expand its legal structure as needs became evident. Moreover, as that chapter noted, Shanghai's land use planning process has become considerably more transparent in recent years, in the face of widespread public concerns about corruption and cronyism. The initial process was apparently adequate to stimulate considerable real estate development, but the government improved that process due to continuing concerns about its impartiality and fairness.

By contrast, Chapter 6 raised ongoing questions about the ability of developers to use government coercion to requisition land that is currently occupied by others. Here is a case in which adequate legal protections may not yet be present, and

---

440 Charles Lindblom argues that this type of economic development cannot exist without support from the government. CHARLES E. LINDBLOM, THE MARKET SYSTEM: WHAT IT IS, HOW IT WORKS, AND WHAT TO MAKE OF IT 42 (2001) ("If the market system is a dance, the state provides the dance floor and the orchestra.").

the result has been widespread protests and calls for greater legal protection. Urban residents worry about the security of their land tenure, which reduces their willingness to invest and places a drag on the economy, and the government is becoming increasingly aware of the need to act to resolve this problem. Similarly, occupants of collectively owned land, on which land use rights may not be granted, have little incentive to invest in their property, and there have been growing calls to provide rural residents with property protections similar to those now enjoyed by city dwellers.

Chapter 7 described the Guaranty Law and the Property Rights Law—which became effective twelve years apart—each of which includes provisions addressing the validity and enforceability of mortgages. Again, the level of protection of security interests held by lenders increased during the era when China's real estate market was enjoying great gains. And while Chinese lending standards seem somewhat less demanding than those seen in the West, this may reflect the fact that China's lending industry still is dominated by state-owned or state-controlled banks that are heavily motivated by political considerations.

The uncertainty surrounding the ability to renew land use rights when they expire and the price at which any such renewal will occur, discussed in Chapter 3, and the cumbersome nature of transfers involving residential real estate, described in Chapter 8, present more troublesome counter-examples. In both instances, an apparent market failure does not seem to have slowed the real estate industry. One possible explanation is that the markets would have grown at an even faster rate had the legal structure provided investors with greater certainty. This argument is probably impossible to prove or disprove and could just as easily be made in the cases where the market does seem to be functioning smoothly.

There are other, more likely, explanations. With regard to the renewal of land use rights, participants in the new Chinese real estate markets may simply have been unfamiliar with the idea of discounting future interests to present value. Forty, fifty, or seventy years probably seemed like an incredibly long time to the new Chinese investment community of the 1980s—think about how much had happened in China during the previous seventy years—and these pioneers simply may have adopted an attitude of, "What, me worry?" Those who entered the market later may have assumed that the deal structure had already been vetted by more experienced market participants and that it was not their place to raise concerns that did not seem to bother their mentors. This attitude may change as the first round of land use rights begins to approach its expiration date and as Chinese real estate professionals continue to become more experienced and sophisticated in their business dealings.

With regard to acquisitions of residential real estate, purchasers may have had little choice but to buy on the terms described in Chapter 8, and may have observed numerous previous instances in which any risks that might potentially have led to disaster had not actually done so. Faced with the imminent demolition of an inadequate former dwelling, a fast-disappearing opportunity to buy a newer and more modern residence at an acceptable price, and few purchase and financing options that were less risky, and aware of numerous similar transfers that had occurred without incident, these less sophisticated borrowers apparently chose to close their eyes and dive in. Although existing statutes did provide some level of legal protection, these buyers' lack of knowledge of the risks they were taking, or their willingness to take them anyway, has paid off in nearly all cases. In short, out of a combination of luck, naiveté, and skill, they took perilous actions which the law and development model predicts they should have been less willing to take, and their gambles largely paid off.

The Law and Development Model Cannot Be Transplanted from the West to China

A fourth possible explanation of why the law and development model might not apply well to China can be summarized in four words: China is too different. Models that were developed by Westerners might transfer well into nations that follow Western traditions, and perhaps reasonably well into some nations that suffered through a Western colonial history. But they simply do not translate as readily into cultures that are further removed from those of the West, and particularly not into a nation as huge and distinctive as China. Given how dramatically different Chinese cultural and historical assumptions and traditions are from those in the West, it is too difficult for this Western transplant to take root.

Pitman Potter, for example, describes the ways in which the Chinese concepts of public responsibility and collective interest generally triumph over the more Western values of liberty and economic utility.[441] Similarly, Kenneth Dam praises China for not adopting Western norms as wholeheartedly as some might have preferred. "The Chinese have no doubt been wise to avoid a legal transplantation strategy in view of the distinctive social norms and culture that China's long history, its relative isolation from outside influences, and its internal twentieth century upheavals have produced."[442]

Frank Upham argues that the rapidity of China's economic growth makes it difficult to apply the law and development model there. The best way to initiate such dramatic changes quickly is to tear down existing institutions of property rather than buttressing them.[443] In fact, Upham warns more generally of the risks of transferring legal institutions to new environments, noting that dissimilar social

---

441   Potter, *supra* note 374, at 56.

442   DAM, *supra* note 353, at 275–76; *see also* Michael Trebilcock & Paul-Erik Veel, *Property Rights and Development: The Contingent Case for Formalization*, 30 U. PA. J. INT'L L. 397, 402 (2008) (recognizing the importance of pre-existing social norms to the success of a property system).

443   Upham, *supra* note 344, at 597; *see also id.* at 599 ("Instead of preserving existing property rights [at other times of rapid change], the legal system legitimated their destruction.") (footnote omitted).

contexts can lead to unintended results, a particular risk for nations that are still developing their legal systems.[444] And Francis Fukuyama observes that ideas can be successfully transplanted to other societies only if one considers the underlying support for those ideas:

> It requires a great deal of hard work to persuade people that institutional change is needed in the first place, build a coalition in favor of change that can overcome the resistance of existing stakeholders in the old system, and then condition people to accept the new set of behaviors as routine and expected.[445]

David Kennedy suggests that China is different not so much because of its unique culture and history, but rather because of the rate at which it is transforming its legal system. If anything, this rapid change should help us focus our thinking on issues such as the importance of property rights: "Property law—and private law more generally—is a particularly important site for thinking about social, political and economic strategy in a developing society at moments in which the legal and economic order is being reorganized in what is likely to be a once-in-a-generation way."[446] Changes in property rights always raise issues of who benefits and who suffers, and formalization of any system of property rights is a political decision, a point that is highlighted in nations that are changing as rapidly as China. "The ongoing allocation and definition of property entitlements is part of the social and political history of any market economy,"[447] and rapid economic change necessarily creates a need for rapid rethinking about property rights.

Mo Zhang focuses more specifically on the importance of personal relationships in Chinese culture. Given this distinction, China is more inclined to employ rule *by* law principles than it is to conform to the more Western rule *of* law. To some in China, the Western concept of rule of law cannot be grafted onto China's legal system. "China does not regard the rule of law as having universal application. Instead it insists that the rule of law in a country is determined by and conforms to its national conditions and social system."[448] Yet if China wishes to continue to integrate itself into the global marketplace, it faces a dilemma when the rules of that market are largely dictated by the West: "China's

---

444 Upham, *supra* note 368, at 100.
445 FUKUYAMA, *supra* note 407, at 478–79.
446 Kennedy, *supra* note 384, at 36.
447 *Id.* at 20.
448 Zhang, *supra* note 368, at 6 (footnotes omitted); *see also id.* at 41 (describing China's unique Confucian tradition and its ongoing influence today); *id.* at 42 (discussing the strong desire in China for political and social stability, even at the expense of reductions in personal liberty); Zhang, *supra* note 439, at 328 (emphasizing the importance to the Communist Party of maintaining tight control over China).

discourse for the rule of law is heavily influenced by its legal tradition and yet closely interwoven with the country's modern reform initiatives."[449]

Randall Peerenboom considers, and largely rejects, the possibility that China is too different from the West for law and development theory to apply. He initially raises the possibility that perhaps "because China is so different from other countries, it is likely to develop its own long-term, stable alternative to rule of law—a different kind of legal system that does not comply with the requirements of a thin theory."[450] Western nations have had centuries to evolve toward their current systems of rule of law, so it might be unrealistic to expect China to arrive at the same destination so quickly. "Rapid change may lead to chaos and confusion."[451] Peerenboom ultimately discounts this suggestion, however, arguing that China is not as different from Western nations as many suggest. If anything, China should seek to benefit from the missteps and false starts that Western nations have suffered and survived, so that it need not repeat those errors as it follows a similar development path.[452] These commentators all intimate, in somewhat different ways and to somewhat different extents, that China is a unique case and that models devised to predict outcomes in more typical economies cannot be expected to function as well when applied to such a large and atypical nation.

The facts do offer some support for this view. Western companies were initially attracted to China because of the potentially enormous market of buyers there. Early on, though, these companies began to recognize that most Chinese citizens had not yet accumulated the capital necessary to consume large quantities of Western goods. However, this same population quickly evolved into the world's factory, producing low-cost goods and enthusiastically exporting them, aided by an exchange rate that the Chinese government has kept artificially low. Given China's ability to produce tremendous quantities of goods at low cost, more and more Western companies began to shift production there. Chinese exports have grown at a remarkable rate, and China has managed to maintain that rate over a prolonged period because of the very large number of rural workers willing to relocate to work in urban factories.

These facts point out another variation of the "China is different" argument, namely the belief that the investment gains potentially available there are so huge that investors are willing to take much larger investment risks, including those that result from the weaknesses of legal institutions. It is not that foreign or domestic investors fail to undertake the same type of cost–benefit analysis they would pursue anywhere else, although some of them might. Rather, it is that the potential benefits are so enormous that they often outweigh even huge potential costs, such as a high likelihood of failure, the large scale of any failure, and the uncertainty

---

449 Zhang, *supra* note 368, at 6.
450 PEERENBOOM, *supra* note 2, at 141.
451 *Id.* at 156.
452 *Id.* at 159–60.

that might result if a dispute ever arises.[453] A 1 percent chance of making a killing in a nation containing nearly one-fourth of the world's population may be a better risk-adjusted investment than a 70 percent chance of earning a modest and steady return elsewhere. Nations such as Vietnam may also offer competitive advantages for production of export goods, but they may also be too small to have a significant impact on any large company's overall worldwide balance sheet. China, by contrast, is not.

Related to this variant is the existence of a possible lemming effect. Corporate leaders would rather make the same mistake as their competitors than miss an opportunity that most others are pursuing and that might not knock again in their lifetimes. It is far easier to explain a loss to your shareholders by saying, "We fell for the same story as everyone else and performed no worse than they did," than it is to justify having made a safer alternative investment and missed the opportunities available in China while all your competitors profited far more handsomely from their Chinese ventures.[454]

All of these iterations are variations on the theme that China is just too large and different to conform to any pattern designed for more typical nations. To the extent that recent Chinese development seems to contradict the traditional theory of law and development, the response is that a theory that might explain the performance of many other nations does not fit China as well. This section has shown that there is some support for that view.

It Makes Little Sense to Apply the Law and Development Model to a Nation that Is Still Communist

Another possible explanation for why the law and development model does not seem to work in China is the argument that the model was not developed for application within Communist nations. We should no more apply the model to China today than we would have applied it to the former Soviet Union or the nations of Eastern Europe before 1990, or to Cuba or North Korea today, or, for that matter, to China during Mao's reign. This argument differs from the one in the previous section, which focused on China's unique size, culture, history

---

453 *See, e.g.*, Carothers, *supra* note 420, at 17 ("It is clear that what draws investors into China is the possibility of making money either in the near or long term. Weak rule of law is perhaps one negative factor they weigh in their decision of whether to invest, but it is by no means determinative.").

454 For a discussion of this type of "decision regret," see PETER L. BERNSTEIN, AGAINST THE GODS: THE REMARKABLE STORY OF RISK 286 (1996) (quoting a *Wall Street Journal* article, uncited, that refers to an investment manager who "'is plunging into long-term bonds again despite her reckoning that value isn't quite there, because not to invest would be to momentarily lag behind the pack.'").

and traditions. By contrast, the argument set forth in this section is that China's economy is not a suitable subject to which the traditional model can be applied.

China may have undergone an economic revolution since Mao's death, but under this view, China's transformation is seen as just a second Communist revolution. Stated more strongly, the new China is just an unusual and unexpected contemporary version of its former self. This section addresses the argument that China has not departed sufficiently from its past to be a suitable test case for the traditional law and development model. In addition, this section introduces the related question of how to coordinate economic reforms that lead to growth with political reforms that lead to democratization and greater individual freedom.

Some of the law and development commentators seem to agree with this view, at least in part. For example, Clarke, Murrell, and Whiting note that, unlike Eastern Europe and the former Soviet Union, which rapidly abolished many of their former legal structures, China kept many of its earlier institutions in place while allowing new ones to arise in tandem.[455] And in another work, these same authors note some of the ways in which little has actually changed legislatively in China since reform:

> Indeed, Chinese legislation is often remarkable for its lack of institutional anchoring. Like the policy documents it has come largely to replace, it is often evidently intended more for edification than for litigation, and continues, a quarter of a century into the reform era, to contain broad statements of policy and legally unenforceable norms.[456]

A notable example of the various ways in which China has maintained many of its old restrictions is in its attitude toward the alienability of rural land. Although the government is permitted to grant land use rights on state-owned land, it is not permitted to do so on collective-owned land, which is largely agricultural. This land can be transferred only if it is first converted to state-owned land, as discussed earlier.

The reason the government prohibits farmers from owning their own plots, as Peter Ho observes, is that "the central government fears the rise of a new class of impoverished and landless farmers should rural land rights become freely

---

455 Clarke, Murrell & Whiting, *supra* note 350, at 404.
456 Clarke, Murrell & Whiting, *supra* note 417, at 43–44; *see also* Ryan Van Steenis, *From Mao to Madison and Back: An Examination of China's National Property Law and its Diminished Potential*, 23 TEMP. INT'L & COMP. L.J. 35, 58 (2009) (footnote omitted):
> Although the NPL [National Property Law] attempts to protect the assets of ordinary Chinese, the ideological tug of Marxism won out against the practical necessity of greater property rights and undermined the NPL's significance. This resulted in a compromised law, which enshrined Marxist concepts of private property as one of the NPL's fundamental principles.

tradable."[457] Thus the government is protecting rural peasants' ability to continue to use the land they have farmed in the past, much as it did during Mao's rule. The government may want to experiment to some extent, as it has done through the Household Responsibility System,[458] but it also feels constrained by the underlying Marxist–Leninist principles of collective ownership of agricultural land.[459]

For the most part, though, the law and development commentators acknowledge the progress China has made as it moves, however haltingly, away from a strictly socialist system. Rather than denominating China's system as a socialist one and then rejecting the applicability of law and development theory to a socialist China, these commentators seem to view China's economic and legal progress as more dialectical. Government policy veers away from socialism, snaps back in response to criticism from traditionalists, adopts an intermediate approach that synthesizes the two more extreme ones it just unsuccessfully attempted to employ, and then veers further away from that approach only to recoil again. This view largely parallels the observation made earlier in this chapter that it is difficult to transplant Western law and development theory to a non-Western nation, but here with the additional wrinkle that this non-Western nation also retains at least some of its socialist attributes.

The Co-opting of Chinese Entrepreneurs

Bruce Dickson, much like Kellee Tsai in her work discussed above,[460] describes how the Communist Party has managed to keep China's budding entrepreneurial class largely within the fold, contrary to the predictions of those who thought that rising wealth in China would lead to greater demands for legal protection of personal freedoms. The very title of one of Dickson's books, *Red Capitalists in China: The Party, Private Entrepreneurs, and Prospects for Political Change*, indicates the degree to which he views the entrepreneurial class and the Chinese Communist Party (CCP) as converging.[461] Dickson focuses on the ways in which the CCP has sought to co-opt China's new entrepreneurs. He observes that China's growing class of business people is not simply a passive group on which pre-existing laws and norms act. Rather, this new class is a group that interacts with other groups in Chinese society, thereby influencing future legal and economic

---

457 Peter Ho, Institutions in Transition: Land Ownership, Property Rights, and Social Conflict in China 39 (2005).

458 The Household Responsibility System was adopted to allow rural peasants to use a designated piece of agricultural cooperative land and to keep some of the proceeds attributable to that land. *See* Qinglan Long, *Reinterpreting Chinese Property Law*, 19 S. Cal. Interdisc. L.J. 55, 58 (2009) (describing this system).

459 Ho, Institutions in Transition, *supra* note 457, at 41.

460 *See supra* notes 339–42, 424–25 and accompanying text.

461 Bruce J. Dickson, Red Capitalists in China: The Party, Private Entrepreneurs, and Prospects for Political Change (2003).

development. Thus, it is overly simplistic merely to assume that the government adopts laws in a vacuum and citizens then act in response to those laws; rather, the process is considerably more interactive, as some of the other commentators discussed above have also noted.

Dickson's focus in *Red Capitalists in China* is on whether China's economic boom will ultimately lead to the democratization that many observers have been predicting for years. His expressed concern is not that the lack of clear property rights will slow China's economic growth, which it does not appear to have done so far, but rather that the absence of these rights will impede political liberalization. "Among the factors that may prevent liberalization in China," he writes, "are unclear property rights, the state's ambivalence over privatization, local protectionism, labor unrest, and the common backgrounds and shared interests of the emerging middle classes and state officials."[462]

Dickson's concern is that China's entrepreneurs are profiting quite nicely under the current system of murky laws and uneven enforcement and that they will use their positions and their connections to maintain things as they are. Kenneth Lieberthal makes a similar point, noting how private entrepreneurs in the West seek to minimize their contact with government officials while their Chinese counterparts view these contacts as providing them with a competitive advantage.[463] If laws are unclear and *guanxi* still matters, those who enjoy the strongest personal connections will continue to thrive under the regime as presently constituted and will have little motivation to seek change. Dickson examines this point further in a follow-up work, *Wealth into Power: The Communist Party's Embrace of China's Private Sector*, where he continues his discussion of the extent to which China's capitalist class may prefer the current regime under which it has prospered to a more democratic one.[464]

In both works, Dickson is pessimistic as to whether China's rising entrepreneurial class will lead a movement to expand individual and political rights. "[M]ost people make the rational decision to tolerate the status quo, even if they are not fully satisfied with it. This is not a ringing endorsement of the CCP's right to rule, but it may be sufficient to remain in power indefinitely."[465] This echoes Tsai's view that "should democratization occur in China, it will not be led by a disgruntled horde of private entrepreneurs."[466]

---

462   *Id.* at 12 (footnote omitted).
463   LIEBERTHAL, *supra* note 109, at 21–22.
464   BRUCE J. DICKSON, WEALTH INTO POWER: THE COMMUNIST PARTY'S EMBRACE OF CHINA'S PRIVATE SECTOR (2008).
465   DICKSON, *supra* note 461, at 167 (footnote omitted).
466   TSAI, *supra* note 339, at 5; *see also id.* at 148 ("there is little evidence to suggest that assertive entrepreneurs would advocate a transition to democracy as the most desirable means for satisfying their interests"); *see generally* Matthew Stephenson, *A Trojan Horse in China?*, *in* PROMOTING THE RULE OF LAW ABROAD: IN SEARCH OF KNOWLEDGE, *supra* note

Dickson, then, views China as still having an inadequate property rights system, even after the passage of much recent legislation in that area and related business fields. Nonetheless, China's economic system has developed rapidly, seemingly unimpaired by this absence. And China's new political and entrepreneurial leaders have conspired, with some degree of intention, to leave things as they are. The CCP acts in a manner that is designed to reduce citizen demands for greater political and social rights, while the business class seems largely satisfied with the current arrangement, under which it is faring well.

As another group of authors points out, "Social change, demographic inevitabilities, and the downside consequence of unprecedented economic growth preoccupy Chinese leaders by day and keep them awake at night. Understanding these domestic developments and the Chinese authorities' response is the most critical part of the China puzzle."[467] By following the course Dickson has described, China's leadership can maintain the social stability that the citizens and the government both appear to crave more than personal liberty. Democratization, in this view, is a luxury that must wait until after economic development occurs. Even then, a more developed China may decide not to purchase this particular luxury with its newly obtained wealth.

Dickson thus has moved beyond the question of how China can have prospered economically in the absence of clear property rights. He recognizes this anomaly, but chooses instead to focus on the reasons why this economic growth has not then led to political transformation. Incremental legal adaptation has been sufficient to foster economic growth, and there is now no group within Chinese society that has both the desire and the means to initiate further legal changes.[468] In Dickson's view, China has initiated the smallest amount of legal change necessary to catalyze fast-paced economic development, and it plans to go no further. Moreover, the Party must maintain the fiction that it adheres to its traditional ideology, or else its justification for retaining power evaporates.[469] In short, the traditional theory of law and development seems to have overlooked the extent to which a determined

---

368, at 191 (expressing skepticism as to whether China's recent economic transformation will lead to democratic and human rights reforms).

467 BERGSTEN, GILL, LARDY & MITCHELL, *supra* note 12, at 40; (2006); *see also* Zhang, *supra* note 439, at 328 (describing China's twin goals of demonstrating to the world that it protects private property rights and maintaining the Communist Party's unchallenged authority over the country).

468 Note that Dickson spends little time discussing whether those who have not benefited greatly from economic reform might be the social class to lead the charge for liberalization. Recent upswings in social protests raise the question of whether China might face another revolution from below. *But see* DICKSON, *supra* note 464, at 27 ("The emphasis on creating a 'harmonious society' may be meant to placate nonbeneficiaries without jeopardizing the benefits enjoyed by cronies.").

469 DICKSON, *supra* note 461, at 165–71; *id.* at 171 ("Most observers expect that a thriving market economy and a Leninist political system will inevitably prove to be incompatible, but the CCP's strategy has been to try to make them coexist.").

government can employ the bare minimum of change and use it to motivate and then co-opt an entire class of entrepreneurs.[470]

Dickson is not alone in holding this view. Writing about China's unwillingness to allow private ownership of land, Peter Ho notes that "the central government's decision to maintain the Marxist–Leninist principle of state and collective ownership has to date also avoided the large-scale land-related grievances over pre-revolutionary ownership that ruptured transitional economies such as parts of the former Soviet Union, East Germany and Kyrgyzstan."[471] In part, Ho believes, this was done to undercut any claims that pre-Communist owners might have to be compensated for the loss of their property.[472] China, in other words, has avoided some of the problems other Westernizing nations faced by Westernizing less than they did.

The Lending Industry and Government Pressure

My research in China provides considerable support for the view that it might not be appropriate to apply the law and development model to China, given the many attributes of Communism that still characterize its evolving economic system. One of the most notable features of the Chinese real estate market is the extent to which the lending industry is owned or controlled by the state. As Chapter 7 repeatedly emphasized, Chinese banks are not private enterprises that respond to the profit motive and the demands of shareholders. Rather, they are controlled by the government, which often has other reasons for encouraging specific developments.

For example, the government might pressure a lender to extend credit to a money-losing state-owned enterprise (SOE). Even though there is a strong likelihood that the borrower will default and never repay its debt to the bank, the government might well wish to prop up this enterprise anyway. SOEs of this type provide their employees with housing, education, health care, and employment. If the enterprise were to fail, thereby depriving its workers of the protection of the "iron rice bowl," the government might have to assume these social welfare costs more directly. From the government's perspective, it might be less expensive to support the company's workers indirectly, by encouraging a government-controlled lender to extend a loan that is unlikely ever to be repaid, than it would

---

470 Tsai is more inclined to attribute this development to the initiative of the entrepreneurial class. She argues that business owners took the lead when their profit-making activities were still highly controversial and found creative ways to circumvent legal restrictions existing at the time, though often with assistance from local officials. Tsai, *supra* note 339, at 11–12.

471 Peter Ho, *Introduction: The Chicken of Institutions or the Egg of Reforms?*, in Developmental Dilemmas: Land Reform and Institutional Change in China 1, 12 (Peter Ho ed., 2005).

472 *Id.* at 17.

be to provide direct benefits to these workers after they lose their secure jobs and benefits.[473]

Even if it is more expensive to act in this fashion, the government nonetheless may wish to avoid the social disorder that might follow if thousands of workers were suddenly to lose their jobs, their homes, their health care, and educational opportunities for their children all at once. The Chinese government fears the type of unrest that such rapid change could engender, and might prefer to wind down these doomed SOEs more gradually. A profit-oriented bank is unlikely to make a loan to a failing SOE such as this. But a government-controlled lender is acting more like a municipal agency than a private bank. Thus Chinese banks bear little resemblance to the lending institutions with which Westerners are accustomed to dealing.[474] In this sense, there is considerable merit to the criticism that the law and development theory should not be applied to China because China still supports, in some significant ways, an economic system that retains many essential features of its recent past.

Just as the government may wish to prop up failing SOEs, it may also wish to encourage noteworthy new developments in major areas. Anxious to attract foreign tourists and to show the world that it has become a major economic force, China has been building office towers, hotels, and shopping malls at a truly staggering pace. In some cases, little market research is conducted before these buildings are designed and built. They exist not because the market demands them, but because government officials wish to showcase them.

Journalist Jan Wong recalls a conversation with an architect friend in which she asked him why anyone had built the underutilized new shopping mall they were visiting. He replied, "'They don't do a feasibility study or a marketing analysis .... They got a lot of money and they don't know what to do with it, so they build a mall.'"[475] Later, she describes the mall:

> The 5.8-million-square-foot New Yansha has six floors, a thousand stores, a hundred restaurants, 20,000 employees, 230 escalators, a climbing wall and an ice rink. People stroll up and down the air-conditioned halls, but most don't even glance at the $500 cashmere sweaters or $10,000 golf clubs. Some people even bring their own snacks. No one is making money, including at the climbing wall.[476]

---

473   *See also* LIEBERTHAL, *supra* note 109, at 32 ("China is now trying to create, within ten or fifteen years, institutions to provide a social safety net on a governmental basis that took most Western countries fifty to a hundred years to develop.").

474   Note, for instance, the considerable public resistance in the United States to the government's temporary acquisition of stakes in major lending institutions during a time of severe economic crisis. *See supra* note 274.

475   JAN WONG, A COMRADE LOST AND FOUND: A BEIJING STORY 131 (2009).

476   *Id.* at 157.

It is difficult to apply law and development theory to a nation in which non-economic government incentives such as these lead to the construction of projects that do not appear to be meeting any market demand.

The Business of Real Estate Development

In a similar fashion, Chapters 3 and 4 illustrate the considerable direct role the government plays in much Chinese real estate development. The government owns the land on which it will grant land use rights, and thus has largely unfettered power to determine the identity of the user and the type of use to which the land will be put. The entity that acquires the land use right is itself often partially owned by the government, which can thereby profit from the development. In fact, the government partner's equity investment in the partnership may take the form of a contribution of the right to use the land that is to be improved. Private parties often are able to acquire desirable land use rights by virtue of their personal contacts with the government officials who possess the power to determine the disposition of the land. And Chapter 5 illustrates the ways in which the government, by virtue of its ownership of the land, can direct certain industries toward or away from specific geographic locations, thereby directly controlling the future course of development. Western nations are often heavily zoned and regulated, but not to the degree routinely seen in China.

Demolition and Relocation

Most important, perhaps, is the manner in which the government can remove current occupants from land by paying them the value of their property for its current, low-intensity use, as discussed in Chapter 6. The government can then expand the range of permitted uses of the property and convey land use rights to real estate developers at a much higher price, reflecting the land's newly increased highest-and-best use. In this way, the government alone can profit from intensifications in permissible land uses over which it has complete control. Former owners are removed by the government at a modest cost determined by that same government, the land is then sold by the government to a developer that is willing to pay the higher price that the new, government-determined use merits, and the same government retains the difference between the high sale price for the land use right and the much lower acquisition cost. In many cases, the government also holds an equity interest in the development entity.

Similarly, if the land is collective-owned, the collective cannot grant land use rights. The government must acquire the land from the collective, at which point the land—now state-owned—can be subjected to land use rights. Once again, the amount the collective receives from the government is often considerably lower than the price that will later be paid to the government by the party acquiring the land use right.

A relocation process such as this can work only when the government has an extraordinary measure of control over a nation's land. In China, the government owns all land other than that owned by collectives and is the sole party that can initially grant use rights on land. This power over land, coupled with the government's control over the lending industry just described, illustrates the wide variety of ways in which China's real estate market, though much freer than it was two decades ago, is anything but a free market. In this regard and others, the criticism that China still exhibits many of the attributes of a Communist nation has considerable merit and helps to explain why the traditional law and development model may not apply well to China.

No Model Applies Perfectly to Any Nation, and Every Country Is Unique

As the previous chapter and this one have shown, commentators have been struggling to explain how China has maintained its rapid pace of economic development without necessarily following the predictions of traditional law and development theory. Some commentators have argued that the theory is incorrect. Others believe that the theory is partially accurate but needs refinement. Some interpret the evidence in a way that suggests that China is, in fact, following the traditional theory. Others claim that China's unique size, history, and culture make it an inappropriate nation for the application of a model that was developed to explain more conventional economies. Still others believe that China has not yet steered its economy far enough from its Communist past and thus is an unsuitable test case for the law and development model. Evidence from China can be found to support each of these arguments, but none of them conclusively.

Can We Synthesize these Possibilities?

This final section suggests that it might be possible to synthesize portions of all of these arguments into a workable, if more complex, explanation of China's recent growth. The apparent disharmony between the traditional law and development model and China's recent history—if there truly is any disharmony—can be attributed to imperfections in the model, to misperceptions of the data, and to some of the unique features that China exhibits. More broadly, any generalized explanatory model that seeks to be applicable across so wide a range of international economies inherently must oversimplify. This means that application of the model to any particular nation, especially one as distinctive as China, will necessarily be imperfect. Every country is a case unto itself, and no generalized model can be expected to apply flawlessly anywhere.[477]

---

477 *See, e.g.*, Guo, *supra* note 199, at 66 ("All in all, the CPC [Communist Party of China] has incorporated various elements of Confucianism, Marxism–Leninism, Darwinism, its own ideology, and economic liberalism, and so on."); Upham, *supra* note

In recent years, the oversimplified assumptions and analysis of neoclassical law and economics have been criticized by the behavioralists, whose insights have enriched the field. The more expansive perspective provided by behavioral law and economics scholars has added depth and color to neoclassical economic theory by making it both more detailed and more universal. Behavioral analysis has increased the breadth of neoclassical theory and the accuracy of its predictions, but it is more difficult and complicated to apply.[478] In similar fashion, it might be possible to improve traditional law and development theory by factoring in additional components that the theory may have overlooked and that China now demonstrates it must include. As Douglass North noted even before the behavioralists had begun to criticize neoclassical theory, "There is nothing the matter with the rational actor paradigm that could not be cured by a healthy awareness of the complexity of human motivation and the problems that arise from information processing."[479] A realistic acknowledgement of detail, nuance, and subtlety will make the law and development model more accurate, but the extra precision comes at the cost of additional complication.

In Part II, I analyzed the actual practices of Chinese real estate professionals operating today under China's evolving legal system. In Chapter 11, I sought to apply traditional law and development theory to many of those real estate practices in order to determine whether the practices comported with the predictions of the theory. As I have shown in Chapter 11, Chinese real estate practice meets the expectations of the theory only to a limited extent. And each of the justifications that I have proposed in the current chapter as possibly accounting for the limited explanatory power of the traditional theory is partially accurate and partially misplaced as applied to modern China.

Any theory that succeeds in explaining modern China more completely will most likely incorporate insights from each of these criticisms. By doing so, the improved, China-specific version of the theory will highlight a variety of ways in which the traditional theory must be modified to account for the particular Chinese example. This revised application of the theory to China will be more detailed and precise, less transferable to other settings, and more challenging. And this refinement is likely to emphasize uniquely Chinese attributes that are inapplicable elsewhere, in much the same way that behavioral law and economics scrutinizes and incorporates actual behaviors of actors in particularized settings within an

---

344, at 593 (asking why China does not appear to act in the manner that traditional law and development theory predicts and concluding "that much of the explanation lies in the way economists understand the world. Put starkly, they simplify and generalize.").

478 *See, e.g.*, Christine Jolls, Cass R. Sunstein & Richard Thaler, *A Behavioral Approach to Law and Economics*, 50 STAN. L.R. 1471, 1473 (1998) ("Our goal in this article is to advance an approach to the economic analysis of law that is informed by a more accurate conception of choice, one that reflects a better understanding of human behavior and its wellsprings.").

479 NORTH, *supra* note 348, at 111.

economic system. It will cease to be the traditional theory of law and development and will become instead an explanation of how China has managed to progress in light of its own unique background and history. As Kevin Davis and Michael Trebilcock have noted:

> Optimal institutions generally, including legal institutions in particular, will often be importantly shaped by factors specific to given societies, including history, culture, and long-established political and institutional traditions. This in turn implies some degree of modesty on the part of the external community in promoting rule of law or other legal reforms in developing countries and correspondingly a larger role for "insiders" with detailed local knowledge.[480]

Randall Peerenboom notes that an observer might attempt to apply various existing theories to China, to test the explanatory value of each one. But these theories draw on experiences from other countries, and applying them thus creates the risk of missing features that are uniquely Chinese.[481] Instead of trying to come up with a grand unifying theory of development applicable to all nations, it will be more productive to acknowledge that China has been forging its own, culturally directed path. This will be an enormous and complicated task, but the findings described in Part II and the discussion in this Part III suggest at least some of the contours of a more precise theory of law and development for China.

Even after Douglass North's new institutional economics had been widely accepted, he recognized its limited explanatory power. Writing in 2005, he noted that there is "no set formula for achieving economic development. No economic model can capture the intricacies of economic growth in a particular society."[482] A model cannot predict outcomes with great accuracy, although a society can use suitable models to make educated guesses. Better yet, that society can allow its citizens to figure out for themselves how to adapt to change through "the maintenance of institutions that permit trial and error experiments to occur .... Adaptive efficiency evolves only after a relatively long period of evolving informal norms and we know of no shortcut to this process."[483] Writing at about the same time, Jeffrey Sachs concurred: "Dozens of recent statistical studies have shown that difference in economic growth rates across countries depends on a multiplicity of factors .... The real challenge is to understand which of these many

---

480   Davis & Trebilcock, *supra* note 418, at 945–46.
481   PEERENBOOM, *supra* note 2, at x–xi. Peerenboom also warns against going to the opposite extreme: one should not conclude that China is so different that none of the old rules or models apply. *Id.* at xiv.
482   DOUGLASS C. NORTH, UNDERSTANDING THE PROCESS OF ECONOMIC CHANGE 165 (2005).
483   *Id.* at 163.

variables is posing particular obstacles in specific circumstances—what I mean precisely by 'differential diagnosis.'"[484]

In other words, models may be useful when viewing an economy from afar. But as the observer zooms in and can perceive the more precise contours and greater levels of detail of a society, the predictive value of any theory diminishes. I have raised several possible explanations for why China seems to challenge traditional law and development theory, some of which are inconsistent with others. The reason why so many seemingly contradictory explanations all seem to make some sense is that they all might be partly true within a large, complex, and rapidly changing China. Different rationales have varying amounts of explanatory power in different contexts, and China provides a huge number of different contexts.

Weaving the Strands Together: An Illustration

Traditional law and development theory suggests that no real estate entity would ever build a 50-story office tower on land that it does not own, that it may use for only forty years without any assurance that the use right can be renewed, in a nation without a formal law of property, and with new and barely tested statutes in other areas of business law. Yet hundreds of such buildings were constructed in China before the 2007 effective date of the Property Rights Law. In this regard, the traditional theory was wrong, or at least needed significant modification, failing to explain how something that actually did occur repeatedly could ever have happened.

Conversely, one can legitimately argue that China was, in fact, following traditional law and development theory during this period. China did have a growing body of business laws during this era of reform. And even though it had no formal property law until 2007, other related laws did an adequate job of satisfying those who sought to invest. The Company Law allowed the necessary business structures to exist. The Guaranty Law provided some basis for using property as security for the repayment of debts. And in areas where the law was inadequate, such as protecting citizens from having their residences requisitioned for commercial development, public outrage—far riskier and more rare in China than in the West—has been leading to increasing protection of residential property rights. In these respects, China was following the traditional theory, and is doing so more and more as time goes by.

And there is considerable support for the argument that China is too different for Western norms such as the theory of law and development to take root. For example, China places considerable emphasis on avoidance of social unrest and on communitarian concepts of collective benefit, and historically has provided far lower levels of protection for individual rights.[485] These particularized traditions

---

484 SACHS, *supra* note 392, at 322.
485 *See, e.g.*, Wuquan Fa [Property Rights Law], art. 7 ("The attainment and exercise of property rights shall comply with laws, social morality and shall not do harm to the

suggest that it is inappropriate to apply the traditional theory to China. In addition, Western investors have proved willing to take risks in China that they would decline to take anywhere else, because the potential benefits are so much larger there than in any other market. To some degree, then, China is sufficiently distinctive from all other nations, both in cultural background and in size, that models with high predictive value elsewhere can fail there.

Moreover, China still is a Communist nation in many respects. Most rural land remains owned by collectives, and individual farmers cannot obtain land use rights to their cropland, let alone fee simple title. The Chinese Communist Party is making great efforts to work closely with entrepreneurs, some of whom are actually Party members. Lending institutions are still largely controlled by the government. The government also controls how all land can be used, who can use it and for how long, and whether prior occupants will need to relocate. Citizens of most Western nations would strongly reject most of these features in their own economies, and yet China's economy is booming despite the presence of all of them.

In short, China does contradict the traditional law and development theory in some ways. In other regards, China demonstrates how the model needs to be refined. China does follow the theory in still other respects. And in yet other ways, the model simply cannot be expected to apply readily to China, both because of its particular size and history and because of the many attributes of Communism that remain in place.

China's Other Path Moving Forward

And yet, there China is. The only way to explain accurately how China has managed to accomplish so much in recent decades—all traditional models aside—is to recognize that in different regards, each of these possible explanations for China's failure to adhere strictly to the model is partly correct. Through a combination of drive, ambition, luck, borrowing from other nations, bottom-up experimentation that is later blessed by the government, and top-down declarations that are grudgingly accepted by the populace, China has managed both to prove and to disprove features of traditional law and development theory. It has embraced some rule-of-law features while still relying heavily on *guanxi*. It has headed off some of the dilemmas faced by other formerly Communist nations that reformed too quickly but faces criticism for not restructuring quickly enough. It has invited Western observers and advisers without always accepting their advice. It has undergone economic, political, and legal change concurrently; in

---

public interests and the legitimate rights and interests of others"); *id.* art. 84 (2007) ("In the spirit of providing convenience for production, life of the people, enhancing unity and mutual assistance, and being fair and reasonable, neighboring users of the real property shall maintain proper neighborhood relationship.").

fact, "[e]conomic transition is the essence of social and cultural transformation."[486] As Deng Xiaoping recommended from the outset, Chinese reformers truly have been crossing the river by feeling for each stone.

China is thus following a path that its leadership—and perhaps, indirectly, its people—has willingly chosen, even as it is criticized abroad for manipulating exchange rates, failing to ensure product safety, neglecting to safeguard intellectual property, and taking inadequate care of the environment. In the near term, the domestic benefits of Chinese development have probably outweighed the costs. In the long term, as Zhou Enlai noted about the consequences of the French Revolution, it is too soon to tell.[487]

Many of the commentators discussed above have either stated or alluded to the different ways in which traditional law and development theory and the Chinese experience might be harmonized. Donald Clarke has suggested that property rights may have been significantly more important to Chinese success than contract rights, because property rights protect citizens against government intrusion while contract rights merely regulate relationships among private parties.[488] Clarke, along with Peter Murrell and Susan Whiting, argue that China's political structure has managed to serve as a viable alternative source of stability even when formal laws remained more unpredictable.[489] Kenneth Dam submits that nations can achieve rapid growth with weak institutions only when they are still at a low level of economic development, but that strong institutions are necessary for an economy to develop beyond that point.[490]

Edward Steinfeld believes that China is actually doing a better job than most people acknowledge of following the American path of development. In his view, China has made an express decision to emulate the American model while also seeking to transform it to advance its own interests.[491] In contrast, Albert Chen suggests that some Chinese may be becoming resistant to Western norms, viewing them as subtle attempts to destroy traditional Chinese culture while reaffirming Western hegemony.[492] And Frank Upham argues that China's modern transformation has actually been advanced by an uncertain legal system that threatens the stability of property rights. In Upham's view, "rapid economic development requires changing underlying structures, not preserving them."[493]

---

486 Daniel W. Bromley, *Property Rights and Land in Ex-Socialist States: Lessons of Transition for China*, in DEVELOPMENTAL DILEMMAS: LAND REFORM AND INSTITUTIONAL CHANGE IN CHINA, *supra* note 471, at 35, 55.

487 *See supra* note 427 and accompanying text.

488 Clarke, *supra* note 57, at 93–100.

489 Clarke, Murrell & Whiting, *supra* note 350, at 403.

490 DAM, *supra* note 353, at 277.

491 STEINFELD, *supra* note 68, at 18.

492 Albert H.Y. Chen, *Legal Thought and Legal Development in the People's Republic of China 1949–2008*, in LEGAL REFORMS IN CHINA AND VIETNAM: A COMPARISON OF ASIAN COMMUNIST REGIMES, *supra* note 377, at 51, 66–67.

493 Upham, *supra* note 344, at 597.

Still other commentators focus more closely on norms and behavior, in much the way that the behavioral law and economics scholars have done.[494] Amartya Sen emphasizes "the role of social values and prevailing mores, which can influence the freedoms that people enjoy and have reason to treasure .... The exercise of freedom is mediated by values, but the values in turn are influenced by public discussions and social interactions, which are themselves influenced by participatory freedoms."[495] And Kevin Davis and Michael Trebilcock recognize the difficulty of transplanting Western legal models into cultures with differing norms, given that norms derive from underlying cultural assumptions that may not be found in the receiving culture.[496]

In each of these examples, a commentator knowledgeable about both law and development theory and Chinese growth has suggested ways in which the traditional model and actual Chinese development may not be as divergent as they seem to be at first. By assessing arguments such as these, and many others, it should be possible to transform a generalized model that does not adequately describe China's recent experience into a more precise and more complex model that better describes modern Chinese society. These commentators have sought to expand and rethink the traditional model, thereby moving toward a more refined description of the modern Chinese experience. They have succeeded, in large part, by accounting for the behavior of actual people on the ground. I have tried to advance that process in this book, by providing numerous examples of how Chinese and foreign real estate investors have acted in the face of considerable legal uncertainty. I have then tied many of these illustrations into a gradually more refined model of development in China.

It is easy to say that "China cannot possibly exist in its current form" or "the model is wrong," but it is more productive to examine what has actually happened in China. From these observations, one can assess which factors have contributed to China's actual accomplishments, attempt to use these components to forge a particularized model of law and development for China, try to determine how this model's best features can be replicated and its worst features avoided in China and elsewhere, and use past performance as a rough method of predicting the future. Those three lost economists are not really on the mountain their map tells them they are on. Either the map is wrong, or they are misreading it, or a little bit of both.

---

494 *See supra* notes 478–79 and accompanying text.
495 SEN, *supra* note 378, at 9.
496 Davis & Trebilcock, *supra* note 418, at 904.

PART IV
Conclusion

Chapter 13
Will the Miracle Continue?

China's recent modernization would be remarkable if the nation had merely spent huge sums of money quite rapidly to replace crumbling buildings and infrastructure. The fact that China has accomplished these feats with support from its new private sector—and despite the nation's prohibition of the private ownership of land, its stated adherence to Marxist principles, and its absence of a comprehensive property law until 2007—makes these successes even more incredible. By allowing state-owned land to be controlled by private parties for extended time periods, China was able to ignite private investment.

Entrepreneurial Chinese have been willing to use their resources to develop property with only a vague idea as to how their private arrangements would be enforced in the event of disagreements. Anxious to modernize quickly while improving living standards, the government has allowed these experiments to proceed. Legal structures that developed hastily and through trial and error often have become blueprints for the formal laws to follow. Perhaps these unofficial trials have helped persuade the government that there is strong public support for laws that might otherwise have been viewed as contrary to socialist dogma. China's leaders have been willing to look the other way, while China's citizens have enthusiastically gambled that the nation's legal development will eventually catch up with its economic growth. So far, the private sector has not been disappointed. But the job of law reform is far from complete.

This book has attempted to show how real estate professionals in China have been functioning in this vibrant but uncertain legal world. China's real estate sector still is in an early stage of development, but it is nonetheless more mature than China's real estate law. Despite its youth, and despite the fact that it largely developed in the absence of a formal real estate code, the Chinese real estate industry has fared remarkably well since the government began reintroducing free market concepts in the late 1980s. Through a combination of resourcefulness, willingness to experiment, tolerance for risk, and desire for material wealth, Chinese investors have fashioned a new and unique real estate system. It possesses some features familiar to Westerners, others that are derived from Chinese history and culture, and still others that these new capitalists have invented on the fly as their legal system matures rapidly.

By engaging in field research in China, I have attempted to describe and analyze the current state of Chinese real estate law. China's laws pertaining to real estate are both new and relatively scarce. This means that the only way to develop a more complete picture of the current state of Chinese real estate law is by determining how real estate professionals are actually functioning in an unsettled legal climate.

My interviews with dozens of Chinese real estate professionals have helped to fill in the gaps left by the published sources. They also paint a picture of a nation making a halting transition from its socialist past to a future it calls "socialism with Chinese characteristics."

In the introductory chapter of this book, I set forth two goals. First, the book would describe how the Chinese market actually functions in practice, given the high level of background uncertainty inherent in the current Chinese legal system. Second, it would attempt to ascertain how China has managed to grow so dramatically in the absence of this legal certainty. The traditional law and development model suggests that China could not have modernized so quickly. China thus challenges the validity of the model.

In Chapter 2, I set forth my preliminary conclusions, so that the reader could assess their validity while reading the more detailed chapters that followed. I suggested that most Chinese legal structures and institutions are still in the midst of an ongoing evolutionary process. The unsettled status of the law causes legal and business professionals to operate by experimentation. I noted that many of these professionals are new to their fields, given how recently many of these legal developments have occurred. The modern Chinese real estate market is, after all, only a quarter-century old.

I observed that Chinese professionals place great emphasis on personal relationships. The rule of law is a new concept in China and is viewed with considerable misgivings. Even as China continues to transform itself, *guanxi* is likely to continue to play an important role in Chinese business relationships. I also stressed how relatively undeveloped the Chinese legal system is when compared to the reality of Chinese property markets. Investors have taken the lead in inventing new business structures, and the legal system is doing what it can to keep up.

Chapter 2 also emphasized the ways in which China calls traditional law and development theory into question. China appears, at least on the surface, to have been able to expand economically before establishing a modern legal system based on rule-of-law principles. Meanwhile, as I also noted, China is still a heavily regulated economy. The Chinese government intrudes into economic matters to a far greater degree than its Western counterparts do, and transparency is in short supply. China is spending enormous amounts on modernizing the nation's infrastructure. Finally, China remains a work in progress that continues to evolve rapidly. Thus, there is tremendous opportunity for interested outsiders to offer insights and suggestions.

Part II then sought to break the Chinese real estate system down into its constituent parts. Each of the chapters in this Part examined a particular facet of Chinese real estate law and practice. In each, I sought to unite the provisions contained in published laws and regulations with the insights offered by those actually working in the industry. This process was designed to portray the current state of Chinese real estate law as fully and accurately as possible. From the land use right to Chinese corporate structure, from site selection to demolition and relocation, from lending to the presale of residential units, and then from commercial construction and leasing to the development of infrastructure, these eight chapters examined the most significant components of China's modern real estate system.

These chapters also emphasized the fact that the continued success of China's economy depends, to a large degree, on the ability of local governments to sell land use rights to real estate developers. The developers upgrade China's commercial and residential real estate stock, while the government uses the proceeds from these sales to continue to build infrastructure. As one government official reminded me, the Chinese economy thus is modernizing by selling to private developers the right to use land that the government seized from its prior owners without fair compensation. In this sense, the Chinese miracle is being financially supported by the previous two generations of China's citizens. They suffered mightily and lost a great deal after 1949. But this unusual type of forced savings is benefiting their children and grandchildren in ways they never imagined.

Finally, Part III offered a discussion of the law and development model, along with numerous illustrations of the ways in which China appears to be departing from this model. Those illustrations are drawn from the discussion in Part II and raise the question of whether the more general model is applicable in light of China's recent experience. Finally, I offered numerous possible explanations of how the model and recent Chinese growth might be reconciled.

In the coming years, China's business and legal systems will almost certainly continue to develop. China's huge population, rapidly expanding economy, and increasing interrelationships with other nations virtually ensure that the process that began in the late 1980s will proceed further. It is possible that the Chinese legal system will be more fully articulated within its body of published laws and regulations. However, as the preceding chapters have suggested, it is also possible that a country with a civil law system and a strong emphasis on interpersonal relationships will remain one in which actual practice diverges greatly from published law.

The preceding chapters have highlighted numerous areas in which reform, or at least more clarity, is necessary. Those who own land use rights in China need greater certainty as to whether they have the legal right to renew these rights, and at what price. Less affluent Chinese, both urban and rural, need stronger assurances that they will not be displaced from their homes and farms. To the extent that they do continue to be relocated, they need to receive compensation that more fairly represents the current market value of the land they are losing.

China's lending industry needs to focus more closely on whether individual borrowers are creditworthy and whether they will repay their loans. There is considerable need for reform of the process of preselling new residential units in urban areas. Some of these transformations have already begun, and the Chinese public is calling out loudly for others.

There are also warning signs of potential future problems. Most Chinese probably agree that greater certainty and security of property rights and stricter lending standards will benefit the Chinese real estate industry in the coming years. At the same time, Western nations advocating for economic reform have lost much credibility in the eyes of the Chinese government and public during the past several years, and deservedly so. Many of these nations have long lectured the Chinese as to how they ought to modernize their economy and further integrate it into the global financial system. Now that the economic systems of these Western nations have slid into global recession, many Chinese are rightly questioning whether they should heed this advice.

To many Western observers, it might appear that the Chinese real estate market should have collapsed years ago. Yet this market seems to be thriving, and the level of confidence in the stability of real estate investments is extremely high within China. Western observers and participants are sure to monitor China's real estate markets with great interest in the coming years, as the Chinese economy continues to grow and becomes more closely joined to the economies of other nations. An improved understanding of China's legal and business systems will benefit real estate market observers and participants within China and elsewhere.

China's leaders and citizens seem to want to rebuild an entire country in just a few decades. Considering that they began this task recently and that the starting point was an economy that had been stagnant for half a century, China has made striking progress. For the interested observer of contemporary real estate markets, China is the most fascinating place in the world, and the coming years promise to be no less exciting.

Index

agricultural land 55, 63, 94, 138
    collective ownership of 4, 30, 35, 68–73
    displacement of farmers 22, 58–60, 68–72, 136–7
    distinguished from urban land 4, 30, 35, 41–2, 63, 68–72, 94–6
    expropriation of 59–60, 63, 68–72, 136–7
    inalienability of 68–72, 185–6
    preservation and reclamation of 58–60, 95–6
    quotas on transfer of 60, 95, 135–7
    self-sufficiency and social security function of 58–60, 68–72, 95–6, 136–7, 185–6
    transfer of 30, 41–2, 68–72
    valuation of 22, 69–70
    see also demolition and relocation; "iron rice bowl"; land use controls; protest in China; zoning
Amsden, Alice 155, 162

banking system
    asset-management companies 100–101
    concentration in a small number of state-owned or -controlled banks 13, 81, 85–8, 93, 101–2, 121, 125, 180
    focus on social and political viability of projects 13, 121
    nonperforming loans 79, 87, 99–102, 111, 122, 125–6
    regulation of 83, 86, 99, 101, 108–9, 126, 142, 202–3
    stability of 99–102
    State-Owned Enterprises (SOEs) as drag on 46–8, 87, 111, 125–6, 189–91
    see also Chinese government; law and development theory; lending, real estate; presales; state-owned enterprises (outside of the real estate and lending industries) (SOEs)
behavioralism 176, 193, 198
Beijing 10, 30, 43, 57–60, 67, 95, 110–1, 172
bond financing 97, 101
Build–Operate–Transfer (BOT) process, *see* public and private sectors

Carothers, Thomas 159–60, 174, 184
cash-flow loans, *see* construction process; lending, real estate
Chen, Albert H.Y. 11, 20–21, 28, 35, 45, 149–50, 160, 197
Chinese Communist Party (CCP), *see* Communism
Chinese government
    central government desire to slow real estate market 32, 39, 43, 52, 55, 72, 74, 80–81, 84–5, 88–9, 95, 110–11, 116–7, 138
    control of real estate market 11, 13, 18, 22, 35–7, 51–7, 62–72, 83, 87, 94, 99, 129–30, 135–40, 144–6, 162, 190–2, 201–2
    provincial and local government need to sell land use rights rapidly 29, 33, 41–3, 110–11, 134–5, 137–8, 144, 203
    provincial and local government support for local real estate development 45–8, 95, 110–11, 133–5
    tensions between central and provincial governments 27, 41–3, 57–60, 72, 94–6, 110–11, 138

see also banking system; corruption; land use controls; land use rights; lending, real estate; transparency
Chongqing 39, 136
City Planning Law 53, 134–5, 179
Clarke, Donald 8–9, 29, 158, 170–71, 173–4, 197
Clarke, Donald, Peter Murrell, and Susan Whiting 155, 172–3, 185, 197
commercial construction, see construction process
commercial leasing, *see* leasing
commercial lending, *see* lending, real estate
Communism 3–4, 7, 11, 15, 17, 28–31, 40, 47, 50, 52, 96, 102, 139, 144, 160, 171, 179, 182, 184–92, 196–7, 201
  see also Socialism
communitarianism 5, 160, 166, 195
Company Law 45–6, 179, 195
condominiums, *see* residential apartments
Constitution, Chinese 3, 9, 11, 18, 27–9, 31, 62, 139, 164, 178–9
  amendments to 18, 27–9, 31, 164, 178–9
  provisions relating to property 18, 27–9, 31, 62, 164, 178–9
construction process 4, 14, 18–19, 32–5, 58, 62, 72–3, 76–102, 127–8, 150, 203
  as not always driven by profitability 13, 191
  commercial construction 119–32
  contrasts between American and Chinese approaches 76, 82, 84, 119–28, 135, 140
  government influence over 48, 54, 85, 101
  infrastructure construction 4, 53–4, 133–46
  project loans and cash-flow loans 76–9, 126–7
  quality of construction in China 40–41, 129
  residential construction 106–17
  see also contracts; lending, real estate; mortgages; public and private sectors; real estate developers; residential apartments
contractors 40, 127–8
  as co-owners of real estate ventures 51–2, 84–5
  as unwilling lenders to developers 51–2, 80, 84–5, 114–15, 127–8
  lien rights of 114–15
contracts 5, 14, 28, 33, 66, 105, 110, 115, 119, 120, 123, 127–8, 132
  relationship of contracts to land use rights 28–9, 33–4, 38, 55, 164
  relationship of contracts to zoning 41
  rule of law and 149–58, 169, 171, 173, 175, 178, 197
  see also construction process; land use rights; presales
corruption 11, 14, 28, 36–7, 49–50, 87, 99, 111, 126, 145, 179
  see also Chinese government; lending, real estate
Criminal Law 96

Dam, Kenneth 155, 157, 175–6, 181, 185, 197
Davis, Kevin 173–4, 194, 198
demolition and relocation 13, 37, 61–74, 83
  government role in 61–8, 72–4, 136, 191–2, 202–3
  housing construction as increasing the incidence of 61–5, 72–4, 180–81, 191–2
  retention of profit by government 65–8, 191–2
  transfer of cleared land to developers 37, 62–8, 72–4, 83, 136, 191–2
  urban residents, displacement of 61–8, 72–4, 136, 180–81, 191–2
  see also agricultural land; land use controls; law and development theory; protest in China
Deng Xiaoping 11, 18, 21, 197
Dickson, Bruce 177, 186–9

Ellickson, Robert C. 8–9, 136
Ellickson, Robert C. and Vicki L. Been 136

entities, ownership 13, 32, 45–52, 53, 63, 83, 84–5, 90, 125, 127–8, 130, 135–6, 138–42, 165–6, 191, 195
  see also joint stock limited companies; law and development theory; limited liability companies; public and private sectors; real estate developers
evolution of legal and business systems 6–7, 11, 19, 23, 28–9, 80, 106, 144, 155–6, 158, 161, 172–3, 175–6, 183, 189, 193–4, 202
  see also law and development theory
exchange rate of renminbi 104–5, 174

field research methods 7–12, 173–4, 178–81, 183–4, 189–92, 201–4
foreigners, influence of 10, 20–21, 23, 41, 46–8, 50–51, 77, 79, 125, 145, 178, 183, 198
Fukuyama, Francis 171, 182

General Principles of the Civil Law 27, 149–50, 178
granted land use rights, see land use rights
green space, increase in 42, 73, 134, 136
guanxi 5, 20, 36, 49–50, 83, 102, 135–6, 187, 196, 202
Guaranty Law 34, 42, 75–6, 81–2, 127, 150, 180, 195

historic preservation, see urban land
history, Chinese, and its influence today 17–19, 94, 172, 176, 181–4, 192, 194, 196, 201
Ho, Peter 185–6, 189
housing stock, see residential apartments
Huang, Yasheng 60, 145, 177
Huangpu District 55
Huangpu River 14, 18, 144–5

income inequality 65, 153–4, 161–2
inflation 92, 97
informal economy 108, 115, 121, 151, 154–9, 164–6, 169–70, 173, 175, 177, 194
  see also de Soto, Hernando

infrastructure construction, see construction process; public and private sectors
investment opportunities for ordinary Chinese 90–2, 104–6, 108, 180–81
"iron rice bowl" 47, 102, 189
  see also agricultural land

Japan 17, 59, 143
joint stock limited companies 45–6
  see also entities, ownership

Kennedy, David 162, 172, 182

Land Administration Law 18, 23, 33, 38, 41, 57–8, 69–72, 96, 135, 137, 143, 150
land shortages 61–2
  see also land use controls; population and density
land use controls 53–60, 179, 185
  conflicts of interest between government and developers 41–50, 55–7, 86–7, 106–7, 136–8, 141
  exactions and impact fees, analogies to 37, 136
  government incentives and pressure 41–8, 55–60, 86–8, 135–8, 140, 191
  government taking of property and compensation requirement 22–3, 27–8, 59–71, 94–6, 116, 136, 138, 149, 179, 189, 203
  public input 53–5, 133
  Shanghai procedures 35–7, 54–6, 179
  see also agricultural land; Chinese government; demolition and relocation; land shortages; land use rights; population and density; protest in China; Shanghai; zoning
land use rights 12–13, 27–43, 63–4, 150, 164–5, 173–5, 203
  allocated land use rights 68–9
  as alternative to private ownership of land 4, 7, 12–13, 27–9, 189, 201
  attributes of 31–5, 88, 150, 179
  distinguished from Western ground lease 34–5, 39, 81, 120

fear that government will run out of
   desirable land 72–4, 97
grant of by government 27–8, 35–7,
   45–6, 49–51, 98, 141–2, 191
land use control function of 41–3, 48,
   53–7, 87, 135–8, 140, 185–6, 191
legal basis for 27–8, 164
mortgageability of 30, 35, 75, 79–83,
   113, 119–23
precursors to 28, 164, 173–4, 179
registration of 33–5, 120, 157
renewability of and price of at end
   of initial term 37–40, 98, 164–5,
   173–5, 180
revenue source for government 29,
   41–3, 48, 65–72, 101, 110–11,
   134–9, 143–4, 203
tensions with Marxist doctrine 12–3,
   18, 28–31, 70–71, 81, 94–6
transfers by private rights holders
   32–3
see also Chinese government;
   contracts; land use controls; law
   and development theory; leasing;
   mortgages; presales; zoning
law and development theory 12, 14–15, 22,
   152, 169–71, 202–4
   ambiguity of and uncertainty within
      China's legal system 5, 28, 149–52,
      157–8, 164–5, 167, 180, 197–8,
      201–2
   application of theory to various
      Chinese legal structures 163–7,
      178–81, 189–92, 195–8
   Chinese departures from traditional
      model 163–7
   co-opting of Chinese entrepreneurs
      186–9
   possibility that China is following
      traditional model 176–81, 195
   possibility that China is still too
      Communist for traditional model to
      apply 184–92, 196
   possibility that no model applies well
      in any nation 192–8
   possibility that traditional model is too
      Western to apply in China 181–4,
      195–6
   possibility that traditional model is
      wrong 171–4, 195
   possibility that traditional model needs
      refinement 174–6, 195
   poverty and 153–4, 161–3
   sequencing of economic and legal
      development 152, 160–61
   social norms and customs, relevance
      of 8–9, 154–9, 165–6, 169, 173,
      175–7, 181, 185–7, 194–8
   traditional model 153–63
   see also banking system; demolition
      and relocation; entities, ownership;
      evolution of legal and business
      systems; land use rights; presales;
      rule-of-law standards
Law on the Administration of Urban Real
   Estate 28, 31–3, 35, 38, 62, 68–9,
   81–2, 106, 108, 110, 113, 135, 143,
   150
law professors 6, 8, 19
law students 6, 8, 20, 54
leasing 14, 28, 34–5, 76, 81, 120, 128–32,
   203
   see also land use rights; lending, real
      estate
lending, real estate 5, 13–14, 180, 202–4
   cash-flow loans 76–9, 126–7, 131
   commercial rental property 124–6,
      128–31
   contrasts between China and the West
      123–6
   corruption in credit decisions, role of
      87–9, 99, 126
   government's ownership of lenders,
      significance of 47, 85–90, 125–6,
      135–7, 142, 189–92, 196
   incentives facing loan officers 88, 111
   prevalence of domestic lenders 77
   project loans 76–9, 126–8
   security interest in tenant rents,
      unavailability of 85
   security that developers can offer to
      lenders 32–3, 79–83, 164–5, 167
   sources of funds 84–5, 90–8
   stability of banking sector 99–102
   standards for lending in China 39, 75,
      77–8, 85–90 108–16, 119–26

see also banking system; Chinese government; construction process; corruption; leasing; mortgages; presales; real estate developers; residential apartments
Lieberthal, Kenneth 46, 70, 172, 187, 190
limited liability companies 45–6, 48, 52, 110, 179
   see also entities, ownership
Lindblom, Charles 161–2, 179
Lou Jianbo, *see* Randolph, Patrick A., Jr. and Lou Jianbo
Lubman, Stanley 6–7, 10–11, 19–21, 29–31, 47, 67, 151, 154

Mao Zedong 17–18, 21, 87, 94, 154, 166, 184–6
mentors, professional 11, 20, 180
migration within China 4, 70, 73, 95–96, 128, 134
modernization of China 3, 6, 14, 21, 23, 30, 86, 95, 133, 139, 145–6, 178–9, 201–4
mortgages 75–117
   commercial lending standards, problems with 85–90
   default rate, residential 77–79, 89–90, 109, 111
   definition of in China 75–6
   foreclosure of 89–90
   leasehold mortgages, absence of 76
   mortgageable property 30, 32, 35, 42, 75–6, 79–85, 111–15
   registration of 33–4
   residential lending standards, problems with 77–9, 180, 203–4
   residential lending, timing problems with 14, 84, 87, 106–15
   residential leveraging opportunities 103–6
   secondary market, absence of 78–9
   see also construction process; land use rights; lending, real estate; residential apartments
Murrell, Peter, *see* Clarke, Donald, Peter Murrell, and Susan Whiting

National People's Congress 30, 71, 144, 149

Nationalists 17, 59
nationalization of land after 1949, 17–18, 23, 94, 97
   as source of revenue for current government 23, 94–8, 203
new institutional economics, *see* North, Douglass
North, Douglass 154–6, 158, 160, 169–70, 173, 175–6, 193–4

Peerenboom, Randall 3, 5, 9–11, 19, 21, 58–9, 74, 96, 159–62, 169–71, 174–5, 177–8, 183, 194
Peru 156–9, 172
population and density 55–6, 61–2, 72–4, 95, 105, 111, 134, 144, 183–4, 203
   see also land shortages; land use controls; Shanghai
Potter, Pitman 160, 181
presales 14, 84, 103–15, 167, 203
   buyers as unwilling lenders to developers 14, 84, 105–109, 115
   difficulties facing buyers as a result of 14, 84, 105–9, 111–15, 167
   restrictions on 105–8
   speculation, relationship to 105–7
   timing problems with 14, 84, 107–9, 111–15, 167
   see also banking system; contracts; land use rights; law and development theory; lending, real estate; residential apartments
private ownership of land, *see* land use rights
profit motive, private 7, 12–13, 53, 86, 98, 101, 106–7, 116–17, 119, 121, 126, 129–31, 135–6, 138–9, 149–51, 166–7, 184, 187, 189–90
project loans, *see* construction process; lending, real estate
Property Rights Law 5, 28, 30, 32, 33–42, 59, 62, 70–1, 75–6, 80–2, 89, 96, 105, 112–13, 119–20, 123, 127, 130, 133, 136–40, 150, 164–6, 178–80, 195–6
property taxes 39–40, 57, 60, 94, 116–17, 142
   see also taxes

protest in China 13, 59–60, 67, 179–80, 188
  see also agricultural land; demolition and relocation; land use controls; social stability
public and private sectors 133–46
  Build–Operate–Transfer (BOT) process 14, 98, 140–42
  distinctions between, murkiness of 90–3, 133–42
  public–private joint ventures 13, 46, 49, 130, 139–42
  see also construction process; entities, ownership
Pudong New Area, *see* Shanghai

Randolph, Patrick A., Jr. and Lou Jianbo 18, 27, 31–4, 38, 41–2, 46, 59, 63, 68–70, 76, 82, 94
real estate developers
  bureaucracy as an impediment to 83, 141
  disadvantages facing smaller developers 83, 130
  early entrants, advantages of 49–51, 83
  high cash outlays required of 79–85, 113–14, 119–23
  market analysis by 85–90, 122, 126
  preference for selling completed projects 85, 123, 128–30
  see also construction process; entities, ownership; lending, real estate
relocation, *see* demolition and relocation
renminbi, *see* exchange rate of renminbi
residential apartments 14, 103–17
  affordability of 58, 64–8, 87, 95–6, 108–9
  condominiums, similarities to 105, 123–4
  high demand for 103–6, 111–12, 116–17, 129, 180–81
  investment vehicles, apartments as 64, 78, 87, 89–92, 101, 103–6, 108–9, 123, 129
  overseas investment in 50–51, 104–5, 178
  proximity to jobs 56
  resales of 116
  see also construction process; lending, real estate; mortgages; presales
rule-of-law standards 2, 5–6, 11, 14, 20–21, 74, 152–6, 159–61, 169–71, 174–8, 182–4, 187, 194, 196, 202
  see also law and development theory
Russia 42, 74, 163, 184–5, 189

Sachs, Jeffrey 163, 194–5
Santos, Alvaro, *see* Trubek, David and Alvaro Santos
savings and savings rate 48, 79, 87, 89–93, 98–9, 103, 111, 203
securitization 78–9
Sen, Amartya 161, 198
SEZs, *see* Special Economic Zones (SEZs)
Shanghai 4, 7, 10, 14, 18–19, 77, 78, 80, 82, 83, 93, 103, 130–31
  ad valorem property tax trial in 39
  Expo 145
  land reserve system 68
  Pudong New Area 18, 30, 41, 51, 56–7, 59–60, 73, 86, 103, 133, 136, 139–42, 144–6
  redevelopment since 1990s, 4, 7, 14, 18–19, 42, 45, 48, 51, 54, 66–7, 73, 105, 141, 145–6
  skyscrapers and skyline 4, 18–19, 21, 40
  stock market 91, 103
  transfer of land use rights by 35–7, 49–50, 71–2, 95, 107, 110, 138
  Xintiandi project 56–7, 98
  see also land use controls; population and density
Shenzhen 80, 91, 103, 144
social stability 22, 43, 67, 70, 72, 95–6, 115, 182, 188
  see also protest in China
Socialism 3, 11, 29–31, 133, 139, 160, 186, 202
  socialist market economy (socialism with Chinese characteristics) 6, 11, 30, 53, 202
  see also Communism
SOEs, *see* banking system; state-owned enterprises (outside of the real estate and lending industries (SOEs)

de Soto, Hernando 156–9, 163, 169, 172, 175
  see also informal economy
Soviet Union, former, *see* Russia
Special Economic Zones (SEZs) 139–40, 144–6
Spence, Jonathan 17–18
state-owned enterprises (outside of the real estate and lending industries) (SOEs) 3, 46–8, 71, 87, 91, 102, 111, 125–6, 189–90
  see also banking system
Steinfeld, Edward 31, 151, 178, 197
Stiglitz, Joseph 162–3
suburban expansion 42, 64–5, 73

taxes 29, 57, 60, 66, 73, 78–9, 88, 93–4, 97, 98, 101–2, 110, 116–17, 139–40, 144
  use of to slow real estate market 57, 88, 116–17
  see also property taxes
trade imbalance with West 3, 93
transparency
  business standards 88, 107
  government processes 37, 49–50, 54, 107, 111, 179, 202
  legal standards 5, 11, 22, 159–60
  see also Chinese government
Trebilcock, Michael J. 173–4, 181, 194, 198
Trubek, David and Alvaro Santos 153–4, 161

Tsai, Kellee 151, 166, 175, 177, 186–9

Upham, Frank 153, 159, 171–2, 181–2, 192–3, 197
urban land 27, 30, 68–70, 94, 104, 143
  historic preservation 67, 98
  redevelopment of older buildings 62

valuation of land in China
  problems with valuing Chinese land 35–40, 42, 49–51, 59–60, 63–73, 81, 87, 96, 131, 174, 180, 191, 203
  real estate bubble, possibility of 4, 22, 52, 58, 105–6
Vietnam 160, 163, 184, 197

Wenzhounese investors 52, 165–7
Whiting, Susan, *see* Clarke, Donald, Peter Murrell, and Susan Whiting
Wong, Jan 190
World Trade Organization (WTO) 3, 50, 92

Xintiandi project, *see* Shanghai

Yangtze River 4, 72, 145

Zhang, Mo 149, 159, 178, 182
Zhou Enlai 176, 197
zoning 41, 53, 55, 82, 120
  see also agricultural land; land use controls; land use rights